Grave Matters

Grave Matters

*Death and Dying in Dublin,
1500 to the present*

Lisa Marie Griffith & Ciarán Wallace

EDITORS

FOUR COURTS PRESS

Typeset in 11pt on 14pt AGaramondPro by
Carrigboy Typesetting Services for
FOUR COURTS PRESS LTD
7 Malpas Street, Dublin 8, Ireland
www.fourcourtspress.ie
and in North America for
FOUR COURTS PRESS
c/o ISBS, 920 NE 58th Avenue, Suite 300, Portland, OR 97213.

A catalogue record for this title is available
from the British Library.

ISBN 978–1–84682–601–6

Printed in Spain
by Castuera, Pamplona

This book is dedicated to all who lie in unmarked graves in Dublin's many burial grounds, and to those Dubliners who were unable to make their native city their final resting place.

Foreword

This collection of essays is the result of a conference entitled 'Death and Dying in Dublin' held in the Glasnevin Cemetery Museum in April 2014 by the Dublin History Research Network. At that event, members of the general public, research students and established academics gathered to hear a fascinating variety of talks on issues relating to illness, dying, burial and commemoration in the city. The success of the conference showed us, once again, the enduring concern that people have with death – the one truly universal fact. This fact is at the centre of all our activities in the Glasnevin Trust, whether at Newlands Cross, Dardistown, Palmerstown or Glasnevin. It is a topic that touches everyone in more ways than we may realize, just as it did for the countless generations before us. These essays deal with a broad range of topics across many centuries. Some examine the ways in which the people of Dublin prepared for death and the medical efforts they made to avoid it. Others look at the customs and traditions around burial and the impact of death on those left behind. Political campaigns to immortalize the elite dead and legal attempts to prevent judicial killing are considered alongside sectarian divisions and a forgotten pandemic. Many of the essays deal with the response of ordinary individuals and families to the reality of death, individuals much like the million Dubliners buried in Glasnevin. They remind us that we are part of an endless series of generations each with its own fears and hopes around the grave.

As the current custodians of many of Dublin's major cemeteries, we are keenly aware of our responsibility to preserve the heritage of Dublin's past generations. Serving the present generation is also part of our mission and we host thousands of visitors, from school groups and overseas visitors to dignitaries and mourners, at the popular Glasnevin Cemetery Museum. Our commitment to providing a legacy for future generations involves major conservation work on the physical fabric of the cemetery – but it also includes this volume. The exciting new research being carried out by these authors enhances our understanding not just of death and dying, but also of daily life and social attitudes in the past. We are proud to sponsor this valuable addition to the research on the history of Dublin city and its people.

GEORGE McCULLOUGH
Chief Executive, Glasnevin Trust

Contents

Illustrations

PLATES APPEAR BETWEEN PAGES 96 AND 97

Abbreviations

BMH	Bureau of Military History, Ireland
CSPI	Calendar of State Papers of Ireland
DCLA	Dublin City Library and Archives
DIB	*Cambridge dictionary of Irish biography*
JRSAI	*Journal of the Royal Society of Antiquaries of Ireland*
MA	Military Archives, Ireland
MC	Dublin Municipal Council minutes
NAI	National Archives of Ireland
NLI	National Library of Ireland
ODNB	*Oxford dictionary of national biography*
PRIA	*Proceedings of the Royal Irish Academy*
RCBL	Representative Church Body Library
RSAI	Royal Society of Antiquaries of Ireland
TCD	Trinity College Dublin

Contributors

PATRICIA BEDLOW is a qualified archivist and has an MPhil in public history from Trinity College Dublin; currently, she is a museum assistant in Glasnevin Cemetery Museum.

EAMON DARCY lectures in early modern Irish and European history at Maynooth University. He is the author of *The Irish rebellion of 1641 and the Wars of the Three Kingdoms* published by Boydell and Brewer and has published extensively on early modern Ireland. His next work is a history of Ireland from 1485 to 1695, which will appear with Collins Press in 2016.

SIOBHÁN DOYLE is completing a PhD in Museum Studies & Commemorations at Dublin Institute of Technology. She has presented her research at international level in Radboud University Nijmegen (Netherlands), the University of Stockholm (Sweden) and Columbia University (New York); her research interests include the historiography of visual culture, commemorative practices, notions of national identity and dark tourism.

ORLA FITZPATRICK is a PhD researcher at Ulster University working on the topic of modernity and the Irish photographic book. She has worked as a librarian since the early 1990s. Her publications include articles on Irish photographic history and material culture for *Source: Photographic Review, Éire-Ireland* and *Irish Architectural and Decorative Studies*. She has also curated several photographic exhibitions and edited a photographic book for the National Library of Ireland. Her blog www.jacolette.com covers vernacular Irish photography.

PHILOMENA GOREY was awarded her doctorate at University College Dublin in 2014 for her thesis entitled 'Managing midwives in Ireland: from ecclesiastical regulation to state registration, *c.*1600–1918'. Her research interests include the development of man-midwifery in Dublin in the eighteenth century, the initiatives of the Local Government Board to introduce maternal care in nineteenth-century Irish dispensaries, the early education of midwives and nurses and the incidence and treatment of puerperal fever. She is a registered general nurse and midwife at the Rotunda Hospital.

PAUL HUDDIE is a graduate of University College Dublin. He was awarded a PhD by Queen's University Belfast in 2014 for research on Irish society during the Crimean War. He is a researcher of war and society in Britain and Ireland in the long nineteenth century, has presented widely on this subject and has been published in several journals including *Irish Sword*, *Quaker History* and the *British Journal of Military History*. His monograph, *The Crimean War and Irish society*, was published by Liverpool University Press in December 2015.

BRIAN HUGHES is an associate lecturer in modern history at the University of Exeter's Cornwall Campus. He is the author of *16 lives: Michael Mallin* (Dublin, 2012) and editor of *Eoin MacNeill: memoir of a revolutionary scholar* (Dublin, 2016). A monograph based on his PhD thesis, entitled *Defying the IRA? Intimidation, coercion, and communities during the Irish Revolution*, is forthcoming with Liverpool University Press.

CIARÁN MAC MURCHAIDH is Head of School in Fiontar at Dublin City University. His research interests are in the area of eighteenth-century religious literature in the Irish language, especially the sermon genre. He has written widely on aspects of this topic and his most recent publication, co-edited with Professor James Kelly of St Patrick's College, Drumcondra, is *Irish and English: essays on the Irish linguistic and cultural frontier, 1600–1900* (Dublin, 2012).

JAMES MCCAFFERTY DSM, PhD is a veteran of the UN operation in the Congo, having served with three Irish battalions there in the period 1961–4. His doctoral thesis, 'Political and military aspects of the Irish Army's service in the Congo, 1960–64', was supported by a John & Pat Hume scholarship at Maynooth University.

IAN MILLER is a Wellcome Trust Research Fellow at the Centre for the History of Medicine, Ulster University. He is the author of *A modern history of the stomach: gastric illness, medicine and British society, 1800–1950* (London, 2011), *Reforming food in post-Famine Ireland: medicine, science and improvement, 1845–1922* (Manchester, 2014) and *Water: a global history* (London, 2015). He is currently writing a monograph on the force feeding of English and Irish hunger strikers between 1909 and 1981.

IDA MILNE is a social historian whose principal research interest is in the effect epidemic disease has on societies. She was awarded a PhD from

Trinity College Dublin in 2011 for her work on the 1918–19 influenza epidemic in Ireland. She is currently a research fellow at Queen's University Belfast and Maynooth University, working on a project about the changing landscape of childhood illness in twentieth-century Ireland; this research is co-funded by the Irish Research Council and Marie Curie Actions.

SEAN J. MURPHY holds a BA and MA in history from University College Dublin. He teaches genealogy to UCD's Adult Education programme as well as working as a historical researcher, lecturer and author. His broad research interests include Dublin graveyards and their memorial inscriptions.

FIONNUALA PARNELL studied archaeology in University College Dublin. Her MA thesis on the eighteenth-century headstones of Fingal led her to continue her research into the trades and occupations found inscribed on Irish headstones. She is currently extending this research into Scotland and the rest of the UK. Fionnuala works for the Office of Public Works.

RAYMOND REFAUSSÉ is the Librarian & Archivist of the Church of Ireland based in the Representative Church Body Library, Dublin. He has published extensively on the archives of the Church of Ireland. Among his publications are, with Mary Clark, *A catalogue of maps of the estates of the archbishops of Dublin, 1654–1850* (Dublin, 2000), with M.J. Mc Enery, *Christ Church deeds* (Dublin, 2001) and *Church of Ireland records* (2nd ed., Dublin, 2006). He is series editor of the RCB Library's *Texts and Calendars* series, published in association with Four Courts Press, which seeks to publish critical editions of important Church of Ireland archives.

PATRICK WALSH is an Irish Research Council/European Commission funded research fellow in the School of History and Archives at University College Dublin. Among his many publications are *The making of the Irish Protestant ascendancy: the life of William Conolly, 1662–1729* (Woodbridge, 2010) and *The South Sea Bubble and Ireland, money, banking and investment, 1690–1721* (Woodbridge, 2014).

EDITORS

LISA MARIE GRIFFITH has written extensively on Dublin's social history from the eighteenth century; her most recent publication was *Stones of Dublin: a history of Dublin in ten buildings* (Dublin, 2014). Lisa is a co-founder of the Dublin History Research Network and she is a frequent contributor to broadcast and social media on the city and its story.

CIARÁN WALLACE lectures in Irish history and Irish studies at Dublin City University, Mater Dei campus. He has written on the social and political history of Dublin city and suburbs in the nineteenth and twentieth centuries. His latest publication was the co-authored *Thomas Fitzpatrick and the Lepracaun Cartoon Monthly: 1905–1915* (Dublin, 2015). Ciarán is a coordinator on the Dublin History Research Network.

Acknowledgments

This collection arose from a one-day symposium arranged by the Dublin History Research Network which was hosted by Glasnevin Trust at the cemetery's museum. We would like to thank all of those at Glasnevin who assisted with the preparations running up to this event and on the day. We would also like to thank the speakers who participated in the symposium including Mary Ann Bolger, Siobhán Doyle, Orla Fitzpatrick, Paul Huddie, Brian Hughes, Stuart Kinsella, Ciarán Mac Murchaidh, Doireann Markham, James McCafferty, Ian Miller, Ida Milne and Sean Murphy. Luke Portess was kind enough to provide an image of Glasnevin Cemetery for our poster, and for the cover of the book. We are grateful to David Dickson and Ciaran O'Neill of Trinity College Dublin, coordinators of the Dublin History Research Network, who supported the symposium. The enthusiasm for this topic which we received on the day from contributors, attendees and Glasnevin Trust encouraged us to follow the event with this collection of essays. Patricia Bedlow, Raymond Refaussé, Patrick Walsh, Fionnuala Parnell and Eamon Darcy kindly agreed to contribute to the volume.

There were a number of people who assisted us in putting this volume together. The Dublin City and County Heritage Officers kindly provided information on cemeteries within their jurisdiction. Mary Clark, Archivist at Dublin City Library and Archives (DCLA), provided us with information on sources and pointed us towards the very useful Graveyard Directory, which is located on the DCLA website. Dublin City Council is responsible for more historic graveyards than any other Dublin institution and DCLA is an invaluable repository for the study of death. Gus Nichols from Nichols' Undertakers opened up his company archives to us. Gus also answered questions about the history of his family's firm and about his profession. This was hugely valuable and allowed us to gain a better understanding not just of the undertaker's work within the city, but also about records and locations in the city connected to death. William Laffan, Joe Brady, Pól Ó Duibhir, Aida Yared, and Luke Portess allowed us to reproduce their images, or images from their own collections, for the purpose of this book and we are very grateful as they provide valuable insights on the city and illuminate the text.

The staff at Four Courts Press, and in particular Martin Fanning, have supported this project from very early on; they encouraged us to expand the volume and to include a large number of images in the text. This would be a very different collection without their expert guidance and help.

Finally, our thanks to the Glasnevin Trust who gave vital financial support, and to George McCullough, Mervyn Colville, Luke Portess, Conor Dodd and the rest of the team at Glasnevin who supported and encouraged this volume. Glasnevin is a unique cemetery within Dublin and nationally. The Trust is also responsible for a number of cemeteries city-wide and it is their commitment to the preservation of the graves, the grounds and cemetery records that makes a volume like this, and research on this topic, possible.

Death and the city: an introduction

LISA MARIE GRIFFITH & CIARÁN WALLACE

> So many belonging to me lay buried in Kilbarrack, the healthiest
> graveyard in Ireland, they said, because it was so near the sea.
> Brendan Behan, The Borstal Boy.

Even in daily life, death and dying are all around. This is especially true in the
city where memorials, graveyards and cemeteries surround us, where a passing
ambulance may briefly hold up traffic or a public funeral close the streets. Like
any older city, Dublin has amassed centuries of ordinary and extraordinary
deaths, sad family burials, humble and heroic commemorations; but the city's
particular social and political history have produced a unique geography and
culture of dying, death and remembering. Looking at Dubliners' efforts to
delay the inevitable or to prepare for the afterlife tells us much about medical
developments and social attitudes; examining the commerce and creativity
surrounding burial and bereavement deepens our understanding of the city's
trade and craftsmanship. Memorialization, both private and political, reveals
how the dead are incorporated into the identity of the surviving family,
community or state.

Several studies on the topic of death and dying have been published in
Ireland in the last fifteen years, such as Clodagh Tait's *Death, burial and
commemoration in Ireland, 1550–1650*, Greta Jones' study on the history of
tuberculosis in nineteenth- and twentieth-century Ireland, Viven Igoe's *Dublin
burial grounds and graveyards* or James Kelly and Mary Ann Lyons' recent
collection of essays *Death and dying in Ireland, Britain and Europe: historical
perspectives*.[1] While this undoubtedly reflects the growing academic interest in
the field of medical history, it might also reflect a particular Irish interest in
death. In autumn 2014 *One million Dubliners*, a documentary about Glasnevin

---

[1] Clodagh Tait, *Death, burial and commemoration in Ireland, 1550–1650* (Basingstoke, 2002); Greta Jones,
The captain of all these men of death: the history of tuberculosis in nineteenth- and twentieth-century Ireland
(New York, 2001); Vivien Igoe, *Dublin burial grounds and graveyards* (Dublin, 2001); James Kelly & Mary
Ann Lyons (eds), *Death and dying in Ireland, Britain and Europe: historical perspectives* (Sallins, 2013);
Harold Mytum, *Mortuary monuments and burial grounds of the historic period* (New York, 2003); Anne
Ridge, *Death customs in rural Ireland: traditional funerary rites in the Irish midlands* (Galway, 2009). For a

Cemetery, was released in cinemas throughout Ireland before being broadcast that November on RTÉ1. As well as attracting large audiences, the documentary received critical acclaim. This broad popular interest in the topic of death in Ireland extends beyond the deaths of historic or sensational figures to an interest in the death of ordinary everyday people; the title of *One million Dubliners* tells us just this – the cemetery commemorates all the lives and stories of those buried within its walls, not just those who are celebrated in history books. This is reinforced in Shane MacThomáis' volume *Dead interesting: stories from the graveyards of Dublin*, which takes a broader view of those buried in Glasnevin, seeking out the stories of ordinary, and not so ordinary, Dubliners interred there.[2]

There are a number of reasons for this particular Irish interest in death. The Great Famine, which saw the death of around one million Irish people over a period of just five years, has cast a long shadow over our national consciousness. The memory of these traumatic years was kept alive in Ireland and was brought by immigrants to the new countries in which they settled, ensuring that the famine was not forgotten. There is also a strong cult of death that focuses on nationalist leaders who gave their lives for Irish independence. The deaths of key revolutionary leaders like Lord Edward FitzGerald, Robert Emmett and the 1916 signatories meant a cult of martyrdom was founded, maintained and then embedded in the nationalist movement. Dates linked to their failed rebellions were marked in the nationalist political calendar.[3] These commemorations continued when the new state was founded in 1922. While the Civil War created a gulf in Irish social and political life, events like the 1916 Rising and the 1798 Rebellion could still be commemorated. This tradition has continued to the present day as national and local authorities sponsor and support the commemoration of historical events through lecture series, trails, re-enactments and exhibitions. The most extensive commemoration of this kind to date is the Decade of Centenaries (2013–23), which aims to bring historical context to a decade of events (global, national and local) that culminated in the creation of the Irish state. It is through the commemorations for those events that we can get a sense of the Irish preoccupation with our dead and how their lives shaped our country. Studies

more comprehensive list please see the bibliography. **2** Shane MacThomáis, *Dead interesting: stories from the graveyards of Dublin* (Cork, 2012). **3** This occurred outside the official state and could take various guises. For instance, in the 1890s the playwright W.J. Whitbread wrote plays to commemorate the 1798 Rebellion that proved hugely popular with Dublin audiences; these plays include *Lord Edward* (1894), *Theobald Wolfe Tone* (1898), *The insurgent chief* and *The Ulster hero* (1902). Also, see Christopher Morash,

focusing on the leaders of the 1916 Rising, which remained popular through the twentieth and into the twenty-first century, have shone a spotlight on the idea of martyrdom, on the sacrifice that they made, and this has made us think about death in a national sense. (For a less familiar view of the 1916 executions see Brian Hughes' essay on the private reactions of the bereaved families.) Two of our most important national heritage sites, both located in Dublin, became pivotal to this cult of death; Kilmainham Gaol was where the leaders of the 1916 Rising were executed before being buried in Arbour Hill Cemetery, and Glasnevin Cemetery was where Irish nationalist figures dating back to the nineteenth century were laid to rest. These sites have become political and national shrines.

It perhaps follows that there is also a strong historic interest in the locations associated with death. The work undertaken by local historical associations, religious groups and individual scholars reflect this interest.[4] This can also be seen as far back as the nineteenth century and highlights a concern to preserve the graves of previous generations at a time when the political and social landscape was undergoing a momentous shift. Some scholars and associations set out to chronicle the burial sites of the Protestant community. This was a population which was losing its grip on power from the mid-nineteenth century and which, by the foundation of an independent Irish state, was experiencing a decline in numbers. Other groups such as the National Graves Association sought to commemorate and preserve the grave sites of those who had died fighting to create an independent Ireland. In the aftermath of the Civil War such activities could be contentious. That it took so long to establish a museum at Kilmainham Gaol, the site of executions during the 1916 Rising and later the Civil War, and to commemorate the Irish dead from the Great War, shows how politically contentious these sites of death could be.[5]

In more recent times technology has facilitated a greater access to records about death and this has brought us closer to our ancestors than ever before. The digitization of census and parish records has meant that these files, previously available only by visiting the archives, can now be accessed online. Large digitization projects, like the National Library of Ireland's Catholic

A history of Irish theatre (Cambridge, 2002), p. 113. **4** For example, Danny Parkinson, *Donnybrook Graveyard, c.800–1993* (Dublin, 1993), or the records collected in 'Association for the Preservation of Memorials of the Dead in Ireland' between 1888 and 1920 and which are now available in the National Library of Ireland or through local libraries. **5** Rory O'Dwyer, '"The wilderness years": Kilmainham Gaol, 1924–1960', *History Ireland*, 18:6 (Nov./Dec. 2010), pp 41–3; Richard S. Grayson, 'From genealogy to reconciliation: public engagement with remembrance of the First World War in Ireland', *Nordic Irish Studies*,

Parish Registers launched in 2015, are state sponsored and access to them is free of charge. This has meant that amateur researchers can access the records and create their own histories. Through the National Archives of Ireland's 1901 and 1911 Census Online project we can track where our relatives were at historic moments and appreciate what they would have seen or participated in. These digitization projects are now starting to focus on graveyards, going beyond birth, marriage and death records to digitize the location of interment as well. It is important to note the part that emigrants have played in the preservation of these records. Genealogists from Britain, Australia, North America and elsewhere have returned to Ireland throughout the twentieth century to trawl the archives and trace their ancestry. Researchers' interest in these records has contributed to their preservation and subsequent digitization.

This collection of essays seeks to bring together some of the themes that surround death and dying in Dublin, including how people died, what happened when epidemics or crises hit the city, the impact of revolution, how and where people were buried, how they were remembered, how we marked death both in private and publicly as a state. The topic of death is far-reaching and rather than attempting to cover it exhaustively we have focused here on the stages of death – dying, death, burial and commemoration. We hope in this way to draw out how the city and its inhabitants dealt with death during normal times, but also in times of crisis. The reaction of the city to these events can tell us much about society's morals and values as well as about the politics of the day. They also allow us to see how much the city and its inhabitants have changed.

* * *

The church governed all aspects of life from celebrations in the annual calendar to births, marriages and deaths. They taught people not just how to prepare for the afterlife (see Ciarán Mac Murchaidh's essay) and what happened after death, but how people should be buried and commemorated. The city of Dublin was divided into a number of parishes, many such as St Michan's and St Audoen's dating back to the medieval period. Parish churches had graveyards attached to their grounds and while many of these churches had facilities to bury their poorer parishioners, Bully's Acre (located in Kilmainham, just outside the city limits) became the site of burial for Dublin's poorest. Marking the last resting place of an individual was not standard practice in the medieval and early modern period. Dublin's wealthiest citizens were usually buried in crypts or within the main church. 'People of quality, and they are, for the most part, those for whom there are records, were buried within the walls of the cathedrals and parish churches, and just as there was a hierarchy of where people sat in church so there was a hierarchy of where people were laid to rest.'[6] These burials can still be found within the city's churches and cathedrals. Memorials like these were the preserve of the city's wealthiest and most powerful citizens. As such 'there are no graveyards in the conventional sense to visit' up to the seventeenth century.[7] The area around the altar was reserved for the clergy, bishops and archbishops, and radiating from there the space was dedicated to important members of the congregation. Examples of these types of commemorations can be found in Christ Church Cathedral and, more prominently, in St Patrick's Cathedral.[8] The political and social importance of these monuments can be seen in Eamon Darcy's examination of the Agard family memorial, erected in Christ Church Cathedral in the sixteenth century. The middling and lower orders, however, did not erect headstones until the eighteenth century, as Fionnuala Parnell's essay shows, which suggests a greater disposable income in a period when Dublin was booming financially. Funerals of all ranks of citizens were, however, a common site on the city's streets. Patrick Walsh looks at the pomp and ceremony surrounding the funeral of William Conolly, one of the most influential politicians of his day. Hugh Douglas Hamilton, the eighteenth-century Irish artist, trained in Dublin and his sketchbook from this time includes images of the funerals of what he termed 'upper', 'middle' and 'lower rank' citizens (see p. 135 and plates 2 and 3).[9]

The issue of religious worship, and consequently burial, was complicated in the sixteenth century with the Reformation. The state's view of the Reformation was not that a church split had taken place, but that the Reformation was righting the wrongs of a rotten Catholic Church. Consequently, they supported the removal of bishops and priests who did not believe in the reforms from Dublin churches, and their replacement by those who did. Catholic worship moved underground with worship taking place in secret. Nevertheless, the Catholic Church survived and as the penal laws

13:2 (2014), pp 99–113. **6** Raymond Refaussé, 'Gone but not forgotten: the Church of Ireland graveyards of the city of Dublin', *Dublin Historical Record*, 68:1 (Spring/Summer 2015), p. 86. **7** Ibid. **8** During the renovation of Christ Church Cathedral, George Edmund Street banished many memorials to the crypt. While some were later rescued and returned to their original positions, many still remain below ground (Kenneth Milne, *Christ Church Cathedral Dublin: a history* (Dublin, 2010), p. 325). **9** Hugh Douglas Hamilton, *The cries of Dublin: drawn from the life by Hugh Douglas Hamilton, 1760* (Dublin, 2003), pp 184–5.

gradually fell into disuse new churches were discreetly built in the old parishes, mirroring the Protestant places of worship and often in close proximity. St Mary's parish, which was founded in 1679, is a case in point. John Rocque's 1756 map of the city (see fig. 1) shows the original Anglican St Mary's Church facing onto St Mary Street, while the more discreet Catholic Church in the parish was situated to the rear of Middle Liffey Street and seems to have been accessed through a dwelling house. Even its marking on the map is discreet as the building is not named, is heavily shaded and noted only with a cross.

While these new Catholic churches emerged slowly to serve the Catholic population of the city, the Catholic dead needed to be buried. They continued to use the old graveyards they were most familiar with and that were now in the hands of the established Anglican churches. This shared use of city graveyards can be seen in Sean Murphy's essay on St James' Graveyard; Murphy points out that although many believed there was direct legislation prohibiting the burial of Catholics in their own graveyards, this was not the case. The burial of Catholics in Protestant graveyards emerged from this period when the Catholic Church was still recovering from the reformation and had not yet established a built presence in the city's parishes. Raymond Refaussé's essay in the appendices looks at the parish records of these Protestant churches, which date back to the early modern period, and contain the records of Catholic as well as Protestant burials. On the condition of the city graveyards and their records Refaussé says 'the Church of Ireland has been providing for the burial of the citizens of Dublin from medieval times right up to the present day'.[10] These records, which are often overlooked, are an important source for the history of Dublin's population. City graveyards from this period can also tell us about newcomers to the city. Dublin was a capital city and was connected to many parts of the world through trade. Its population was religiously, as well as culturally, diverse. The Huguenot Cemetery on Merrion Row (see plate 6) was founded in the late 1690s for the new French Protestant community that fled to Ireland to avoid persecution in Catholic France. Ireland's oldest Jewish cemetery was founded in Ballybough, Co. Dublin, in 1718.[11] The existence of such cemeteries highlights the movement of groups into the city.

Mortality rates show us that city residents experienced different living conditions and challenges than their rural cousins. The density of population

---

10 Refaussé, 'Gone but not forgotten', p. 84.   **11** Another Huguenot Cemetery, at Peter Street, was in use up to 1879. Legislation passed in 1966 authorized the removal of all remains and the transfer of the land to W. & R. Jacob & Co., for an extension to their premises. Huguenot Cemetery Dublin (Peter Street) Act, 1966.

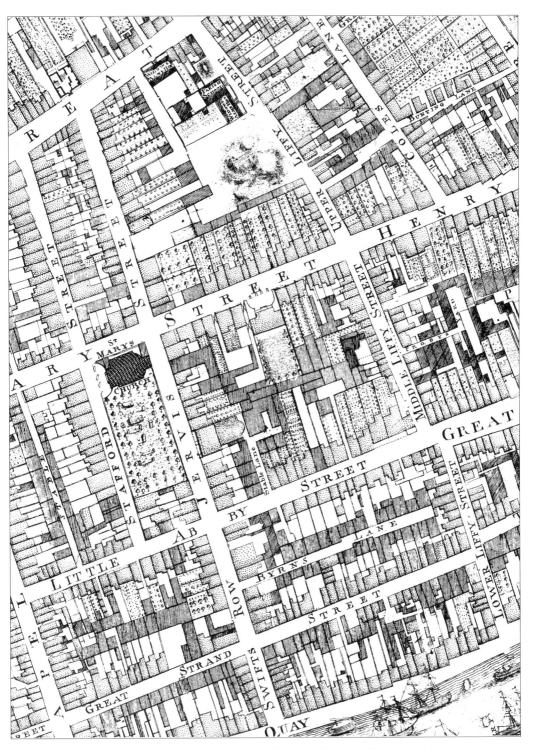

1 Detail of John Rocque map, 1756, showing St Mary's Church of Ireland parish and St Mary's Roman Catholic parish (reproduced courtesy of Joe Brady).

that existed in Dublin, as well as the polluted and unhygienic nature of the environment, meant that disease spread quickly and life in a city could be far more dangerous than in the countryside. Rates of death remained high in the medieval and early modern periods. Thomas E. Jordan has examined the quality of life in seventeenth-century Dublin by looking at extant parish records of births, deaths and marriages, and the work of contemporaries such as William Petty who made their own estimates on city mortality. Jordan has found that although 'not every birth and death was recorded in the accounts of the vestry … it is evident that the parish-born population was not replacing itself through births, although it was expanding.'[12] This population decline can be linked in part to successive wars that occurred in the seventeenth century while the expansion can be explained by the arrival of settlers from other parts of Ireland and from England. While war was one way in which Dubliners lost their lives, disease, illness and accidents also took many lives in the early modern city. Survival was particularly difficult for children. Jordan has found 'mortality after birth has historically been greatest to age five years' but life expectancy improved dramatically after this.[13] The very act of childbirth was dangerous for women and mortality rates among mothers remained high as well. Philomena Gorey's essay on puerperal fever, or 'childbed fever', reminds us how the very act of producing life could result in death.

Early modern Dubliners died from a variety of accidents and illnesses that their healthcare was not equipped to deal with. While individuals had to contend with everyday illnesses, epidemics could grind whole parishes to a halt. Fevers, smallpox and plagues travelled from parish to parish and affected whole communities. One early-nineteenth-century Dublin doctor believed that the flu struck in spring, while 'pestilential disease' was a midsummer illness, 'dysentery and cholera' hit in 'autumn, with typhus fever and malignant cholera occurring during both summer and autumn'.[14] These epidemics could leap social boundaries striking both the rich and poor, who often lived in close proximity to each other. While the wealthy could pay for doctors, surgeons and apothecaries, the poor often utilized 'empirics'.[15] These healers ranged in ability and their skills included setting bones and prescribing 'nostrums' and 'tonics'. Remedies were advertised in the Dublin press and boasted a range of healing abilities. They usually had a high alcoholic content with the rest of

---

12 Thomas E. Jordan, 'Quality of life in seventeenth-century Dublin', *Dublin Historical Record*, 61:2 (Autumn 2008), p. 148. 13 Ibid., pp 149–50. 14 Diarmuid Ó Gráda, *Georgian Dublin: the forces that shaped the city* (Cork, 2015), p. 147. 15 Jordan, 'Quality of life in seventeenth-century Dublin', p. 143.

their dubious and even dangerous ingredients remaining a secret to the general public.[16] Part of the difficulty was that doctors and authorities did not understand how these diseases were spread. The theory of contagion was not accepted and many believed illnesses were spread by bad air, not by people themselves.[17]

City hygiene was a huge problem for parish and civic authorities. They attempted to regulate the disposal of waste by appointing a city scavenger who was responsible for the removal of rubbish, but it remained a major problem throughout the early modern period. Commercial activity took place alongside ordinary dwellings and Dublin supported a wide range of noxious industries from tanneries and slaughterhouses to brick and glass factories. All of these industries created by-products that polluted both air and water in their neighbourhoods. City residents were also responsible for the creation of unhygienic waste. Household rubbish, including sewage, was dumped on the streets and in back gardens: 'Mounds of muck filled up backyards and alleyways. Congested districts had no sewerage system and their water was rotten'.[18] Dunghills developed that were so sizeable they were noted on maps. John Rocque's 1756 map of the city shows four sizeable rubbish piles behind Dunghill Lane and Dirty Lane, off Thomas Street (see fig. 2).[19]

Hospitals, in the modern sense of places where people go to be cured, did not exist for most of the early modern period. The Royal Hospital at Kilmainham, for instance, was completed in 1684 and its purpose was to provide a home for retired soldiers. Throughout the eighteenth century, the number of city hospitals increased but they often functioned as places where the sick and poor went to die. The Foundling Hospital opened its doors in Dublin in 1704. It acted as an orphanage rather than a children's hospital. The Charitable Infirmary opened in 1721 in Cook Street and later moved to Jervis Street.[20] Dr Steeven's Hospital, which opened in 1733, was the first Irish hospital in the modern sense, a place where people went for medical treatment.[21] St Patrick's Hospital was established in 1746 to treat psychiatric patients, being founded and supported through a bequest from Jonathan Swift. These two institutions quickly found that their facilities were inadequate and they could not support the large number of people being referred to them. The Richmond Lunatic Asylum followed a century later and was opened in 1815 in an attempt to meet this demand. Psychiatric care was rudimentary and 'it

---

16 Ó Gráda, *Georgian Dublin*, p. 147.   17 Ibid.   18 Ibid.   19 Ibid., p. 152.   20 Maurice Craig, *Dublin, 1660–1860* (Dublin, 2006), p. 162.   21 Ibid.

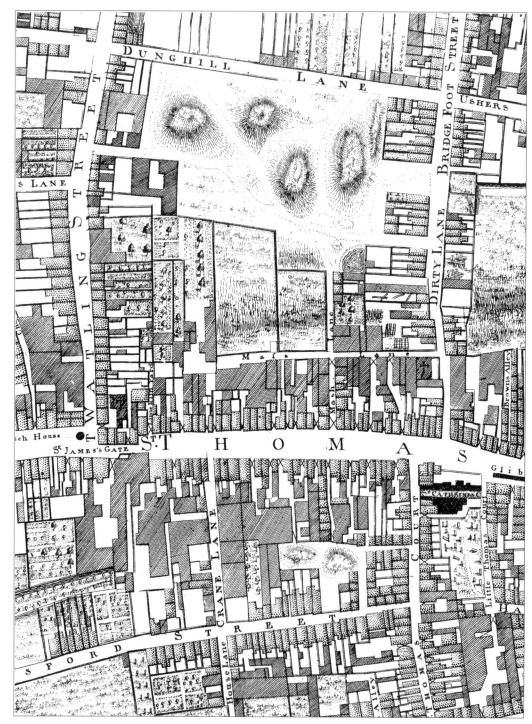

2 Detail of John Rocque map, 1756, showing rubbish mounds in the city. Large dumps developed in the city and could be located in close proximity to residential areas. Waste disposal was a huge problem and caused or worsened epidemics when they broke out (reproduced courtesy of Joe Brady).

employed physical restraints such as straitjackets and solitary confinement in dark cells'.[22] The city Locke Hospital was where Dubliners with venereal disease could go to be treated but they too were incarcerated during this treatment. The Dublin Lying-In Hospital (the Rotunda) was founded by Bartholomew Mosse in 1745 and it moved to its current site in 1757. It was the first maternity hospital in Britain and Ireland and was pioneering in its attempts to improve conditions for pregnant women, and to assist them during labour.[23] By the early nineteenth century, a more effective network of institutions was emerging to treat Dublin's sick. The Cork Street Fever Hospital opened in 1804 in the densely populated Liberties, to contain epidemics and outbreaks. Other institutions followed and with the enactment of the poor law in 1838, and the creation of the Poor Law Unions, there were more medical facilities for Dublin's poor. Despite the growing number of these institutions throughout the early modern period and into the nineteenth century, death would have taken place at home for most people, not in a hospital.

While medical knowledge was poor, Dublin had a large number of anatomy schools and was making a contribution to the expanding medical field. There was a medical school in Trinity College Dublin. The Royal College of Physicians of Ireland was founded in 1654 while the Royal College of Surgeons in Ireland was established in 1784 in Dublin. Medical and anatomy schools needed bodies to practice on and while government legislation supported this work by providing the corpses of executed criminals, this supply could not meet demand. 'Resurrection men' or 'sack-em-ups' stole corpses from graves in 'Donnybrook, Merrion, Kilgobbin, Cruagh near Rockbrook, Kill-o'-the-Grange, Drumcondra, Kilbarrack and Killester, as well as Glasnevin, the city churchyards of St James and St Andrew, and, of course, chiefly from the paupers' burial ground, the Bully's Acre at Kilmainham'.[24] There are reports of dissected body parts being disposed of on city dunghills.[25] In Dublin death, and its aftereffects, were a part of daily life.

Dublin grave robbers were so prolific that they exported bodies to medical schools in England and Scotland. Robert Knox, the doctor at the centre of the notorious Burke and Hare killings, spoke of importing bodies for dissection from Ireland.[26] Efforts to protect bodies were taken by families, some of whom sat by the graves in the early days of interment. Wealthier Dubliners could

22 Ó Gráda, *Georgian Dublin*, p. 162. **23** Craig, *Dublin, 1660–1860*, p. 122. **24** A.C.B. Hooper, 'Dublin anatomy in the 17th and 18th centuries', *Dublin Historical Record*, 40:4 (Sept. 1987), pp 130–1. **25** Ó Gráda, *Georgian Dublin*, p. 152. **26** John F. Fleetwood, 'The Dublin body snatchers: part two',

afford better protection and 'many pre-1832 graves are covered by heavy stone slabs, Drumcondra churchyard has a mortsafe, while the watch-towers at Cruagh and Glasnevin were functional rather than decorative.'[27] Body snatching remained a problem until the Anatomy Act of 1832, which allowed anatomy schools to use donated bodies.[28]

Death was something that the state could inflict as a penalty, a person's life being the ultimate price they could pay. Courts dealt harshly with those accused of theft of private property, in the hopes that severe punishment would act as a deterrent; the death penalty could be imposed for theft of goods to the value of £5. Executions were carried out on a Saturday and were common sights on the streets of Dublin. Hamilton captured the image of criminals on their way to the gallows in one of his street sketches. These executions were a form of entertainment for Dubliners, an indication of attitudes towards death at the time. The executions were usually preceded by a public confession, or speech, which justified the correctness of the sentence, or which highlighted the precarious nature of eighteenth-century justice. This may have been the attraction for many people and, just as we are drawn to crime stories and mystery dramas today, crowds flocked to these executions to be reminded that justice worked or that the city was being made safer. James Kelly's *Gallows speeches from eighteenth-century Ireland* brings together the printed confessions and speeches of criminals who were executed in this period and highlights the allure which these executions had for ordinary Dubliners.[29]

As the political capital of Ireland, executions of political prisoners usually occurred in Dublin. This was established from early in the colony's history. Images from the Tudor re-conquest of Ireland show the heads of executed Gaelic rebels on spikes outside Dublin Castle (see fig. 3). This was a clear political statement to the citizens of Dublin and a reminder of what the consequences of rebellion would be. This message was replayed numerous times in the city's history. In 1803, Robert Emmet was executed in a very public manner outside St Catherine's Church on Thomas Street. Images from the time show a large and unruly crowd attending the grisly event. The last political prisoners to be executed publicly were members of the Invincibles, a radical Fenian group charged with the assassination of the chief secretary and under secretary of Ireland in 1882. This public execution took place outside

Dublin Historical Record, 42:2 (Mar. 1989), p. 51.   **27** Hooper, 'Dublin anatomy in the 17th and 18th centuries', pp 130–1.   **28** Ibid.   **29** James Kelly, *Gallows speeches from eighteenth-century Ireland* (Dublin, 2001).

3 Sir Henry Sidney, lord deputy of Ireland, rides through the gates of Dublin Castle past the heads of executed Gaelic rebels, *c.*1580 (from John Derricke *Image of Ireland*).

Kilmainham Gaol where large groups gathered to watch the spectacle. While the British government began to question the effectiveness of these public executions, they continued to execute political criminals behind prison walls until the end of the War of Independence. (For more recent changes in attitude, see Ian Miller's essay in this volume on the twentieth-century campaign to abolish hanging.)

* * *

What did people die of, where did they die, how and where were they buried?; these same questions regarding death and dying produce different answers as we move into the nineteenth and twentieth centuries. In the modern period, changes in popular practices were matched by changing attitudes towards death, as medicine increasingly won the battle (but not the war) against mortality. New landscapes of death developed, as burial grounds surrounding the old city churches filled up and modern cemeteries were laid out. Memorials to those who died on military service overseas became more common. Erected by the friends and families of the fallen, these plaques and stained glass windows were reminders of Dublin's link to imperial and global affairs (see Paul Huddie's essay on Dublin's Crimean War memorials). As the nineteenth century progressed, the spread of the suburbs presented challenges and opportunities for bereaved families, and for those selling services to them. The role of the state expanded, with deaths being officially recorded under the Births and Deaths Registration Act (Ireland), 1863.[30] Even ancient sectarian tensions, usually hidden beneath a veneer of civility in Dublin, underwent profound changes as burial became more open and democratic.

Dublin's overcrowded tenements were renowned for their squalor. Through the nineteenth century the city's poor still died from the same diseases as they had a hundred years before. Mortality statistics record deaths from zymotic, gastric and bronchial ailments but, essentially, they were diseases of poverty and neglect. The failure to tackle problems in the city's water supply and sanitation services lay behind these deaths, as did the municipal council's inability to enforce proper housing regulations. In the 1880s, death was more prevalent in Dublin than in any other city of the United Kingdom. The average number of deaths per thousand of Dublin's population for the ten years to 1888 was 28.8, higher than that of the great crowded industrial centres of Manchester and Glasgow and even London. Dublin had the highest infant mortality rates in the kingdom, and it was the poorest citizens who suffered the worst.[31] But advances were being made: the opening of the Vartry reservoir supply in 1868 removed a serious threat to public health in the city centre, and from the mid-1880s the new reservoir at Bohernabreena supplied the large population of Rathmines and Rathgar township with clean water. The process of rehousing the tenement-dwellers took decades; philanthropic organizations such as the Iveagh Trust, the Dublin Artisans' Dwelling Company and the Alexandra College Guild joined the municipal council in building workers' cottages and flats. These advances gradually reduced the mortality figures, but poverty could still kill. People died in 1907 and 1913 when houses collapsed from sheer decay, and as late as 1902 an outbreak of smallpox killed thirty-three Dubliners. In this instance the city was better equipped to respond to a health crisis, and the alarmed municipal council built an emergency isolation hospital out by the Pigeon House. By quickly closing up infected houses and putting the families of the sick into quarantine,

---

30 This initial act (26 & 27 Vict. c. 11) was revised by the Births and Deaths Registration Act (Ireland), 1880 (43 & 44 Vict. c. 13) and a series of subsequent acts: the Registration of Births and Deaths Act, 1936; the Vital Statistics and Births, Deaths and Marriages Registration Act, 1952; and the Births, Deaths and Marriages Registration Act, 1972.   **31** Thomas Wrigley Grimshaw, 'Child mortality in Dublin', *Journal of the Statistical and Social Inquiry Society of Ireland*, 9 Appendix (1889), pp 1–19, tables iii, vii, viii.

the council prevented a serious epidemic on the scale of those seen in London and Liverpool that year.[32] Some causes of death were harder to defeat. The national scourge of tuberculosis would require an intensive state effort before it was brought under control, but nothing could stop the terrifying sweep of the Spanish flu through the city in 1919 (see pp 61–76 for Ida Milne's essay on the Spanish flu pandemic of 1918–19).

International scientific developments resulted in more hygienic hospitals, and fewer deaths from infection meant that the public came to regard hospitals more favourably (see pp 46–60, Philomena Gorey's essay on Puerperal Fever in Dublin's Rotunda Hospital). The success of hospitals in combatting disease produced an interesting change in where people actually died. As hospitals were increasingly able to cure serious ailments, people were more likely to turn to them in their final illness. It became more common, when the inevitable did happen, for people to die in hospital rather than at home. To an extent this removed death from the domestic sphere, and, gradually, the need for a local woman to prepare the body, and the opportunity to wake the deceased in their own home, decreased. As one type of death receded during the twentieth century, newer ways of dying become more common. Sudden deaths due to motor accidents or drug-addiction,[33] or slower deaths from coronary disease or obesity, became phenomena of the modern age.

A forgotten feature of death and burial up to the 1820s was the legal prohibition on Catholic clergy saying funeral prayers in churchyards. Catholics, and all non-Anglican congregations across the United Kingdom, were obliged to bury their dead in parish graveyards belonging to the established church; there were no Catholic graveyards. The Anglican Church of Ireland administered Dublin's parish burial grounds and all burials, of whatever denomination, paid a fee to the local minister. With goodwill and discretion Catholic interments could be conducted – the priest wearing ordinary clothes and the vicar turning a blind eye. As Daniel O'Connell's campaign for Catholic emancipation gained strength, however, some Dublin Protestants became alarmed and sought to enforce the letter of the law. On

32 Ciarán Wallace, 'Feverish activity: Dublin City Council and the smallpox outbreak of 1902–3' in D.S. Lucey & V. Crossman (eds), *Healthcare in Ireland and Britain, 1850–1970: voluntary, regional and comparative perspectives* (London, 2015), pp 199–216. **33** The average number of deaths due to road accidents in Dublin between 2009 and 2014 was 20: the Road Safety Authority, *Deaths on Irish roads*, http://www.rsa.ie/en/RSA/Road-Safety/Our-Research/Deaths-injuries-on-Irish-roads/, accessed 12 Feb. 2016. Deaths related to drug use averaged 178 in the Dublin region for the five years to 2013. Health Research Board, *Drug-related deaths and deaths among drug users in Ireland: 2013 figures from the national*

9 September 1823, the funeral of a prominent Catholic merchant took place in St Kevin's Graveyard off Camden Street. Proceedings were interrupted when the Protestant sexton instructed the Catholic clergyman to cease offering the graveside prayers. In the heated sectarian and political atmosphere of the time, the sexton's offensive and insensitive action – and the law which he sought to enforce – became the subjects of press comment and parliamentary debate.[34] Further obstruction of Catholic burial rites kept public attention on the issue. In September 1823, in an early reference to a future transformation in Dublin's burial practices, O'Connell insisted that there was no legal obstacle to Catholics establishing their own cemeteries.[35] To ease tensions, parliament repealed an old statute preventing Catholics from burying their dead in suppressed monasteries,[36] but by introducing the Easement of Burials Bill (1824) they actually introduced restrictions where, O'Connell argued, none had existed.[37] The situation would not be resolved until 1828 when O'Connell's Catholic Association established a special committee, and loaned £600, to purchase land for a new cemetery at Goldenbridge. It is interesting to note that its origins involved the help of a Protestant supporter:

> Several overtures for land had been made and failed, until at last, at the instance of Mathias O Kelly, a kindly Protestant took the matter in hand … A tract of land near Kilmainham, over-looking the Phoenix Park, close to the Richmond Barracks, in the suburbs of Dublin, and situated on a rising ground, near the south side of the Liffey, was secured.[38]

A new era in Dublin burials had begun; the success of Goldenbridge prompted the purchase of extensive lands beyond the city boundary in Glasnevin, where the first burials took place in 1832. Within a few decades the cemeteries were producing a substantial profit, which resulted in the dead funding the living; as a charitable trust the cemeteries' governing committee dispensed grants to dozens of Catholic schools around the city. In 1867, for example, its total donations came to £1,010, the equivalent of €1,118,000 in today's values (see fig. 8).[39]

drug-related deaths index (Dublin, 2015).   **34** John A. Murphy & Clíona Murphy, 'Burials and bigotry in early nineteenth-century', *Studia Hibernica*, 33 (2004/5), pp 125–46.   **35** *Dublin Evening Post*, 20 Sept. 1823, as cited in Murphy & Murphy, 'Burials and bigotry', p. 128, n. 11.   **36** Removing this law (9 Wm III, c. 7) did little to address the wider problem.   **37** Easement of Burials Bill (1824) (5 Geo IV c. 25); Murphy & Murphy, 'Burials and bigotry', p. 138.   **38** H.J. Fitzpatrick, *History of the Dublin Catholic cemeteries* (Dublin, 1900), p. 14.   **39** Current values calculated on measuringworth.com, accessed 26 Feb 2016. Grants to reformatories, orphanages and homes for the deaf and blind are also listed.

4 Engraving of O'Connell's tomb in its completed form, surrounded by images of the round tower, Celtic cross and harp – essential nationalist iconography. The presence of such a significant burial attracted many visitors to Glasnevin, and encouraged the Catholic elite of the city to choose the cemetery for their own burials (reproduced courtesy of Glasnevin Trust).

This major development coincided with wider national and international trends in burial practices. Following the opening of Père Lachaise Cemetery in Paris in 1804, with its influential 'picturesque' style, a series of extensive city cemeteries opened across the United Kingdom. The Rosary Cemetery in Norwich (1819) was Britain's first interdenominational burial ground; Manchester's Chorlton Row Cemetery (1821) and Low Hill Cemetery in Liverpool (1825) also catered for the diverse religious populations of their growing cities. Established by philanthropists, they served a social need, but as joint stock companies they also produced a profit for their founders. During the 1830s, Birmingham, Newcastle, Sheffield, York and Leeds all opened large urban cemeteries, London established six in this one decade.[40] The dominant

40 https:// darlingtonhistoricalsociety. wordpress.com/general-information/the-historic-development-of-cemeteries-in-england/, accessed 15 Feb. 2016.

style was the garden cemetery, a layout that was so popular that we now regard it as the quintessential Victorian cemetery. Graves were laid out in numbered rows and named sections, enabling mourners to easily locate any plot. Wide and well paved paths were lined by sombre evergreen trees, their geometric patterns creating interesting vistas with dignified memorials as their focal points. These cemeteries aimed to create an atmosphere of mourning and reflection, but they were also part of the public parks movement, providing open spaces for appropriately regulated recreation.[41] A leading commentator of the day described the garden cemetery as 'the most convincing token of a nation's progress in civilization and the arts'.[42] Such cemeteries were, he argued, 'not only beneficial to public morals, to the improvement of manners, but are likewise calculated to extend virtuous and generous feelings'.[43]

Dublin's garden cemeteries emerged as part of these trends in sectarian relations and landscape design. Goldenbridge Cemetery's wide circular path inside its perimeter wall, central neo-classical temple and numbered rows make it an early Irish example of the type. The success of this first effort produced Dublin's largest garden cemetery, at Glasnevin. By resolving the sectarian tensions of the earlier period, and creating an architectural parkland for the expanding city, Glasnevin Cemetery was a model of garden cemetery design. It had all the essential features – watch towers, a grid layout and evergreen trees, as recommended by John Claudius Loudon, perhaps the most prolific garden and cemetery designer of the Victorian age.[44] The original entrance on Prospect Square had a gate lodge, an essential feature of a proper garden cemetery in Loudon's opinion. The new entrance on Finglas Road opened in 1879 and the designers included a new lodge and chapel, additional pathways arranged in an appealing pattern, and the O'Connell Tower, surely the most striking focal point of any cemetery vista. Intended as the burial place of nationalist Ireland's most prominent figures, Glasnevin became the stage for many important public funerals from that of O'Connell himself, to Charles Stewart Parnell, Jeremiah O'Donovan Rossa and Michael Collins (see figs 4 and 6). (For an examination of Irish military funerals see James McCafferty's essay on the Niemba funerals, pp 86–93.)

41 James Stevens Curl, 'John Claudius Loudon and the Garden Cemetery Movement', _Garden History_, 11:2 (Autumn 1983), pp 133–56. **42** John Strang, _Necropolis Glasguensis: with observations on ancient and modern tombs and sepulture_ (Glasgow, 1831), p. 62. **43** Ibid., p. 58. **44** J.C. Loudon, _The gardener's magazine_ (1842), p. 666. Although he was writing after the Anatomy Act (1832), which ended the scourge of grave-robbing, Loudon had dealt with Scottish cemeteries which needed to guard against 'Resurrection Men' who supplied Edinburgh's prestigious medical schools with cadavers.

THE GLASNEVIN SHYLOCK, OR THE POUND OF FLESH.

PORTIA—"Can no prayers pierce thee? for thy desires are wolfish, bloody, starved and ravenous."
SHYLOCK—"No, none that thou hast wit enough to make; till thou canst rail the seal from off my bond thou but offend'st thy
lungs to speak so loud."—*Merchant of Venice, Act iv; Scene 1.*

5 Cartoon from *The Leprechaun Cartoon Monthly* criticizing the cost of burial which was
imposed on poor communities by Glasnevin Trust. The cemetery board is depicted as
Shylock from Shakespeare's *Merchant of Venice*. The cartoon appeared in the magazine in
September 1909 (reproduced courtesy of the Board of Trinity College Dublin, the
University of Dublin).

It is also the site of many public memorials, but commemoration can be
controversial. In northern France the new Ring of Remembrance lists all the
soldiers – of whichever army – who fell in the region between 1914 and 1918.
Whether in Europe or Dublin, remembering former combatants on a shared
memorial is a challenging idea; the Necrology Wall unveiled at Glasnevin
Cemetery in April 2016 does just this. It records all those killed during the
fighting of Easter Week 1916, civilians and those who served with rebel units
or crown forces, grouping them by the date they died. Dublin has witnessed
many changes in the style of memorials, often inspired by developments
abroad; it will be interesting to see how the public respond to this latest
innovation.

Mount Jerome Cemetery, on the south side of the city, opened in 1836,
with almost a hundred shareholders subscribing £12,000. Established as a

6 Parnell's funeral crossing O'Connell Bridge, 11 October 1891. Like O'Connell's funeral before it, Parnell's cortège took a circuitous route through the city, allowing vast numbers to witness the spectacle (reproduced courtesy of Glasnevin Trust).

non-denominational cemetery it contains 250,000 burials in forty-eight acres, the majority of its nineteenth- and early twentieth-century interments being Protestant. This reflects the particular local interpretation of 'non-denominational' in Victorian Dublin; Glasnevin was commonly seen as non-denominational but really for Catholics and Mount Jerome as non-denominational but meant for Protestants.[45] With fewer trees, the garden element is perhaps less pronounced at Mount Jerome, but its formal pathways and impressive range of tombs and statuary create the required mournful and morally uplifting atmosphere. Deansgrange Cemetery opened in 1865. Established by Rathdown Poor Law Union, its tree-lined walkways and gate

45 Mount Jerome website. http://www.mountjerome.ie/?content=history, accessed 12 Feb. 2016.

lodge marked it as a garden cemetery, but its separate areas for Catholic and Protestant burials reflected the social concerns of the time.[46]

Moving burials from the inner city neighbourhoods to the outer suburbs of Glasnevin, Harold's Cross for Mount Jerome and Deansgrange near Monkstown, made the services of a funeral director or undertaker essential. As far back as 1819, elite funerals had involved professional arrangers, with cabinetmakers and upholsterers providing superior coffins, black drapery and theatrical staging.[47] With the advent of garden cemeteries, however, the general population needed professional assistance, and full-time commercial undertakers emerged to meet this demand. Arranging suitably dignified transportation for the coffin and mourners was the primary concern, but undertakers' services gradually expanded to include dealing with the payments and paperwork at the church and cemetery, arranging for flowers, organists, newspaper announcements and memorial cards. (See Appendix 3 on Nichols' Funeral Home.) Of course not all Dubliners could afford such dignified ceremonials, and a public controversy arose between the municipal council and Glasnevin Trust over its policy on burying the poor. Following initial complaints in 1901 about the high cost of burial and limited opening hours, by 1909 the criticism had widened to the overall management of Glasnevin Cemetery.[48] With presumably unintended humour, city councillors complained of the 'grave hardship' that this imposed on the poor and called for elected representatives to be appointed to the Trust.[49] Dublin's Poor Law Unions, its nationalist members of parliament and the emerging Sinn Féin movement all called for reform.[50] A cartoon from the time illustrates popular attitudes towards the cemetery's policies (fig. 5). Briefly, the possibility of establishing a municipal cemetery was discussed, but the dispute fizzled out with the start of the Great War in August 1914.[51]

Into the twentieth century the effort and expense involved in maintaining garden cemeteries led to the development of the lawn cemetery. The regular

---

46 Belfast City Cemetery (1869), a classic garden cemetery in all other respects, carried this concern further by constructing a sunken wall separating Protestant and Catholic burials. Belfast City Council, *Cemeteries of Belfast* (Belfast, 2006), p. 4.　**47** See the description of the elaborate funeral of Frances Thomasina, wife of the Viceroy Earl Talbot, at the Chapel Royal in Dublin Castle. Angela Alexander, 'Cabinetmaking, upholstering and undertaking at the viceregal court' in M. Campbell & W. Derham (eds), *The Chapel Royal, Dublin Castle: an architectural history* (Dublin, 2015), pp 71–82.　**48** Newspaper accounts of a coffin being left abandoned outside the gates, and public unease at common-plot burials were discussed at council meetings. MC, 29 Jan. 1912, item 144.　**49** The cemetery's governing committee replied that its founding legislation did not allow for such representation, and that committee members had tenure for life. MC, 10 May 1909, item 360.　**50** MC, 9 Aug. 1909, item 519.　**51** MC, 8 May 1911, item 396.

7 Unveiling of the O'Sullivan monument in Glasnevin Cemetery, *c.*1890s
(reproduced courtesy of Glasnevin Trust).

rows of uniform headstones above graves planted with manicured grass reflect, perhaps, the great military cemeteries in Europe following the two world wars. The visual impact is quite different from the garden cemetery, and only a motorized lawn-mower is required to keep it in good order. Newlands Cross, Dardistown, St Fintan's, Bohernabreena, Saggart and Esker are examples of this arrangement in Dublin, but the city's bereaved families do not always conform to the designer's minimalist layout. Harking back to the earlier garden cemetery, some families continue to place surrounds, plants and memorabilia on the graves. Just as the novelty of the garden cemetery layout must have seemed strange to a population used to crowded medieval graveyards, so the lawn cemetery has taken time to become established as the norm.

Daily life is affected by technological developments; in a similar fashion death and the commercial practices surrounding it have moved with the times. Studio photography was a popular novelty in late Victorian and Edwardian Dublin, but taking a formal post-mortem portrait of a loved one may strike the modern reader as macabre. Orla Fitzpatrick's essay on this short-lived practice reveals that even in death, modernity makes itself felt. Arguably the most significant change in funerary customs in recent decades has been the introduction of cremation. Glasnevin began offering the cheaper option of cremation in 1982, additional crematoria opened at Newlands Cross and Mount Jerome in 2000, Dardistown crematorium will open in 2016. With this new practice came memorial urns for the ashes of the deceased, the columbarium wall for memorial plaques and a quite different final ceremony at the crematorium chapel. Instead of standing by an open grave as the coffin is lowered into the earth, mourners sit in a crematorium chapel (or temple, as one cemetery describes it) for a short ceremony of prayers or reflections which ends with the coffin being gradually veiled from view, or lowered into the catafalque. The business of death continues to change. Just as the tranquility of nature played a part in nineteenth-century cemeteries' advertising, so today Mount Jerome promotes its environmentally friendly crematorium with its low carbon footprint, where heat and waste metals from the cremation process are recycled.[52] Another recent change is the decline of the removal, the practice of removing the coffin from the hospital or family home to the church the night before the funeral. In a short ceremony, usually held in the early evening, the remains were welcomed into the church while friends, neighbours and workmates could offer their condolences to the family. Typically, closer friends and relatives would also attend the funeral ceremony the following morning, with immediate family following the hearse to the cemetery and the actual interment. The removal, once universal in the city, is now a rare occurrence; this has changed the undertakers' standard business model, reducing the amount of attendance and transportation required.[53]

* * *

52 http://www.mountjerome.ie/?content=most-environmentally-friendly-irish-crematorium, accessed 13 Feb. 2016.   **53** Nichols' Undertakers estimated that, in 2016, perhaps 10% of their funerals involved a removal.

CATHOLIC CEMETERIES' COMMITTEE.

LIST OF GRANTS

Made by the Committee of the Dublin Catholic Cemeteries' to Charitable Educational Institutions.

1865.

	£	s.	d.
Reformatory, Glencree	25	0	0
Christian Brothers' Schools, Richmond-street	40	0	0
Christian Brothers' Schools, Westland-row	15	0	0
Christian Brothers' Schools, St. Lawrence O'Toole	15	0	0
Christian Brothers' Schools, Francis-street	15	0	0
Christian Brothers' Schools, Synge-street	15	0	0
St. Vincent de Paul Male Orphanage, Glasnevin	35	0	0
The Daily Poor Schools of Sisters of Charity, North William-street	10	0	0
St. Joseph's Female Orphanage, Wellington-street	6	0	0
Stanhope-street Industrial School	30	0	0
St. Peter's Schools, Philsborough	20	0	0
St. Paul's Schools	20	0	0
St. Catherine's Schools	20	0	0
St. Audoen's Schools	15	0	0
Sisters of Mercy Schools, Baggot-street	25	0	0
Sisters of Charity Schools, Upper Gardiner-street	30	0	0
Dormitory School, Townsend-street	10	0	0
St. Mary's Schools, Harold's-cross	10	0	0
Golden-bridge Reformatory, under Sisters of Mercy	10	0	0
Reformatory, High-park	10	0	0
Male Blind Asylum, Glasnevin	10	0	0
Female Blind Asylum, Portobello	10	0	0
King's Inns-street Schools, per Mrs. Barrett	30	0	0
St. Patrick's Schools, Lower Mecklenburgh-street	15	0	0
St. Clare's Convent Schools, Harold's-cross	30	0	0
George's-hill Convent Schools	30	0	0
Sisters of Mercy, Golden-bridge, for Industrial Schools	20	0	0
St. Joseph's Industrial School, per Mrs. Woodlock	30	0	0
Whitefriar-street Schools	10	0	0
Lakelands Convent Schools	10	0	0
Deaf and Dumb, Cabra	20	0	0
Fairview and Glasnevin Schools, per Rev. Mr. Rooney, P.P.	20	0	0
St. Michan's Schools	10	0	0
Church-street Schools	15	0	0
Tranquilla Convent Schools, Rathmines	16	0	0
St. Bridgid's Five Catholic Schools	50	0	0
Warrenmount Convent Schools	25	0	0
SS. Michael and John's Schools	10	0	0
St. James's Schools	15	0	0
Orphanage of Mary Immaculate, Inchicore	10	0	0
£762	**0**	**0**	

1866.

	£	s.	d.
Reformatory, Glencree	21	10	0
Christian Brothers' Schools, Richmond-street	34	15	0
Christian Brothers' Schools, St. Lawrence O'Toole	12	18	0
Christian Brothers' Schools, Westland-row	12	18	0
Christian Brothers' Schools, Francis-street	12	18	0
Christian Brothers' Schools, Synge-street	12	18	0
St. Vincent de Paul Male Orphanage, Glasnevin	30	0	0
The Daily Poor Schools of the Sisters of Charity, North William-street	8	12	0
St. Joseph's Female Orphanage, Wellington-street	5	4	0
Stanhope-street Industrial Schools	25	16	0
St. Peter's Schools, Philsborough	17	4	0
St. Paul's Schools	17	4	0
St. Catherine's Schools	17	4	0
St. Audoen's Schools	12	18	0
Sisters of Mercy Schools, Baggot-street	21	10	0
Sisters of Charity Schools, Upper Gardiner-street	25	16	0
St. Catherine's Orphanage	25	0	0
St. Mary's Schools, Harold's-cross	8	12	0
Golden-bridge Reformatory, under Sisters of Mercy	8	12	0
Reformatory, High-park	8	12	0
Male Blind Asylum, Glasnevin	8	12	0
Female Blind Asylum, Portobello	8	12	0
King's Inns-street Schools, under Sisters of Charity	25	16	0
St. Patrick's Schools, Lower Mecklenburgh-street	12	18	0
St. Clare's Convent Schools, Harold's-cross	25	16	0
George's-hill Convent Schools	25	16	0
Sisters of Mercy, Golden-bridge, for Industrial Schools	17	4	0
St. Joseph's Industrial School, per Mrs. Woodlock	25	16	0
Whitefriar-street Schools	8	12	0
Lakelands Convent Schools	8	12	0
Deaf and Dumb, Cabra	17	4	0
Fairview and Glasnevin Schools, per Rev. M. Rooney, P.P.	17	4	0
St. Michan's Schools	8	12	0
Church-street Schools	12	18	0
Tranquilla Convent Schools, Rathmines	13	14	0
St. Bridgid's Five Catholic Schools	43	1	0
Warrenmount Convent Schools	21	10	0
SS. Michael and John's Schools	8	12	0
St. James's Schools	12	18	0
Orphanage of Mary Immaculate, Inchicore	8	12	0
£672	**0**	**0**	

1867.

	£	s.	d.
Christian Brothers' Schools, Richmond-street	40	0	0
Christian Brothers' Schools, St. Lawrence O'Toole	20	0	0
Christian Brothers' Schools, Westland-row	20	0	0
Christian Brothers' Schools, Francis-street	20	0	0
Christian Brothers' Schools, Synge-street	20	0	0
Christian Brothers' Schools, St. Mary's-place, Dorset-street	20	0	0
St. Vincent de Paul Male Orphanage, Glasnevin	40	0	0
St. Vincent de Paul Female Orphanage, North William-street	20	0	0
Stanhope-street Industrial Schools	40	0	0
Presentation Convent Schools, Roundtown	20	0	0
St. Patrick's Schools, Mecklenburgh-street	20	0	0
St. Peter's Schools, Philsborough	20	0	0
St. Catherine's Male and Female Schools, Meath-st.	30	0	0
St. Joseph's Industrial School	30	0	0
St. Paul's Schools	25	0	0
St. Audoen's Schools	20	0	0
SS. Michael and John's Schools	25	0	0
Sisters of Mercy Schools, Baggot-street	30	0	0
Sisters of Charity Schools, Upper Gardiner-street	30	0	0
King's Inns-street Schools, per Mrs. Barrett	30	0	0
St. Catherine's Orphanage	30	0	0
St. Mary's School, Harold's-cross	12	0	0
St. Clare's Orphanage, Harold's-cross	33	0	0
Reformatory, High-park	20	0	0
George's-hill Convent Schools	30	0	0
Orphanage of Mary Immaculate, Inchicore	10	0	0
St. Michan's Schools	20	0	0
The Daily Poor Schools of Sisters of Charity, North William-street	10	0	0
Sisters of Mercy, Golden-bridge Reformatory	30	0	0
Whitefriar-street Schools	20	0	0
Fairview and Glasnevin Schools	30	0	0
St. Bridgid's Five Catholic Schools	50	0	0
St. James's Schools	25	0	0
Warrenmount Convent Schools	23	0	0
Tranquilla Convent Schools	15	0	0
Female Blind Asylum, Merrion	15	0	0
Male Blind Asylum, Glasnevin	10	0	0
Deaf and Dumb, Cabra	20	0	0
Lakelands Convent Schools	22	0	0
St. Lawrence O'Toole's Female Poor Schools	20	0	0
Schools of Oblate Fathers, Inchicore	20	0	0
Church-street Schools	15	0	0
St. Joseph's Female Orphanage, Wellington-street	10	0	0
£1,010	**0**	**0**	

C. COYLE, Secretary.

DUBLIN CATHOLIC CEMETERIES OFFICE,
7, Lower Ormond-quay.

8 The dead aiding the living – of all denominations. List of grants made by the Catholic Cemeteries' Committee to a wide range of schools, charities and other institutions throughout the city between 1865 and 1867 (reproduced courtesy of Glasnevin Trust).

As a theme for research, death is universal in its relevance and wide-ranging in its ramifications. Across the centuries, at whatever age or walk of life, people have lived with the anticipation and reality of death. It touches science, art, commerce and politics; try as we may to avoid it death is always there somewhere in the background. (See Patricia Bedlow's appendix on the research potential of the Glasnevin Trust minute books.) As they age, graveyards and cemeteries become historical resources in their own right; the graves of prominent political and cultural figures attract significant numbers of tourists and school groups. Today, all major burial grounds must welcome the tourist and educate the public, while accommodating burials and facilitating mourners; this is especially true for Glasnevin Cemetery with its unofficial role as the 'national' cemetery. Siobhán Doyle's essay on the work of Glasnevin Cemetery Museum sets out the complexity of this challenge.

Cities provide a special stage for the performance of rituals of private grief and public commemoration. Here you are more likely to encounter aspects of dying, death and remembering on a daily basis, in city centre street names, suburban church bells or road fatalities. In a city as old as Dublin, with such a complex social and political history, the changes and continuities in attitudes and rituals around death are many and varied. This collection, therefore, cannot claim to be a comprehensive treatment of an almost limitless subject. As a cross-section of historical periods and academic approaches, we hope it will spark a wider interest in Dublin's and Dubliners' experiences of death and dying.

Puerperal fever in Dublin: the case of the Rotunda Lying-in Hospital

PHILOMENA GOREY

Puerperal, or childbed, fever was an illness of childbirth in which the uterus became infected, in most cases during labour, as a result of poor standards of hygiene facilitated by clinicians and the cross-contamination of organic matter or infection from one patient to another. The disease became evident with the onset of fever on the second or third day after delivery. The infection spread into the pelvic cavity, resulting in peritonitis and possibly septicaemia. There followed a period of illness during which the patient suffered intolerable abdominal pain. Death usually occurred from between three days to several weeks later.[1] The first recorded epidemic of puerperal fever occurred in Paris in 1746, where the disease proved 'more fatal to those in hospital than to those who were delivered in their own houses'.[2] In the lying-in ward of the renowned Paris hospital, the Hotel Dieu, of twenty women who were confined in February of that year, all but one died. By 1770 lying-in hospitals in the major cities in Europe – Paris, London, Dublin, Manchester, Edinburgh, Vienna and Lyon – had experienced maternal deaths due to puerperal fever.[3] With no knowledge of the origin of disease or the concept of cross-infection, medical men struggled to understand its cause and to halt its fatal effects.

This essay will discuss the incidence and treatment of puerperal fever at the Rotunda Lying-in Hospital in Dublin from the time it was first recorded at the hospital in December 1767, ten years after the facility opened for the reception of patients. It will examine the first initiatives to combat the disease which were taken by Joseph Clarke (Master, 1786–1793), followed by those of Samuel Labatt (1814–21), Robert Collins (1826–33) and Evory Kennedy (1833–40) who were the first Masters to witness annual epidemics and whose terms of office coincided with the debate that began in the early nineteenth century about public health and the contagiousness of disease. It will consider Evory Kennedy's call for closure of the hospital in 1867 as epidemics

1 Irvine Loudon, *Death in childbirth: an international study of maternal care and maternal mortality, 1800–1950* (Oxford, 1992), pp 53–6; Irvine Loudon, *The tragedy of childbed fever* (Oxford, 2000), p. 7.   2 *The Boston Medical and Surgical Journal*, 6 (Boston, 1832), p. 84; Fleetwood Churchill (ed.), *Essays on the puerperal fever and other diseases peculiar to women* (London, 1849), p. 5.   3 Churchill, *Essays*, pp 5–9.

continued to occur at alarming intervals. Finally, it will assess the hospital's response to the germ theory of disease and the aseptic revolution in the 1880s until the disease was finally eradicated with the introduction of the sulphonamide group of drugs in 1936.

An extensive canon of literature dates from the later eighteenth century when hospital physicians first began to record their observations in lying-in wards as puerperal fever occurred in epidemical form among their patients. By this time it was recognized as a separate, distinct disease confined to women in childbirth. John Clarke, lecturer in midwifery in St Bartholomew's Hospital in London, commented in 1793 that one of the first accounts of any epidemics in lying-in women could be found in the *Memoires de l'Academie Royale des Sciences* for the year 1746, which described the epidemic of puerperal fever which had occurred at the Hotel Dieu in Paris in 1745–6.[4] Physicians and teachers of midwifery such as Thomas Denman, Nathaniel Hulme, John Leake, Charles White and Alexander Gordon, who practiced in the major lying-in hospitals and dispensaries such as the City of London Lying-in Hospital, the Westminster Lying-in Hospital, the Manchester Infirmary and the Aberdeen Dispensary respectively, were among the first medical men to write essays and treatises on their observations and theories as to the cause of the disease.[5] In Dublin, Joseph Clarke, who was Master at the Rotunda between 1786 and 1793, was the first incumbent to record his observations and his endeavours to stem the disease.[6] Throughout the nineteenth century all midwifery texts included a chapter on contemporary theories and treatments of puerperal fever.[7] Medical journals were forums in which doctors put forward their theories on topics such as the causation, prevention and treatment of puerperal fever. The medical historian Irvine Loudon's definitive publications, *Death in childbirth. An international study of maternal care and maternal mortality, 1800–1950* and *The tragedy of childbed fever*, are judicious and comprehensive, providing a model for analysing maternal mortality and the role of intervention in pregnancy and labour. The history of the Rotunda has been recorded in a number of publications that

4 John Clarke, *Practical essays on the management of pregnancy and labour; and on the inflammatory and febrile diseases of lying-in women* (London, 1793), pp 103–5. **5** Thomas Denman, *An essay on the puerperal fever* (3rd ed., London, 1785); Nathaniel Hulme, *A treatise on the puerperal fever* (London, 1772); John Leake, *An introduction to the theory and practice of midwifery* (London, 1787); Charles White, *A treatise on the management of pregnant and lying-in women* (London, 1772); Alexander Gordon, *A treatise of the epidemic puerperal fever of Aberdeen* (London, 1795). **6** Joseph Clarke, 'Observations on puerperal fever; more especially as it has of late occurred in the lying-in hospital of Dublin' in Andrew Duncan (ed.), *Medical commentaries*, decade ii, vol. 5 (Edinburgh, 1791). **7** For example, Fleetwood Churchill, *On the diseases of*

LYING-IN HOSPITAL.

9 The Lying-in Hospital taken from Robert Pool and John Cash, *Views of the most remarkable public buildings, monuments and other edifices in the city of Dublin* (repr. Shannon, 1970).

locate the institution in the medical and social narrative of Dublin since its foundation in 1745.[8]

* * *

The Rotunda Lying-in Hospital holds a significant place in the development of obstetrics in the eighteenth and nineteenth centuries.[9] It was the largest lying-in hospital in the United Kingdom and, in European terms, fourth to the lying-in hospitals in Vienna, Paris and Moscow.[10] Records from the minutes of the board of governors meetings since 1745 are extant. As a charitable foundation where poor women were recommended by the churchwardens of

women (Dublin, 1847). **8** T.P.C. Kirkpatrick, *The book of the Rotunda Hospital* (London, 1913); O'Donel Browne, *The Rotunda Hospital* (Edinburgh, 1947); Ian Campbell Ross, *Public virtue, public love: early years of the Dublin Lying-in Hospital, the Rotunda* (Dublin, 1987); Alan Browne (ed.), *Masters, midwives and ladies-in-waiting: the Rotunda Hospital, 1745–1995* (Dublin, 1995). **9** Philomena Gorey, 'Managing midwifery in Dublin: practice and practitioners, 1700–1800' in Margaret M. Preston and Margaret Ó hÓgartaigh (eds), *Gender and medicine in Ireland, 1700–1950* (Syracuse, 2012), pp 123–37. **10** Denis Phelan, 'Observation on the comparative advantages of affording obstetric attendance on poor women in lying-in hospitals and in their own homes', reprinted from the *Dublin Quarterly Journal of Medical Science*

the surrounding parishes, it was supported by parliamentary grants. Hence, accounts of proceedings at the hospital since the granting of its charter in 1756 were a matter of public scrutiny. Rotunda Masters kept pace with events abroad and were consistently at the forefront of advances in obstetric practice. Puerperal fever first occurred at the Rotunda in December 1767. Between then and May 1768, 360 women were delivered, 16 of whom died. The disease returned seven years later between March and May 1774, when thirteen women perished and again, after an interval of thirteen years, in 1787 when eleven women contracted the infection in March and April of that year and seven died. Between November 1788 and January 1789, 355 women were delivered at the hospital. Of the seventeen women who contracted puerperal fever fourteen died.[11] There is no evidence that incumbent Masters, William Collum, Frederick Jebb and Henry Rock recorded accounts of these epidemics during their terms.[12] The sporadic incidence of these epidemics at the hospital may not have alerted the Masters to seek causes or take remedial measures. Nor were incidents of the outbreaks of fever reported in the minutes of the meetings of the board of governors.

In 1791 Joseph Clarke first described the symptoms he had witnessed since his appointment as assistant master in 1783. He noted,

> By puerperal fever, I mean a disease which generally attacks women on the second or third day after delivery. Its ordinary symptoms are, a cold shivering fit, acute pain in some part of the cavity of the abdomen and great tenderness when pressed externally; a rapid pulse and those soon succeeded by considerable distension of the abdominal cavity.[13]

Similar to many of his contemporaries, Clarke looked for predisposing causes as to why some women should succumb to the disease. Predisposing causes included exposure to cold weather during winter months, poor general health such as 'acute rheumatism' and 'severe pains in the thorax and difficult respiration', which were all thought to hamper the mothers' recovery after delivery, particularly following long and 'tedious' labours.[14] Early understanding

(Dublin, 1867), pp 6–7.   **11** Clarke, 'Observations on puerperal fever', p. 306.   **12** Collum was elected master in November 1766 and remained in office until November 1773; Jebb's term ran from November 1773 until November 1780; Rock was elected master in November 1780, but died in office in July 1786. **13** Clarke, 'Observations on puerperal fever', p. 299. Similar symptoms were described in Hulme, *A treatise on the puerperal fever*, pp 1–2; Denman, *An essay on the puerperal fever*, p. 10; Gordon, *A treatise of the epidemic puerperal fever of Aberdeen*, pp 6–7.   **14** Clarke, 'Observations on puerperal fever', p. 307; Robert Collins (master 1826–33) considered, but dismissed, the possibility that puerperal fever was associated with

of the disease included theories on miasma arising from bad air given off by people in crowded rooms.[15] Clarke suspected that the beds and furniture had acquired 'noxious properties' from constant use.[16] Contemporary speculation also drew attention to environmental factors such as closed rooms and poor ventilation.[17] He appealed to the board of governors for funds to carry out cleansing of the hospital wards, but not before severe weather in early 1787 had obliged him 'to put two mothers in one bed rather than refuse admittance to those who solicited it at our gates'.[18]

Clarke began a system of closing wards in rotation so that walls could be white-washed. Bed-steads and all woodwork were painted. Bedding was 'scoured' and exposed to 'a current of air'. He was most renowned for his initiatives in providing ventilation for the wards. Traditionally, all windows and doors were shut because it was thought a draught was detrimental to both mothers and babies. He insisted on having holes of one inch in diameter pierced in the doors and window frames to allow a circulation of air.[19] Clarke believed that these measures proved to be successful. He stated that 'from having been most disagreeably harassed by disease, the hospital became remarkably healthy'.[20] Yet a return of the disease in the latter stage of 1788 compelled him to conclude that local infection, particularly some form of contagion[21] in the building, ought to be suspected when three or four women died of puerperal fever within a short time of each other.[22] But his only recourse to prevent the disease, given the knowledge that existed at the time, was cleansing the building in an effort to destroy the perceived source.

Epidemics began to occur regularly in the early nineteenth century. Between 1803 and 1829 twelve outbreaks of the disease struck the Rotunda. The number of women delivered at the hospital rose steadily from 2,018 in 1802, to a high of 3,801 in 1818. In the first thirty years of the nineteenth century, there was an average of 2,800 deliveries annually.[23] The next ten years

long labours. See Robert Collins, *A practical treatise of midwifery containing the result of 16,654 births, occurring in the Dublin Lying-in Hospital, during a period of seven years, commencing November 1816* (London, 1835), p. 385.   **15** Christopher Hamlin, 'Predisposing causes and public health in early nineteenth-century medical thought', *Social History of Medicine*, 5:1 (1992), pp 47–8.   **16** Clarke, 'Observations on puerperal fever', p. 312.   **17** Hamlin, 'Predisposing causes and public health', p. 49.   **18** Clarke, 'Observations on puerperal fever', p. 307.   **19** O'Donel Browne, *The Rotunda Hospital*, pp 32–3.   **20** Clarke, 'Observations on puerperal fever', p. 313.   **21** The term 'contagion' was in common use in this period but it did not mean contagious in terms of transmittable from one patient to the other. Doctors used the term to refer to miasma, or a noxious atmosphere, which emanated from the building itself.   **22** Clarke, 'Observations on puerperal fever', p. 319.   **23** Charitable Institutions, *Dublin, Report of the commissioners appointed by the lord lieutenant to inquire into certain charitable institutions in the city of Dublin; viz. 1. Lying-in Hospital; 2. Dr Steeven's Hospital; 3. The Fever Hospital, Cork Street; 4. The Hospital of Incurables; 5. The Westmorland

saw an average of 2,000 women confined.[24] The number of beds had increased to 112 by 1840, but the institution still struggled to deal with the increasing number of deliveries. Both Labatt and Collins linked puerperal fever to typhus and erysipelas, which were endemic in Ireland in the period between 1816 and 1818. At this time unemployment and poverty, food scarcity and persistently wet seasons combined to escalate outbreaks of fever and disease, such as typhus, cholera and smallpox.[25] Women were admitted to the hospital with typhus and died soon after delivery.[26] In February 1820, Labatt presented a report to the board of governors of the hospital, following a particularly severe epidemic of puerperal fever in 1819, where in the latter four months of that year 1,010 women were admitted, 129 developed the fever and 61 died. In January 1820, 171 women were admitted, 63 became infected and 25 women died. These epidemics convinced Labatt that the contagion of typhus fever was capable of giving rise to puerperal fever; that puerperal fever was communicable from one patient to another and also that it could be carried by an attendant from the sick to women about to give birth, who were previously free from the disease.[27] However, no conclusions were drawn from these observations.

The incidence and frequency of puerperal fever at the Rotunda became part of a wider investigation commissioned by the Lord Lieutenant, Charles Talbot, in 1820 and carried out by the General Board of Health into the simultaneous outbreaks of fever and disease prevalent throughout Ireland at the time. The board was charged with identifying the best means to avert the high mortality rates associated with these recurring outbreaks of puerperal fever at the hospital. Contemporary hospital accoucheurs, the term given to men who assisted in childbirth before the title obstetrician came into use *c.*1830, made a distinction between 'casual fever' and 'epidemical fever'. The former lasted from a number of days up to two weeks, whereas an epidemic persisted for a considerable period, possibly up to some months.[28] Casual fever was identified as an occasional occurrence in private practice or in a lying-in a hospital when

Hospital; and 6. The House of Industry, BPP 1830 (7), xxvi:1, pp 22–3.   **24** Evory Kennedy, *Hospitalism and zymotic diseases as more especially illustrated by puerperal fever, or metria* (2nd ed., London, 1869), pp 30–1.   **25** Timothy P. O' Neill, 'Fever and public health in pre-famine Ireland', *JRSAI*, 103 (1973), pp 1–35; F. Barker & J. Cheyne, *An account of the rise, progress and decline of the fever lately epidemical in Ireland*, vol. 1 (Dublin, 1821).   **26** Collins, *A practical treatise*, pp 381–3; Churchill, *Essays*, p. 18. Typhus is a disease caused by the *rickettsia* bacteria characterized by high fever, skin rash and severe headache. Erysipelas is an acute streptococcal infection of the skin, characterized by fever and purplish lesions.   **27** Churchill, *Essays*, p. 20.   **28** John C. Douglas, 'Report on puerperal fever, in answer to queries from the General Board of Health' in *Dublin hospital reports and communications in medicine and surgery*, vol. 3 (Dublin, 1822), p. 141.

it was 'excited by accidental cause, either during labour, or subsequent to delivery'.[29] Then, it was believed that local inflammation caused pyrexia, a dangerously high temperature. During an epidemic, pyrexia was considered to be the primary cause of the disease and the 'local affection to be consequential', suggesting that women were infected from the 'contaminated atmosphere' and that bedding, walls and furniture in wards became tainted with the 'noxious influence' that caused the disease. There was general agreement that the primary cause of puerperal fever was due to overcrowding, and that 'a hurried succession of patients' was highly conducive to the disease.[30] The Board of Health recommended that no more than 2,000 women should be admitted to the hospital annually. Women who applied for relief but could not be accommodated would be attended by male students and female pupil midwives in their own homes, under the supervision of the Master.[31] The necessity for this, however, did not arise as the epidemic passed by May 1820.[32] Following three epidemics in the 1820s the hospital closed in 1829 for cleansing. Poor women were attended in their own homes by hospital staff and supplied with 'gruel, whey and medicines'.[33] By this time Robert Collins was using chlorine gas in a condensed form to 'fumigate' the wards. The floors and all woodwork and walls were covered with chloride of lime before painting. Blankets and bedding were 'stoved' at a temperature of 130 degrees or suspended in the chlorine gas for forty-eight hours. Straw bedding was replaced when a patient died.[34] Clarke's initiatives on ventilation continued. The hospital was free of fever until 1833.

Immediate treatment of mothers, when symptoms occurred, included the administration of repeated doses of purgatives and emetics, such as saline, calomel and ipecacuanha, to induce either diarrhoea or vomiting to purge the body of the fever.[35] The application of 'three or four dozen leeches' to the abdomen in preference to opening a vein (venesection) was the preferred method of drawing blood at the hospital.[36] This was followed by hot baths and the use of 'stupes', which were flannels steeped in boiling water, wrung out and placed over the abdomen at intervals of four to six hours.[37] Blistered skin was

29 Ibid., p. 143.   **30** Douglas, 'Report on puerperal fever', p. 149.   **31** Charitable Institutions, Dublin, *Report of the commissioners*, p. 6.   **32** Kirkpatrick, *The book of the Rotunda Hospital*, p. 143.   **33** Collins, *A practical treatise*, p. 387.   **34** Ibid., pp 387–8.   **35** Clarke, 'Observations on puerperal fever', pp 316–17. Calomel was a colourless tasteless powder consisting chiefly of mercurous chloride. The dried roots of the Ipecacuanha plant were used as a purgative and emetic.   **36** Clarke, 'Observations on puerperal fever', p. 322; Collins, *A practical treatise*, p. 392; Kennedy, *Hospitalism and zymotic diseases*, p. 11.   **37** Collins, *A practical treatise*, pp 393–4.

then dressed with mercurial ointment. Nineteenth-century medical men had few remedial treatments at their disposal and the use of ipecacuanha and calomel persisted into the 1870s. While there was a preference for bringing patients 'under the influence of mercury' practitioners both in private practice and in hospitals were mindful of the debilitating effects of both disease and treatments and cautiously monitored the administration of their pharmacopiae of drugs.[38] Therapy was also directed towards nutrition – broths, jellies, milk and starchy foods that could be retained in the stomach were given freely following the ingestion of such pernicious remedies.[39]

* * *

The miasmatic theory of disease gradually gave way to the notion of contamination by sources of disease other than by noxious atmosphere. Debates arose among medical theorists. Contagionists held that a chemical or physical influence from a sick person was passed to a susceptible victim by contact, fomites or, for a short distance, through the atmosphere. Anticontagionists, associated with Edwin Chadwick and the public health movement, held that diseases could be explained by filth, particularly sewers, overcrowding, dampness, contaminated water and unwholesome food.[40] Whereas contagionist theories advocated solutions to the spread of disease that included isolation, quarantines, government control and interference in trade, anticontagionists focused on sanitation, public health and the prevention of disease.[41] Complex views and debates continued as to the source of puerperal fever – whether it could be attributed to a single cause, such as putrefaction, contagion or germs, or the notion that it could be caused by a group of different diseases. Endogenist theory argued that infection came from within the patient's genital tract, whereas exogenists believed that infection was introduced from outside.[42] Practical sanitary measures, in line with contemporary practice, were taken at the Rotunda. The laundry at the hospital was abolished and the washing was done at a public laundry in the suburbs,

38 W.S. Oke, 'Villitis intestinal puerpera', *Provincial Medical Journal and retrospect of the medical sciences*, 6:156 (23 Sept. 1843), 523–4; J. Carr Bradley, 'Case of enteritis, with observations', *Provincial Medical and Surgical Journal*, 10:6 (11 Feb. 1846), pp 64–5; Edward Blackmore, 'Observations on the nature, origin and treatment of puerperal fever', *Provincial Medical and Surgical Journal*, 9:12 (19 Mar. 1845), pp 173–8; Kennedy, *Hospitalism and zymotic diseases*, pp 12–13. **39** Kennedy, *Hospitalism and zymotic diseases*, p. 13. **40** Erwin H. Ackerknecht, 'Anticontagionism between 1821 and 1867', Reprints and Reflections, *International Journal of Epidemiology*, 38 (2009), pp 7–21, at pp 8, 13. **41** Hamlin, 'Predisposing causes and public health', pp 44–50. **42** Irvine Loudon, *The tragedy of childbed fever* (Oxford, 2000), pp 111–24.

the ash-pit and dead house were removed to a considerable distance from the building, the sewers and drains were reorganized and water closets erected.[43]

Epidemics continued from the 1830s to the 1860s.[44] In 1867, Evory Kennedy and Denis Phelan, poor law commissioner and secretary of the Board of Superintendence of the Dublin Hospitals, called for the closure of large lying-in institutions in favour of small facilities where disease would not easily be transmitted. Phelan undertook a survey comparing the advantages of giving obstetric treatment to poor women in lying-in hospitals or in their own homes.[45] Influenced by recently published returns collected by Leon Le Fort, professor of surgery at the Paris medical faculty, Phelan assembled data of maternal mortality in the larger cities and towns in England, Scotland and Wales.[46] He considered mortality in lying-in and other hospitals in Dublin, Paris, St Petersburg, London, Vienna and Glasgow, examining mortality of mothers under home attendance from the same lying-in hospitals. His conclusions echoed contemporary opinion – women who were confined in lying-in hospitals died in greater numbers than those confined in their own dwellings; the cause of this mortality must be attributed to puerperal fever, which is spread by contagion; it was absolutely necessary to take hygienic measures to prevent it. In an address to the governors of the Rotunda, Kennedy called for the institution to be 'remodelled', citing his belief that,

> like all human institutions, progress and changing circumstances have produced such an influence upon it, that neither the intentions of the founder, the wants and just rights of the public, nor the claims of humanity by securing the greatest preservation of life, are accomplished by its instrumentality.[47]

He suggested erecting thirty cottages in the Rotunda Gardens, each measuring 25ft by 15ft, capable of accommodating three or four beds. In this way, the proper cleansing and ventilation could be secured between each admission, which would result in the reduction of puerperal fever 'to the same level as in

---

43 *Sixth annual report of the Board of Superintendence of the Dublin Hospitals, with appendices*, BPP 1863 [3152] xxviii, pp 433, 11–12.   **44** Fleetwood Churchill, *On the diseases of women* (6th ed., Dublin, 1874), p. 703.   **45** Denis Phelan, 'Observation on the comparative advantages of affording obstetric attendance on poor women in lying-in hospitals and in their own homes', reprinted from the *Dublin Quarterly Journal of Medical Science* (Dublin, 1867), p. 3.   **46** Leon Le Fort, *Etude sur les maternités et les institutions charitable d'accouchement a domicile dans les principaux etats de l'Europe* (Paris, 1866).   **47** Evory Kennedy, 'Important letter to the president, vice president, governors and guardians of the lying-in hospital', *Dublin Quarterly Journal of Medical Science*, 44:87 (Aug. 1867), pp 514–21.

private practice'.[48] Kennedy was among a growing body of international obstetricians in the 1860s and 1870s who, confounded by high mortality in the lying-in hospitals despite the many measures that were taken to avoid infection, began to question the hospital system. While the possibility of contagion was not disputed, the means by which disease was conveyed provoked debate. Practitioners acknowledged the connection between puerperal fever and other diseases, particularly erysipelas and, by this time, scarletina, when such zymotic diseases 'either endemically or accidently have shown themselves' in hospitals, and raised the question as to the propriety of exposing parturient women to such a risk.[49]

* * *

While this debate was taking place, significant findings were emerging from the Vienna Lying-in Hospital which, at this time, was the largest in the world with about 7,000 deliveries annually. The institution was divided into two clinics in 1833. From 1839, for the purpose of teaching obstetrics, one clinic was allocated to the teaching of medical pupils and the second to the training of midwives. After that date the first clinic, where medical students pursued their studies, consistently had a mortality rate three to five times greater than the second clinic where the midwives were taught. Ignaz Semmelweis (1818–65) was appointed assistant at the hospital in 1847. After several months of intensive investigation he concluded that the difference in mortality rates was due to decaying organic matter, communicated by autopsied corpses, by small particles of placenta, by linen or by instruments, which were conveyed to patients on the hands of the medical students in the first clinic and which produced puerperal fever.[50] He insisted that all personnel wash their hands in a disinfectant solution of chloride of lime before examining patients. The introduction of this measure was immediately effective. Mortality in the first clinic dropped significantly. Semmelweis failed to publish his findings or to convince his contemporaries of his theories. Although antisepsis was introduced into surgery in the late 1860s, it was not until the 1880s that it was used in obstetrics.

Carl Mayrhofer (1837–82) was appointed to the same post as Semmelweis in the Vienna Lying-in Hospital in 1862. He was aware of speculation that

48 Ibid., p. 517.   **49** Kennedy, *Hospitalism and zymotic diseases*, p. 8.   **50** F.H. Arneth, 'Evidence of puerperal fever depending upon the contagious inoculation of morbid matter', *Monthly Journal of Medical Science*, 12 (1851), pp 505–11, at pp 508–9. Arneth was a colleague of Semmelweis.

many living diseases were caused by micro-organisms and the belief that fermentation and organic decomposition were closely related processes. He was also familiar with Pasteur's conclusions that fermentation was always due to living ferments.[51] Mayrhofer had the benefit of improving microscope technology. He began looking for living fermenting agents in uterine discharges from the victims of puerperal fever. He observed and described various organisms that differed in shape and size, in their motility, in their reaction to acidic media and in their capacity to ferment liquids. He referred to these organisms as 'vibrions'. He came to the conclusion that puerperal fever was due to tissue decomposition under the influence of vibrions.[52] He also concluded that Semmelweis was correct when he said that infection was conveyed on the hands of doctors and students. Thus he espoused the belief that all cases of puerperal fever were due to vibrions and opposed the view that the disease was due to multiple causes including poor ventilation.[53] By 1879, Pasteur had identified the micro-organism that caused puerperal fever, which he described as resembling a string of beads (it was not yet called the streptococcus).[54]

What saved the lying-in hospitals was the acceptance of the germ theory of disease, and the introduction of Joseph Lister's methods of sterilization with carbolic acid into obstetric practice in the 1880s.[55] Lombe Atthill, Master at the Rotunda, 1875–82, was the first incumbent to introduce carbolic soap as a disinfectant and the use of a carbolic solution (1:40) which was left beside each wash-hand basin so that all staff and students could dip their hands in it before they examined patients.[56] Arhur Macan, who replaced Atthill as Master, extended these precautions by prohibiting students who attended practice at the hospital from undertaking post-mortem examinations, engaging in dissections or attending any other hospital where patients suffered from infectious diseases.[57] Instruments, such as forceps and catheters, which came into contact with the genitals of patients during pregnancy, labour and following delivery, were also disinfected. In cases of post-partum haemorrhage,

51 K. Condell Carter, 'Ignez Semmelweis, Carl Mayrhofer and the rise of germ theory', *Medical History*, 29 (1985), pp 33–53, at p. 37; W.F. Bynum, *Science and the practice of medicine in the nineteenth century* (Cambridge, 1994), pp 126–32. **52** Carter, 'Ignez Semmelweis', p. 37. **53** K. Codell Carter & B.R. Carter, *Childbed fever: a scientific biography of Ignaz Semmelweis* (Westport, CT, 1994), pp 87–8. **54** Loudon, *Tragedy of childbed fever*, pp 120–5. **55** Bynum, *Science and the practice of medicine*, pp 132–7; Loudon, *Tragedy of childbed fever*, pp 134–45. **56** Lombe Atthill, 'On metria (so-called puerperal fever)', *British Medical Journal*, 2:1180 (11 Aug. 1883), p. 260. **57** Arthur V. Macan, *Report of the Rotunda Hospital for the year ending November 1883*, pp 3, 5.

perineal tears or retained placenta, the master or his assistant were the only practitioners who could attend the patient after the vagina and genital area were irrigated with the 1:40 carbolic acid solution. Students were compelled to keep a record of the patients they examined so that the origin of any infection could be traced. Furthermore, pupils could examine a patient only four times during labour.[58] Macan recorded that in the year ending November 1883, 1,090 women were delivered in the hospital, six died, resulting in a maternal mortality rate of 0.55 per cent or 1:182, lower than the average mortality rate which ran at approximately 1.5 per cent. He pointed out that none of the deaths were related to puerperal septicaemia.[59] It was at this time that palpation of the abdomen was introduced routinely to lessen the necessity of making vaginal examinations. Students were taught to recognize the head, back and limbs of the foetus, to know its size, the quantity of fluid and to determine its position and presentation, whether the head of the foetus was engaged and whether the birth would be multiple or not, thereby reducing 'the risk of conveying septic infection'.[60]

Not all deaths in childbirth were as a result of puerperal fever. From the 1880s, maternity hospitals began to record puerperal morbidity – a rise in temperature in the days after delivery – as a sign of puerperal complications such as infection. William Smyly introduced this very important initiative during his tenure, at a time when the hospital was free of epidemics.[61] Mild pyrexia was seen as due to physiological processes. To mark its high limit an arbitrary line was placed at a temperature of 100.4° F by continental authorities. The Rotunda's baseline was 100.8° while some British and American hospitals used a limit of 99°. Earnest Hastings Tweedy (Master, 1903–10) drew attention to these disparities calling for an agreed standard baseline temperature and the introduction of a quickening pulse as a symptom which should be grouped under the heading of morbidity in the days following delivery.[62] At his suggestion, the British Medical Association appointed a special committee to inquire into the matter. From the information received from twenty-nine maternity hospitals in England, Europe, America and Canada in regard to recognized standards of puerperal morbidity, the diversity of the replies suggested that efficient comparison of

---

58 Ibid., p. 5.   **59** Ibid., p. 6.   **60** Arthur V. Macan, *An address delivered at the opening of the section of obstetric medicine, at the annual meeting of the British Medical Association held in Dublin, August 1887* (Dublin, 1887).   **61** William J. Smyly, 'The maternal mortality in childbed', *British Medical Journal*, 2:2067 (11 Aug. 1900), pp 337–40.   **62** E. Hastings Tweedy, 'The high range of normal temperature and pulse throughout the puerperium', *British Medical Journal*, 2:2334 (23 Sept. 1905), pp 704–5.

the statistics of these institutions would be practically impossible. The British Medical Association settled on a morbidity standard of a temperature of 100° and a pulse of 90 or over, recorded at three successive readings. The Rotunda, however, considered that a pulse rising above 90 beats per minute and a temperature of 99° and continuing for twenty-four hours constituted a morbid state.[63]

The *streptococcus haemolyticus*, or the ß-haemolytic streptococcus Lancefield Group A, was classified in the 1920s by Rebecca Lancefield, an American bacteriologist. Puerperal fever was among the diseases that were caused by the bacteria, along with erysipelas, scarlet fever, pharyngitis, tonsillitis and others. By 1935, Dora Colebrook and Ronald Hare had recognized the carrier ability of the Group A streptococcus, providing evidence that organisms were very frequently transmitted, not directly from a primary source such as hands, instruments or clothing, but from an intermediate source – the throat or nose of a healthy individual.[64] Also in 1935, the results of trials with the use of dyes tested for antibacterial activity carried out in Germany by Gerhard Domagk (1895–1964) were published. The dye was named Prontosil.[65] In England, Leonard Colebrook (1883–1967), the brother of Dora, successfully completed clinical trials with Prontosil, followed by the introduction of the simpler and cheaper compound, sulphanilamide, the first of the sulpha drugs.[66]

The last epidemic at the Rotunda occurred between January and April 1936 with a serious outbreak of haemolytic sepsis. Fourteen cases were isolated and four women died – a mortality rate of 28 per cent.[67] The outbreak coincided with a wave of streptococcal throat infections both in the hospital and around Dublin. Throat swabs were taken from the medical and nursing personnel and from ten of the fourteen cases of puerperal sepsis. Seven mothers were found to be positive for haemolytic streptococcus. Among the 25 medical staff, 3 were positive while 8 of the 72 throat swabs from nursing staff grew cultures of haemolytic streprococcus.[68] Customary precautions were taken to halt the epidemic with the use of carbolic acid for washing and disinfecting instruments and the isolation of infected patients. Dettol was first introduced

63 Ernest Hastings Tweedy, *Clinical report of the Rotunda Hospital*, year ending 31 Oct. 1906, p. 9. **64** Dora Colebrook, *Report on the sources of puerperal infection* in Medical Research Council's special report series, no. 205; Ronald Hare, 'The classification of haemolytic streptococci from the nose and throat of normal human beings by means of preceptin and biochemical tests', *Journal of Pathology and Bacteriology*, 41 (Nov. 1935), pp 499–512. **65** Loudon, *Tragedy of childbed fever*, pp 174–7. **66** Leonard Colebrook, 'The prevention of puerperal sepsis', *Journal of Obstetrics and Gynaecology of the British Empire*, 43:4 (1936), pp 691–714. **67** Andrew H. Davidson, *Clinical report of the Rotunda Hospital*, 1 Nov. 1935–31 Oct. 1936, pp 11, 14–15. **68** Ibid., p. 17.

as an antiseptic during that year. The last patient to become infected during the final phase of the epidemic was the first patient to be treated with Prontosil at the hospital and was cured of infection. The Master, A.H. Davidson, remarked in his clinical report, 'It is a matter of regret that Prontosil or a similar preparation was not available earlier in the epidemic'.[69]

* * *

An examination of the outbreaks of puerperal fever at the Rotunda Hospital illustrates how medical men dealt with the stricken maternal body at the most emotive of times, that of giving birth. The limitations of the understanding of disease, and the dearth of curative measures, prompted early practitioners to resort to the most harmful of treatments, which gave mothers little relief from pain and no assurance of recovery. Although Semmelweis failed to adequately communicate his findings, it must be remembered that his assertion that puerperal fever was always due to the transfer of morbid matter appeared too simple a theory to explain the variety of circumstances in which women contracted infection. The idea that an answer lay in the application of a solution of chloride of lime would not be taken seriously. Calls for the closure of lying-in hospitals were no more than a response to the dilemma of maternal mortality confounding all efforts to halt epidemics. Lying-in hospitals, as we know, were not abolished. There was no question of closure based on a number of practical considerations: they provided maternal care that was perceived to offer women the knowledge and skill of trained midwives with the support of accoucheurs; they played an integral role in the education of medical students and pupil midwives, and they were centres for the investigation of abnormalities of pregnancy and the complications of labour and the post-natal period where treatments could be implemented and observed.[70] Appointments to lying-in hospitals enhanced the prestige of accoucheurs and raised the status of man-midwifery, which had an uneasy relationship within the medical hierarchy for much of the nineteenth century.[71] Mothers were content to avail of the sheltered environment of a lying-in facility for ten days where they would be assured of nourishment and rest after confinement. Women themselves chose to attend lying-in hospitals and run the risk of fevers rather than remain at home where they would be deprived of such comforts.[72] The antiseptic revolution coincided with the

69 Ibid., p. 15.   **70** Loudon, *Tragedy of childbed fever*, pp 125–6.   **71** Gorey, 'Managing midwifery in Dublin', pp 132–3.   **72** Churchill, *Essays*, p. 20.

development of laboratories where scientists could experiment with microscopic particles and enhance medical pathology. The late nineteenth century saw the introduction of the 'Lady Superintendent' into Dublin hospitals. Educated women with nursing and midwifery qualifications were appointed to the major hospitals.[73] Miss Sara Hampson was the first such appointment in the Rotunda in 1891.[74] The introduction of sulphonamide was timely. After the epidemic of 1936, and for the remainder of Davidson's term, mortality from puerperal sepsis was virtually eradicated.

73 Gerard M. Fealy, *A history of apprenticeship nurse training in Ireland* (London, 2006), pp 58–82. **74** Mary A. Kelly, 'The development of midwifery at the Rotunda, 1745–1995' in Browne (ed.), *Masters, midwives and ladies-in-waiting*, p. 87.

Stacking the coffins: the 1918–19 influenza pandemic in Dublin

IDA MILNE

In June 1918, as Irish society was preoccupied with the ember days of the First World War, the threat from the government to impose conscription as the British forces ran out of manpower, and the associated growing voice of nationalist Ireland protesting against that imposition, a strange new disease appeared. Described variously as a mysterious influenza or a plague, it was initially reported from the north-east, where Belfast citizens were severely affected, but it quickly emerged in Howth, a small port in north county Dublin. By 24 June, 200 cases had been recorded in Dublin's inner city. Dr Matthew J. Russell, the assistant medical officer of health for Dublin Corporation (the municipal council), told an *Irish Independent* reporter that 60 children were stricken in one city convent, and in one factory 40 employees were down with the disease. The symptoms, Dr Russell noted, seemed mild enough – stiffness, feverishness, distaste for solid food, with vomiting.[1]

Irish newspapers, reflecting the opinions of the public and the medical profession alike, and following the international trend, were initially reluctant to name the disease, instead referring to it as a 'mysterious malady', a 'plague', a 'dread disease' or some other similarly non-diagnostic term.[2] While the symptoms were something like seasonal influenza, this disease was appearing in the summer, and was infecting larger groups of people than the usual winter influenza. This fear to name the disease probably emanated from the expectation that a terrible disease would emerge from the gruesome war conditions. The conclusion of the 1870–1 Franco-Prussian War with a pandemic of smallpox was very much in the conscious memory of the public, the medical professions and the British government; it was often alluded to in official reports and in the newspapers. Informed by this and other post-war disease events and similar incidents, the British government had established a number of interdepartmental committees to cope with the expected increased incidence of infectious disease caused by the First World War in the post-

---

1 *Irish Independent*, 25 June 1918.   2 European mainland newspapers were also reluctant to name the disease: see Wilfred White, 'The plague that was not allowed to happen' in Howard Phillips & David Killingray (eds), *The Spanish influenza pandemic of 1918–19, new perspectives* (London, 2003), pp 49–57.

bellum period.[3] The leader writer of Wexford's *People* echoed the sentiments of many: 'A plague of some kind follows all great wars.'[4]

* * *

The June outbreak was the first and mildest wave of the worst influenza pandemic the world has experienced since the 1500s, a disease that the World Health Organisation estimates killed about 50 million people, but some suggest it may have killed as many as 100 million; 10 million died in India alone.[5] It infected at least one-fifth and perhaps as much as half of the world's population. In Ireland, there were 20,057 deaths officially certified to the influenza, but there is a growing body of evidence to suggest that many deaths went uncertified, as doctors struggled to treat the huge numbers of patients they failed to complete the paperwork. With the help of Royal College of Surgeons in Ireland (RCSI) medical statistician Anthony Kinsella, this author has estimated that it infected about 800,000 people on this island, or one-fifth of the population, with most of the infection concentrated into three waves, this first one in June and July 1918, and two much more severe waves in the autumn of 1918 and the spring of 1919.[6]

Dublin city was badly affected in all three waves. In the entire county of Dublin, 2,866 people are certified as having died from influenza in 1918 and 1919, out of a total population in the 1911 census of 477,196; it is probable that about 114,000 Dubliners suffered from the disease over the two years. Dublin had the second-highest county death rate from the flu in Leinster in 1918, at 3.70 per thousand of the population, second only to Kildare at 3.95; nationally, it was slightly behind Armagh at 3.72 and Belfast (county borough) at 3.85. Dublin's position as a traffic hub, with people – including soldiers – coming and going by sea and by rail, made it particularly vulnerable. Donegal also experienced continual reinfection over the three waves, perhaps because of heavy war traffic passing through the naval base at Lough Swilly. Some parts of the country escaped with minimal damage – Co. Clare, for example, lost only 48 people to the disease in 1918 and 143 in 1919, out of a population of 104,232.[7] The summer wave died down in July; the flu remerged in the capital

---

3 *Annual report of the chief medical officer, 1919–1920* (1920), xvii, cmd. 978; the author attributes the smallpox reference to Prinzing's *Epidemics resulting from wars*. See also *Irish Times*, 31 Oct. 1918.   4 *The People*, 16 Nov. 1918.   5 WHO Report on Global Surveillance of Epidemic-prone Infectious Diseases – Influenza, http://www.who.int/csr/resources/publications/influenza/CSR_ISR_2000_1/en, accessed 6 Jan. 2015.   6 Ida Milne, 'The 1918–19 influenza pandemic in Ireland: a Leinster perspective' (PhD, TCD, 2011).   7 Ibid.

in mid-October 1918, just as the city was reeling from the shock of the torpedoing of the mailboat RMS *Leinster* off the east coast as it was making its way from Kingstown to Holyhead, with the loss of over 500 people, on 10 October.[8] While German torpedo attacks on ships in the Irish sea were frequent during the war, the loss of life on the *Leinster* was exceptional. National and provincial papers devoted hundreds of column inches to this atrocity over the following days, and carried harrowing stories of lives lost and saved, bodies recovered, funerals, memorial services, obituaries and relief funds. The newspapers were still reacting to this impact of the war directly on Dublin's doorstep when the *Irish Independent* reported, on 16 October, that influenza was once again rife in the city. Fourteen deaths from influenza in the city had been recorded at the offices of the Corporation's Public Health Committee the same week, although the reporter pointed out that it was difficult to quantify the real number of deaths from influenza, as it was not a notifiable disease. Doctors were obliged to notify the Local Government Board about deaths caused by certain infectious diseases including cholera, typhoid, measles and smallpox. The same day, a dispensary doctor told an *Irish Independent* reporter that almost three-quarters of the deaths of people up to the age of 30 were either directly attributable to influenza, or to diseases resulting from it. He said that for the previous ten days the number of deaths from pneumonia within the city had been unprecedented. This doctor observed that 'pneumonia followed with startling rapidity the moment the necessary precautions were relaxed'.[9]

Another doctor, who had been working day and night for the previous fortnight treating influenza sufferers in the North Dock district, suggested that the death rate in the poorer quarters from influenza was largely due to malnutrition.[10] The North Dock was one of the poorer areas of the city, with over 1,800 families housed in one-room tenements, according to the census of 1911. The paper reported that some city schools were already closed, and those that remained open were severely affected by the absence of staff and pupils. Outside the city, Bray and Kingstown to the south, and Howth, Grange and Baldoyle on the north side, were all badly affected. Medical officers in Howth spoke of treating between 400 and 500 cases in the previous couple of weeks, with whole families ill with the disease, and there had been many deaths.[11]

8 *Irish Times*, 11 Oct. 1918.   **9** *Irish Independent*, 16 Oct. 1918.   **10** Ibid.   **11** Ibid.

The normally restrained *Irish Times* described, in the issue of 31 October 1918, the dramaturgy of the influenza, as hearse after hearse passed through the streets of the city to the cemeteries:

> Yesterday, from early morning til well after midday, cortège after cortège reached Glasnevin Cemetery, sometimes as many as three corpse-laden hearses being seen proceeding up Sackville Street at the same time. Close on forty orders for interment were issued at the Cemeteries' Office yesterday, and, inclusive of the remains brought for burial on the previous day, which had been temporarily placed in the vaults overnight, there were close on one hundred bodies for sepulture. At Mount Jerome there were eight interments—a number much in excess of the daily average.[12]

By 2 November, the *Irish Times* abandoned all pretences at reserve in its coverage of the epidemic's effects on the capital city. Under headlines of INFLUENZA EPIDEMIC IN IRELAND—HEAVY DEATH TOLL; EFFORTS TO COMBAT THE DISEASE, it documented the challenges faced by traders, as business houses and factories found it difficult to stay open because so many of their staff were ill.[13]

Doctors, nurses and chemists were in heavy demand, and working all hours, and hospital accommodation everywhere was severely taxed. Official figures showed that hundreds of people had died in Dublin during the preceding month, with 231 dying during the week ending 25 October. There was a practically unbroken succession of funeral processions on their way to Glasnevin Cemetery. On several days, the Cemeteries' Committee employees had not been able to complete all the interments, and had to resort to storing bodies overnight in the vault. It was reported that the cemeteries had not been so busy since the cholera outbreak of the 1830s. Mount Jerome had buried 55 for the week ended 29 October, compared with 11 for the corresponding week in 1917. Of these deaths, thirty-four were certified to pneumonia or influenza. Even though cinema houses and places of entertainment were being disinfected, the newspaper noted that there had been a marked drop in attendances. Business people in the city complained of a trade paralysis. One leading grocer remarked that the great bulk of his customers were sending in

12 *Irish Times*, 31 Oct. 1918.   **13** Ibid., 2 Nov. 1918.

written orders by messenger rather than coming to collect them themselves. In turn, he said, this placed a burden on the regular delivery service, as the orders were coming in hundreds rather than in the regular dozens. All sorts of business premises, including solicitors, insurance agents and chartered accountants houses, were being liberally sprinkled with antiseptic fluids. Druggists reported having had such big orders for disinfectant that, in some cases, their stocks ran out.[14] Between 1 and the 21 October 1918, 490 people were buried in Glasnevin Cemetery, compared with 243 in the corresponding period in 1917. The cemetery committee said that this represented a daily average of 23 burials since the epidemic re-emerged in Dublin, as against normal interments averaging 12 a day. Towards the end of this three-week period, as many as forty bodies were buried in the cemetery in a single day. The epidemic was reaching its peak in the city. The following week, 343 were buried in Glasnevin, almost as many as had died on the *Leinster*.[15]

* * *

Eyewitness accounts of the second and third waves tell that the influenza virtually silenced the city as it passed through. If people were not sick themselves, they were staying home to tend to the ill, or not going out to avoid catching it. Many schools were closed, on the advice of the city's veteran and highly respected chief medical officer, Sir Charles Cameron, whose opinion was constantly sought by newspaper reporters during the crisis. Court sittings were deferred, many concerts and sports matches cancelled. Public buildings in the city were disinfected every day. Cinema houses refused to admit children of school-going age; they also closed for half an hour between shows to allow ventilation of the premises, and were disinfected frequently. The corporation's public health department officials inspected city venues to check whether they were taking the proper precautions to curtail the dissemination of the disease in crowded situations. The corporation published posters giving precautionary advice. As an *Irish Times* journalist wrote: 'Disinfection and purification are the watchwords just now with housekeepers and managers of all sorts of business and general establishments'.[16] Disinfectant carts became part of the Dublin street landscape, as the corporation's cleansing department sprayed the main streets daily.

14 Ibid., 2 Nov. 1918.   **15** *Irish Independent*, 4 Mar. 1919.   **16** *Irish Times*, 31 Oct. 1918.

Given the numbers made ill by the disease, it is no surprise that hospitals reported that the influenza crisis placed a great burden on their services, particularly as it came at a time of coal shortages and just as the hospitals' perennial financial crises were exacerbated by extraordinary inflation as the war drew to a close. They faced an additional problem in that wounded or ill soldiers were occupying many of the beds. In both the Dublin Union Workhouse (now St James' Hospital) and the Mater Hospital, several extra medical wards were provided to treat flu patients.[17] In the Dublin Union Workhouse, the Master, on the recommendation of the infirmary doctor, vacated four wards in the male hospital occupied by the 'feeble infirm and ulcer cases', moving them to the workhouse proper, to cater for influenza patients at the end of October 1918. The Master took on extra nursing staff and also appointed a man to ensure the swift removal of the bodies of patients who died during the night. The increased number of admissions also placed an added demand on the workhouse's cab and ambulance service, and extra staff had to be employed to cater for that demand. The ambulance was, when necessary, loaned out to bring flu victims to hospitals. At the Adelaide Hospital, influenza was reported to have caused a severe strain on the hospital accommodation; a reduction in the numbers of soldiers seeking admission enabled the staff to accommodate more influenza patients in the Victoria Home; otherwise even more hardship would have been inflicted on the sick poor.

Hospital reports tell of a high death rate during the pandemic, due to the serious nature of many of the pneumonia cases, some of them dying only hours after admission to the hospital. Although the reports do not list the number of influenza cases treated, Dr George Peacocke, physician to the Adelaide and the King George V hospitals in Dublin, claimed in November 1918 that there had been 497 influenza admissions during the month of October 'in a large hospital with which he was connected,' and to which the milder cases were not admitted, with 32 deaths.[18] Although Peacock did not name the hospital, it might be assumed that he refers to the Adelaide, as it was the larger of the two hospitals. The Adelaide, already in financial crisis to a level that threatened its existence, had been forced to make two extra fundraising appeals in the autumn of 1918 as the influenza epidemic was at its zenith, one to regular subscribers and another, a 'half crown fund', to bring in

17 Dublin Union Board of Guardians minute books, 1918–19. BG series; D.W. Macnamara, 'Memories of 1918 and "the flu"', *Journal of Irish Medical Association*, 35:208 (1954), pp 304–9.   **18** *The Medical Press,*

smaller sums from former patients. From mid-summer, hospital management
had introduced economy measures, rationing heat on the wards and in the
nurses' home and limiting the theatre operating days. At the height of the flu
epidemic in November 1918, hospital management ordered that the coal cellar
under the hospital's dispensary be kept locked to protect coal supplies. Many
of the Adelaide's 10 nursing sisters and 43 nurses and probationers contracted
the disease during the autumn outbreak of influenza.[19]

The Mater Hospital normally had a couple of fever wards in operation, but
during the epidemic almost every ward was transformed into a medical or
fever ward, with just one gynaecological ward and one male and one female
surgical ward retained for emergencies. D.W. Macnamara, then a junior house
doctor in the hospital, wrote that he believed that the number of influenza
patients he had examined at the time must have 'run well into four figures'.
He saw up to fifteen bodies in the mortuary at one time while six or seven
were commonplace. During the influenza, he examined a newly admitted case
at 4 p.m., and another in the same bed three hours later, the previous patient
having died and been removed to the mortuary.[20] As the Adelaide reports
suggest, wounded and ill soldiers were already placing a strain on many
Dublin hospitals before the pandemic occurred. Charles Cameron, his
assistant, Dr Russell, and P.T. Daly, chairman of the Corporation's Public
Health Committee, visited the hospitals on 23 October to assess the
accommodation available for influenza patients. Finding many of the beds
occupied by soldiers, they approached the military authorities and persuaded
them to agree immediately not to send any more soldiers to the civilian
hospitals.[21] Most authorities agreed there was little contemporary medicine
could do to cure the ill, except provide good nursing, keeping patients clean
and well hydrated. In desperate efforts to find something to at least make their
patients more comfortable, doctors tried everything that might possibly help.
The more favoured prescriptions were quinine, which reduced fever, cough
mixtures, linseed poultices, and Calomel, or mercurous chloride, given because
doctors were intent on keeping the bowels moving. Other favoured treatments
included gargling with a tincture of creosote, and an injection of strychnine.[22]
In the Mater Macnamara reported that the older doctors often prescribed what

1 Jan. 1919.   **19** Sixty-first annual report of the Adelaide and Fetherston-Haugh convalescent home,
Rathfarnham, for 1918, Adelaide Archive, Trinity College, Dublin, Adelaide Hospital finance and house
committee minutes, 1918.   **20** Macnamara, 'Memories of 1918 and "the flu"'.   **21** *Evening Herald*, 23
and 24 Oct. 1918.   **22** Milne, 'The 1918–19 influenza pandemic'.

he called 'heroic' doses of whiskey or brandy for patients during the pandemic, which, he suggested, meant that at least they had a 'merrier dance to the hereafter'.[23] The city's morgues, undertakers and cemeteries struggled to cope with the extra numbers for burial, and had a backlog as they were overwhelmed by those needing their services at the peaks of the epidemic. The issue was complicated by a strike involving ten city undertaking businesses, which Lord Mayor Laurence O'Neill stepped in to resolve in mid-October; the dispute was causing extra delays for burials.[24]

* * *

Oral histories collected to document memory of the pandemic in Ireland can be quite detailed. People who lived through it have often observed that the church bells never seemed to stop ringing for funerals. It was not at all unusual to have several dead from the same family. One source recalled that when her mother's sister, brother and father all died from the flu, they were laid out in the front room of the family home in Leeson Park Avenue for some time as the undertakers, Nicholls, could not bury them immediately in Deansgrange.[25] Another interviewee, whose family were involved in the timber business, providing wood for coffins to one of the city's main undertakers, Fanagans, recalled his father telling him that wood for coffins was in heavy demand, and that the coffins were stacked eighteen high with bodies in them, in the mortuary of the South Dublin Union Hospital.[26]

The peak week for deaths from this influenza in Dublin was the week ending 2 November, when doctors certified 287 influenza fatalities. Of these, 32 were children less than 5 years old, and 86 were adults aged 25–34 – more than double the death-rate for any other age category. This statistic points to another unusual feature of this flu – it seemed to particularly strike young adults – whereas the normal winter flu more typically killed infants and the elderly or infirm. That also meant that many families lost fathers, mothers and breadwinners; the Irish mortality statistics are not sophisticated enough to permit a count of the numbers of children orphaned by the disease. The loss of a parent to the flu often had far-reaching consequences for children, as they were either deprived of the carer or the breadwinner, and the remaining

23 Macnamara, 'Memories of 1918 and "the flu"'.   **24** *Irish Times*, 14 Oct. 1918.   **25** Telephone communication with Anne Shankey, Dublin, 31 Mar. 2008. My thanks to Anne Shankey for this account. **26** Telephone communication with Hugh Byrne, 30 Mar. 2008, and my thanks to Hugh Byrne for this account. Fanagan's business records for this time do not survive.

10 James and Margaret Delaney from Kimmage Road West. James was a police constable stationed at Lad Lane; he caught flu in December 1918, returned to work but died from influenzal pneumonia in January 1919 (reproduced courtesy of Ann Burke, granddaughter of James and Margaret Delaney).

parent, if there was one, often had to cover both roles. James Delaney, aged 28, was a Dublin Metropolitan Police constable based at Lad Lane when he caught the flu in December 1918. He seemed to recover, returning to work, but died from influenza pneumonia in January 1919. That was a common feature of this flu – people would catch the flu but die from pneumonia, as in this pre-antibiotic era contemporary medicine had no effective cure for pneumonia. His wife Margaret sent her children, Denis and Beck, to her grandmother's house in Monaghan while she set herself up in a cake shop on Lower Kimmage Road. When she was established, the children came back, but disease was to make another terrible impact on the family, as Beck died from scarlet fever at the age of five.[27] In the 1910s, child deaths from infectious diseases like scarlet fever and measles were a common feature of city life. Stella Larkin McConnon has observed that her mother, Anne Moore Larkin, who was born to a family living in a tenement in Marlborough Street, was the only one of ten children to survive beyond the age of five. This was not uncommon in the cramped and unsanitary tenement conditions that many of the city's citizens occupied. Stella was told by her mother that some of Anne's siblings died during the influenza pandemic.[28]

Catherine Moran Heatley died from influenza pneumonia in her parents' house in Nicholas Street in the Liberties in November 1918. Her three little boys, who were at her bedside as she died, had already lost their father, Lance Corporal Charles Heatley of the Royal Dublin Fusiliers, who was killed on 1 July 1916, at the Battle of the Somme. Her grandson, Fred Heatley, told this author that his father and uncles never knew what had killed her, that it was always a puzzle to the family until it occurred to Fred himself, as a result of finding out more about the pandemic, that it might have been the cause of her death. This was confirmed when he found her death certificate. Charles Heatley's name is inscribed on the Thiepval Memorial to the fallen of the Battle of the Somme, whose bodies were not found. Charles was killed as a direct impact of the war, while his wife Catherine died as an indirect impact of the same war.[29]

Some of the newspaper descriptions paint pathetic tableaux of families' failing struggle to survive when all were struck down with the disease. The *Irish Times* recorded the inquest of Mrs Frances Phelan, 27, who lived with her

27 Interview with Ann Burke, Simmonstown, Celbridge, 6 Feb. 2007. My thanks to Ann Burke for this account of her grandfather's death. **28** Interview with Stella McConnon Larkin, Dublin, 12 Oct. 2012. **29** Series of telephone calls and email correspondence with Fred Heatley, 2008–14.

11 Margaret Delaney, widow of James, in mourning (reproduced courtesy of Ann Burke, granddaughter of James and Margaret Delaney).

husband, child and sister-in-law on Corporation Street, Dublin. Neighbours, noticing the Phelans had not been seen for some time, broke into their rooms and found Mrs Phelan dead in the bed, with her husband, infant son and sister-in-law also lying on the bed, seriously ill. The caretaker of the buildings, John Maguire, said that when he entered, he found the four occupants of the room in the one bed, the baby with a comforter in its mouth. He tried to rouse the man and helped him to dress. The second woman was partly dressed. He wrapped a coat about her, placed her on a chair, and sent a message to the police. The three were removed to Dublin Union Hospital by ambulance, but did not recover.[30] In other parts of the country – notably Dundalk, Athy, Naas, Clonmel, Rathvilly and Clones – communities organized at local level through the Women's National Health Association, the Society of St Vincent de Paul, landlords and local farmers to provide hot soups and stews for families too ill or too poor to feed themselves during the pandemic.[31] Little evidence has emerged to indicate that such supports were given to Dublin sufferers by their communities, or at least the main newspapers do not refer to the setting up of communal kitchens or group feeding schemes in the capital to care for the pandemic ill, which is perhaps surprising given the success soup kitchens played during the 1913 Dublin strike and lockout. The newspapers carry sporadic references to nursing religious orders doing work in some parts of the city. A couple of the statements to the Bureau of Military History mention that members of Cumann na mBan operated a nursing depot out of 6 Harcourt Street, from where members trained by the Red Cross offered their services to the influenza ill. But as this receives little attention in the newspapers, and as Máirín Beaumont describes there being two members on duty each night in case they were needed, it would appear that the help they gave was minimal when compared to the enormity of the problem.[32] Sinn Féin activist and medical doctor Kathleen Lynn, on 'the run' at the time the pandemic first broke out in Dublin, was guaranteed legal immunity following negotiations by Lord Mayor Laurence O'Neill, on condition that she work with the influenza ill. Lynn set up a centre for influenza sufferers on

30 *Irish Times*, 26 Feb. 1919, and *Weekly Irish Times*, 1 Mar. 1919.   **31** See Patricia Marsh, 'An enormous amount of distress among the poor' in Virginia Crossman & Peter Gray (eds), *Poverty and welfare in Ireland, 1838–1948* (Dublin, 2011), pp 207–22; Ida Milne, 'Influenza: the Local Government Board's last great crisis' in D.S. Lucey & Virginia Crossman (eds), *Healthcare in Ireland and Britain, voluntary, regional and comparative perspectives* (London, 2015), pp 217–36.   **32** The Bureau of Military History Witness Statements, WS Ref: 385, Máirín Beaumont (http://www.bureauofmilitaryhistory.ie/, accessed 27 Mar. 2014). See also the Bureau of Military History Witness Statements, WS Ref: 398, Bridget Martin, née Foley (http://www.bureauofmilitaryhistory.ie/, accessed 24 Feb. 2014).

Charlemont St, which later became St Ultan's Children's Hospital. But again, while Lynn's work undoubtedly saved lives, her diaries suggest that the scale of the centre's work was not large.[33] In contrast, the community kitchens in Dundalk, Naas and Athy fed several hundred each day, and Clonmel borstal cooked and distributed fifteen gallons of soup a day when 2,000 fell ill in the town.[34]

Some oral evidence suggests that individual actions by kindly neighbours may have saved lives, despite the personal risk of infection. In Lucan, Co. Dublin, Elizabeth Molloy, whose entire family was unable to function because of the disease, felt an enormous sense of relief when her soldier uncle returned home and took charge of nursing the family. Arriving home from war to find the family ill and the house cold, he lit the fires, made food and treated them with quinine and whiskey, and all survived. A 12-year-old neighbour had been bringing Elizabeth's family and others food and supplies before she became ill herself; Elizabeth painted a vivid word picture of the girl's mother carrying her body along the banks of the Grand Canal pleading with God to give her daughter back.[35]

* * *

In December 1918, the influenza made a forceful and perhaps fateful imposition on national politics. Richard Coleman, one of the seventy-three anti-conscription campaigners detained in mid-May under suspicion of involvement in the so-called German Plot, a government ruse to discredit the campaigners, died on 9 December in Usk, Monmouthshire, where he had been interned. Coleman, already a hero because of his part in the 1916 Rebellion, had now become a martyr in death. His timing could not have been more effective for the cause of Sinn Féin, who claimed his death as a murder in prison. The general election was to be held on 14 December and there is ample evidence to suggest that the party harnessed the opportunity provided by Coleman's death to their election campaign message. At the final pre-election rallies, Sinn Féin's banners and posters were draped with black mourning ribbons. A party advertisement on the front page of the leading daily newspaper, the *Irish Independent*, claimed Coleman had joined the ranks

33 Kathleen Lynn diaries, Royal College of Physicians in Ireland. See also Margaret Ó hÓgartaigh, *Kathleen Lynn: Irishwoman, patriot, doctor* (Dublin, 2006). 34 Milne, 'The 1918–19 influenza pandemic'. 35 Ida Milne, 'Through the eyes of a child: Spanish influenza remembered by survivors' in Anne Mac Lellan & Alice Mauger (eds), *Growing pains: childhood illness in Ireland, 1750–1950* (Dublin, 2013), pp 159–74.

of Irish martyrs, listing him with national heroes such as Fr John Murphy and Thomas Ashe who had died at the hands of the British.[36]

Frank Gallagher, who was working for the interned Sinn Féin director of publicity, Bob Brennan, at the time, evaluated Coleman's death from the perspective of its propaganda value:

> He was but 27 years of age; he was handsome. It was as if a goodly knight had fallen in a crusade. The people's tears came quickly for him. The inquest disclosed the utter neglect of the sick in Usk prison, where there was not even a trained nurse … The disclosure horrified all who had men in prison … The morning after the Coleman inquest canvassers sought out those still doubtful and put straight questions to them. How could any but the heartless stand aside now? All over Ireland that night the 'D's' [for doubtful, 'F': for and 'A': against] were being rubbed out.[37]

Coleman's body arrived back to Dublin on 13 December, was received into Westland Row railway station by leading nationalist activists, and brought to the church next door, pending burial in Glasnevin Cemetery on the day after the election.[38] Members of the Dublin Trades Council, representing 25,000 workers, had been instructed to attend the funeral in full force. Sinn Féin published in the newspapers detailed instructions to its supporters about the roles they were to play in the funeral procession through the streets of Dublin; conveniently, the instructions appeared in the newspapers before and on the day of the election, with the funeral taking place the following day. This level of stage management demonstrates that the organization was keen to exploit the opportunity of Coleman's funeral to make an impression on the government and on the electorate.[39]

Sinn Féin had a resounding victory in the election winning seventy-three seats. P.S. O'Hegarty believed the vote was reactionary. 'The victory of Christmas 1918 was not a victory of conviction, but of emotion. It was a victory occasioned less by any sudden achievement by the majority of a belief in Ireland a nation than by the sudden reaction against various acts of English tyranny.'[40] Whether Coleman's death, and the way he was presented to the

---

36 The postal censor said that correspondence after the death of Coleman showed that it was being exploited as 'a further instance of British inhumanity'. Colonial Office Papers CO904/164. See also Frank Gallagher, *The four glorious years, 1918–1921* (Dublin, 2005) and *Irish Independent*, 12 Dec. 1918. **37** Frank Gallagher, *The four glorious years, 1918–1921*. **38** *Evening Herald*, 13 Dec. 1918. **39** For funeral report see *Irish Independent*, 16 Dec. 1918. **40** P.S. O'Hegarty, *The victory of Sinn Féin: how it won it and*

electorate as a martyr for the cause, were actually effective in increasing the vote for Sinn Féin is open to speculation. Bob Brennan, Sinn Féin director of publicity and also director of elections until his internment in Gloucester three weeks before the election, claimed that he had predicted the number of seats several weeks before, indicating that Coleman's death made little impact on the vote. But there may have been some professional jealousy of his subordinate, Frank Gallagher, who wrote about it having a deep impact on the electorate.[41] In a pamphlet published after the release of the prisoners in 1919, Sinn Féin claimed that Coleman's death was murder.[42]

In March 1919, the flu killed another young light of the nationalist movement, the recently elected Tipperary (east) MP Pierse McCan, while he was interned in Gloucester. The death of McCan was really the final nail in the coffin of the German Plot, which had turned into a public relations disaster for the government.[43] Like Coleman, McCan's body was brought into Westland Row on its return from Britain. This time, the burial was not in Glasnevin, but in his native Duhalla in Co. Tipperary, but the opening scenes of the funeral was a massive parade, effectively a show of force for the nationalist movement, through the streets of the capital city.

If anything, the funeral was even grander than that of Coleman. Some 10,000 people were reported to have followed the hearse to the Pro-Cathedral in Dublin, before another imposing procession through crowd-lined streets to Kingsbridge Station, this time with members of the new Dáil Éireann marching behind the hearse. The corpse was taken by train to Thurles for burial, leaving Kingsbridge in a van draped with an enormous Sinn Féin flag; crowds stood on platforms of stations along the way. Archbishop Harty and sixteen other priests conducted the service in Thurles. The removal to the burial ground at his family home was again an enormous affair, even by the standards of Sinn Féin funerals, with forty-three priests at the graveside. Nationalist politicians once again used the opportunity to lay the blame for the death of another gallant young *Fíor Ghael* at the hands of the government who detained him without trial and refused to release him when the flu presented a dangerous threat to his health.

* * *

how it used it (Dublin, 1924), p. 21.   **41** Robert Brennan, *Allegiance* (Dublin, 1950), p. 167.   **42** Sinn Féin pamphlet collection, 'The case of Ireland' (1919), NLI: Ir 94109/22.   **43** Milne, 'The 1918–19 influenza pandemic in Ireland'.

The influenza pandemic seemed to have spent its worst in Dublin by the middle of April 1919. It has left its lasting physical imprint on the landscape of Dublin necropolises, in the headstones of almost 3,000 citizens of the city. More hidden imprints remain in the many unmarked graves of victims, and in the memories of Dubliners whose families and communities suffered, memories that were sometimes occluded by a lack of a history of the disease in an Irish context, as in the case of the young Heatley brothers. It took almost a hundred years for the family to learn the connection between the outbreak of the disease in Dublin and the mysterious death of their grandmother. Thousands of other Dublin families experienced similar bereavements during the influenza pandemic – losses that affected the rest of their lives.

'That woe could wish, or vanity devise': Crimean War memorials in Dublin's Anglican churches

PAUL HUDDIE

> We have mural tablets, every size,
> That woe could wish, or vanity devise …
> Here, to her spouse, with every virtue grac'd,
> His mournful widow has a trophy plac'd;
> And here 'tis doubtful if the duteous son,
> Of the good father, be in praise outdone.[1]

These lines taken from the 1810 poem by the Revd George Crabbe entitled 'The Church' illustrate that churches can often represent treasure troves of memorials to the dead. Yet due to the lateness in the Catholic, and especially the Presbyterian, churches' development of a tradition of in-church memorialization in Ireland, such memorials are principally relegated to the walls and crypts of the churches of the Church of Ireland. This is something that people can too often forget; some Anglican churches are veritable museums. A prime example of this in the Dublin area is the parish church in Monkstown; there memorial plaques fill the walls of the church from the floor to the ceiling, only interrupted by stained glass windows, which are simply more memorials in an alternative medium. This is due to that denomination's tradition of memorialization stretching back to the seventeenth century, which saw a burgeoning during the Victorian period. As Etain Murphy argues, in the latter case this was due to the great importance that people of that era attached 'to the outward trappings of bereavement'. To them 'death was part of life and they wanted to be reminded every Sunday of their loved ones'. It was as if they were 'bringing their gravestones into church'.[2] In her 2001 study *Dublin burial grounds and graveyards* Vivien Igoe described gravestones as being a 'part of our national heritage' and 'a historical resource of prime importance' by which we can 'unravel our Nation's past'. Although by far the most common, gravestones are not the only form of memorial or 'medium of record' to the dead that can

---

1 Revd George Crabbe, LLB, *The Borough: a poem in twenty-four letters* (Philadelphia, 1810), p. 21.
2 Etain Murphy, *A glorious extravaganza: the history of Monkstown parish church* (Bray, 2003), pp 273–4.

be found in Dublin today.[3] While Igoe was versatile enough to include churchyards and crypts in her work, she naturally omitted the naves and transepts of churches as part of her study of burial. However, these too house a variety of other funerary monuments, namely brass and marble plaques and stained glass windows. They not only form another part of Ireland's heritage and act as a historical resource comparable to headstones, but also represent a discernible sub-section of *ad monumenta mortuorum* – memorials to the dead.

Marble plaques and stained glass windows were regularly utilized for the commemorations of those whose bodies were inaccessible, usually overseas or lost at sea during a conflict of some kind. Hence their prevalence in this essay. Although these memorials are perhaps the most personal of all such monuments to the Crimean War, they do not exist in isolation but rather alongside a variety of other public works. These can be found in town squares, outside courthouse, on bridges and in specially designated parks all over the island of Ireland, in many forms including Russian trophy cannon, a granite obelisk and a replica round tower. Just like headstones and elaborate gravesite monuments of the broader period those Crimean War memorials and monuments, which were purposefully commissioned and erected both within churches and outside, can be used as historical resources. They tell us much about the people associated with them, both explicitly and implicitly through their locations, scale, ornament and especially their inscriptions.

It is the purpose of this essay to not only discuss the symbolism and historical value of these memorials, but to also interrogate their place within the broader contexts of funerary memorialization in Ireland, the memorialization of the war, and the trends of the mid-Victorian period and long nineteenth century. Attention will be drawn to these 'symbols of death' and 'expressions of grief', which can be used, as Igoe argues, to 'gain some understanding' about the attitude of people – the mid-Victorian Irish – towards death, specifically during a time of war.[4]

The Crimean War was a conflict between 1854 and 1856, fought by the alliance of Britain, France, Turkey and Piedmont-Sardinia against Russia. Through the various public celebrations, extensive newspaper coverage and hundreds of poems and ballads, it is clear that efforts were made by a large cross-section of the Irish public to honour the living soldiers between 1854

---

3 Vivien Igoe, *Dublin burial grounds and graveyards* (Dublin, 2001), p. 15.   **4** Igoe, *Dublin burial grounds*, p. 15.

and 1856.[5] Thus, it is unsurprising that the half-decade that followed the cessation of hostilities saw a substantial effort, in both the public and private spheres of Irish society, to memorialize the dead.

The principal period of this memorialization was between 1857 and 1860, and of the 73 known memorials and monuments that were built or emplaced across the island of Ireland, 23 were placed in churches, being primarily commissioned as white marble plaques. There were also three stained glass windows and one brass plaque.[6] Of that total, five were located in Dublin city. At Arbour Hill garrison chapel and St Patrick's Cathedral respectively plaques were erected to the memory of all the officers and men of the 30th (Cambridgeshire) Regiment of Foot and the 18th (Royal Irish) Regiment of Foot who died in action, of their wounds or of disease during the Russian campaign. The latter was an accompaniment to a large stained glass window erected in the north transept of the cathedral next to the regiment's China and Burma monuments. Across the city near Merrion Square in St Stephen's parish church, two additional white marble plaques were erected to individual officers from the locality: Captain Charles T. King, Esq., of the 32nd Regiment of Foot, and Captain Jackson Wray of the 88th (Connaught Rangers) Regiment of Foot. Two additional and similar works can also be found to individual officers in the suburban environs of the city, in the county parish churches of Monkstown and Killiney, to Lieutenant-Colonel William Hoey of the 30th Regiment of Foot and Lieutenant John Sherwood Gaynor of the 47th Regiment of Foot respectively.

* * *

The Crimean War represents a clear midway point in Ireland's funerary monument tradition: from the huge, extravagantly ornate and extremely expensive memorials of the Napoleonic era, which were also limited in number, to those of the latter Victorian era, which were smaller, less ornate, cheaper and far more numerous. Yet the Napoleonic era monuments were in many ways a step down from the overly elaborate, and to quote Homan Potterton, often 'pagan' or Popish Anglican 'funeral monuments' of the later-seventeenth and eighteenth centuries.[7] The change occurred from the 1850s onwards and it may be seen as a manifestation of the rise of the middle classes,

5 For more on this see Paul Huddie, *The Crimean War and Irish society* (Liverpool, 2015), pp 55–91. 6 Huddie, *The Crimean War*, pp 203–5.   7 Homan Potterton, *Irish church monuments, 1570–1880* (Belfast, 1975), pp 63, 80.

and in this case their expansion within the military officer class. The period from the end of the eighteenth century to the beginning of the twentieth also saw a change in the mediums being used in memorialization. Although works had been produced in other mediums (beyond white marble plaques) prior to the Crimean War it was in the 1850s and early 1860s that their usage, especially stained glass windows, gained increasing popularity. This was partly due to the influence of two artistic trends in England. The first was what the 1850s Conservative politician and architectural pundit, Alexander Beresford Hope, called the 'polychromatic architectural movement', and the second was the more general movement in favour of glass. This was championed in the same period by George Chandler, dean of Chichester, and the contemporary English antiquarian, James Heywood Markland.[8] In Hope's opinion, expressed in an article in the *Irish Builder* in 1861, the increased popularity of stained glass at that time was due to a burgeoning popular mentality that churches had become too cluttered with plaques – what he called 'blisters'. Thus a desire emerged to bring more colour into the structures and internal decoration of churches.[9] That being said, Keith Jeffery's argument relevant to Ireland's First World War memorials might also be applied to this changing mentality: people sought to erect something that was a 'practical thing of tangible benefit for the bereaved'.[10] Windows were light sources and could also display a story or message. Regardless of the emerging changes and Hope's assertions in 1861, the marble plaque still remained the most popular form throughout the mid-Victorian period in Ireland, as is evident from its prominence among the Crimean works.

The change in medium, as well as in size and composition, between the French wars and the Great War stemmed partly from a changing social perception of the common soldier. During the Crimean War the common British soldier was transformed from the 'debased creatures' they had been for centuries into an enduring, brave and Christian soldier.[11] These kinds of monuments had begun to emerge just before the Crimean War, but that conflict, simply by causing the deaths of thousands of men and thus inciting their memorialization, acted as an accelerant of the emerging new trend. Although some British Crimean-era works such as the Coldstream Guards' memorial in St Paul's Cathedral, London (erected in 1855), continued to

---

8 *Irish Builder*, 3:14 (1 Sept. 1861), p. 615.   9 Ibid.   10 Keith Jeffery, 'Echoes of war' in John Horne (ed.), *Our war: Ireland and the Great War* (Dublin, 2008), pp 268–9.   11 E.M. Spiers, *The Army and society, 1815–1914* (London, 1980), p. 116; Veronica Bamfield, *On the strength: the story of the British Army wife* (London, 1974), pp 13–14.

include only the names of officers, all Irish regimental plaques included the numbers of NCOs, privates and drummers lost through death and disease in the East. In Dublin there were two: the plaques to the 18th and 30th Regiments, and while they did not give the enlisted men's names, they were still a new departure. These newly inclusive regimental memorials, with the exception of the two Mansfield stone pedestals erected outside of Tralee Courthouse (which list the names of all of the county's Crimean War as well as Indian Mutiny and Second Opium War dead), represent the first step towards the regimental, parish and county rolls of honour that emerged after the Boer War, and which were produced *en masse* during and after the Great War.[12] The composition of the memorials, or specifically the symbols with which they were imbued, conformed to an established tradition. They appeared in a variety of forms that were common by the 1850s, or in the case of the windows and brass plaques, still emerging. These included pagan, heraldic, architectural, medallion and heroic relief styles, all of which were combined with a variety of militaristic symbolism. In the case of the Dublin memorials the pagan, heraldic, architectural and militaristic styles are all evident, and these were often accompanied by scriptural quotations and long biographical obituaries. Extracts from John 11:25, Revelations 14:18 and Malachi 3:17 can be found on the works dedicated to the 18th Foot, Lieutenant-Colonel Hoey and Captain Wray. The medallion and heroic relief styles are absent, being found only in Monaghan and Armagh.[13]

As Etain Murphy also notes, Victorians attached great importance to the manifestations of bereavement and this is nowhere clearer than in the inclusion of 'weepers' in monuments. Such allegories were used to 'emphasize the depth of their sorrow' felt by the bereaved; this emphasis is evident in the memorial to Captain Jackson Wray. Its employment on that particular monument was, as the inscription notes, due to the fact that he was his parents' 'dearly loved and only child' and his loss 'deeply affected' them.[14] While this use of the lamenting figure is unique in the Irish context, being the only Irish Crimean memorial to utilize this funerary element, what makes it even more remarkable is that the lamenting figure is not the traditional female in a classical style, rather it is a soldier of Wray's regiment. Such allegories were uncommon in Irish Crimean monuments, but they were common in regular Irish funerary works. They were also regularly used in British works, being

---

12 Huddie, 'Ireland and the Crimean War', p. 113.   13 For more details see the appendix table of Irish memorials in Huddie, 'Ireland and the Crimean War', p. 227.   14 Murphy, *A glorious extravaganza*, p. 275.

employed in the Guards' plaque in St Paul's Cathedral and, for example, in the plaques to Captain the Hon. Charles Welbore in Harrow Chapel, and to Colonel Mackeson in Canterbury Cathedral.[15] Yet this absence of military weepers in Irish war memorials does not mean that pagan iconography was absent: upturned torches, symbolizing life being 'snuffed out in death', flank the Gaynor plaque at Killiney while the solitary broken column, symbolizing a life cut short, was employed for Hoey (aged 39 on his death) at Monksktown.[16] The cinerarian urn and draped shroud, what Charles Dickens severely described as a 'jug and towel arrangement', were also very common in the Victorian era and were employed in Derry Cathedral.[17] The dominant styles evident in Dublin are the architectural and militaristic; the former is most apparent in the Wray and King plaques in St Stephen's. Both pieces, executed by the same sculptor, William Manderson of Great Brunswick Street, contain two square columns decorated by simple engravings and tiers above and below, producing the appearance of a classical temple or a vault. In King's memorial this is accompanied by an ornamented tympanum, while Wray's, which is more detailed, exhibits a plateau by which a mixture of mediums is employed through the utilization of reliefs executed in brass. Yet of the two Manderson plaques it is only in Wray's that one can see a burst of militaristic paraphernalia common among Ireland's Crimean memorials. This was also evident in the regimental plaque of the 30th Foot at Arbour Hill and in Hoey's monument. Such iconography is noticeably absent from King's piece. This militarism is manifest in both officers' plaques by a selection of flags on staffs, one of which in both cases carries their respective regiment's number: 'XXX' and '88'. Wray's also includes a drum and a banner upon which is blazoned the word 'Sevastopol', the location of his death. At Arbour Hill crossed swords were also included.

It is also worth noting that a more unconventional military element can be found in the aforementioned window to the 18th (Royal Irish) Regiment, in the form of a roundel panorama of the Russian naval base of Sebastopol in the Crimea.[18] This, as Ulrich Keller argues, by referring to the Coldstream Guards' plaque in London, was a mechanism that artists utilized to undertake the 'superimposition' of the battlefield into a memorial, and perhaps of the viewer

15 *Illustrated London News*, 12 July, 23 Aug. 1856.   **16** Murphy, *A glorious extravaganza*, p. 277.
17 *Journal of the Association for the Preservation of the Memorials of the Dead in Ireland*, 1 (1888), p. 1.
18 Ulrich Keller, *The ultimate spectacle: a visual history of the Crimean War* (Amsterdam, 2001), p. 174. The
spelling of Sevastopol with 'v' rather than a 'b' is intentional here; the former being the modern spelling and

into the location where the commemorated lost their lives. At St Patrick's this is done through the inclusion of the fortress of Sebastopol, but it can also include the place where they were buried, such as the officers' communal gravestone near that fortress, which is included in the case of the Guards. Drawing upon the shared features employed by Hope, Chandler and Markland, stained glass allowed the artist and the commemorators to do far more than sculptors and traditional marble plaques ever could. This it did through its visual versatility, namely the use of varieties of colours and tones. In the case of the St Patrick's Cathedral window the utilization of a variety of brown and opaque tones allows for a vividly reconstructed depiction of the location where the commemorated soldiers died. Although such mechanisms were attempted by sculptors after the war, as after previous campaigns, namely Thomas Farrell's China and Burma monuments for the 18th Regiment erected in the vicinity of the Crimean window, such two-dimensional and monochrome works failed to capture the scene or evoke the realism seen in the roundel. The polychromatic versatility of stained glass is also evident in the artist's ability to use colour to better depict elements through a two-dimensional medium, not only the golden harp and green shamrocks so synonymous with Ireland and the regiment, but also the blue chrysanthemums. These were commonly associated with death, and while not overly utilized in Ireland or Britain, without the use of colour their meaning might well have been lost.

To the principal styles – architectural and militaristic – can also be added the heraldic, evident in the inclusion of the regimental crests, symbols and mottos of the 18th and 30th at St Patrick's and Arbour Hill, and the same of the 88th Regiment coupled with the family crest and motto of the Wray family at St Stephen's. In the case of the first regiment this included the common motif of all Irish regiments, a harp surmounted by a crown, under which was placed a scroll bearing the regiment's motto, 'Virtutis Namurcemsis Praemium' ('Namur – the reward for valour').[19] According to Potterton, heraldry was 'highly important for tombs throughout the seventeenth and into the eighteenth centuries', and thus family crests often accompanied memorials.[20] This tradition evidently persisted long after. The value of any and all such memorials is in the detail they include and, like the newspaper death notices and obituaries recently analysed in depth by Ciara Breathnach and David Butler, church monuments often contain lengthy accounts of the life of the

the latter being the Victorian.   **19** This was the regiment's motto, which originated from the storming of Namur in Belgium in the presence of William III in 1695.   **20** Potterton, *Irish church monuments*, p. 8.

'respected and locally eminent' person being remembered.[21] This is evident in the Gaynor, King and Wray monuments, which give detailed accounts of the men's military careers, family backgrounds and the details of their deaths. One learns that Wray was an only child but also who his mother was (always useful in genealogical work). The perception that people had of the person is also potentially evident, with most memorialized persons being referred to as 'beloved', 'esteemed' and 'appreciated' by those who erected the monuments in their memory. Yet, as Breathnach and Butler warned, just like newspaper death notices and obituaries, which are regularly used as a primary source in order to construct a person's biography or reconstruct a family tree, these memorials must be examined with caution. They were often sanitized, with 'embarrassing indiscretions' being conveniently omitted.[22] On a simpler note, the memorials to the 18th and 30th Regiments, and those like them, inform us of who served with a regiment and how they died, as well as the general toll which the campaign had upon a given unit. The inscriptions on church monuments also explain the origins of the memorials, whether an Irish or British sculptor was employed, and, thus, whether it was an original composition, or, as in the case of the plaque to Lieutenant Vincent Mackesy in Waterford Cathedral, a repetition of the plaque to Captain James Armar Butler in Kilkenny.[23] Through the dedication, they also illustrate who (and how many people) erected a given monument and thus how the costs were met: was it one person paying a lot or many people paying a little? While regimental monuments would most likely have been funded by the entire regiment, those to individual officers could, as has been shown, be funded by wives, parents, fellow officers, or, as in the case of Captain the Hon. William Hely-Hutchinson at Wexford and Lieutenant T.O. Kidd at Armagh, by a large number of people in the locality.

* * *

The years that followed the Crimean War was a period in which a large number of memorials were produced in Dublin, and thus they represent a distinct reference point in the long tradition, primarily within the Church of Ireland, of funerary memorialization in Ireland. It may also, as Breathnach and Butler argue, form part of a broader concept in Ireland of 'memorializing the

21 Ciara Breathnach & David Butler, 'Death notices and obituaries in provincial Irish newspapers, 1820–1900' in James Kelly & Mary Ann Lyons (eds), *Death and dying in Ireland, Britain and Europe: historical perspectives* (Sallins, 2013), p. 252.   **22** Ibid.   **23** *Illustrated London News*, 26 Apr. 1856; Huddie, 'Ireland dead through inscription' – something that stretches all the way back to Ogham writing.[24] Beyond all of this, Ireland's Crimean memorials, substantial in number and varied in both composition and geographical location, were also influenced by, and formed part of, a number of other trends, including the steady decline in eighteenth-century ostentation. These were principally the Victorians' preoccupation with the memorialization of the dead but also the social transformation of the common soldier in the mid-Victorian period. As Edward Spiers argues, the Crimean war was 'a watershed in the relations between the army and society' and this was partly expressed through the inclusion of all ranks upon regimental monuments. Additionally, the Victorian preoccupation with death was often manifest through costly and even extravagant memorials, such as can be seen in Arbour Hill, St Stephen's Church, St Patrick's Cathedral and the parish churches of Killiney and Monkstown just outside of Dublin city.[25] Paula Murphy argues that church memorials, especially plaques, had 'a strong functional purpose', being both 'aspirational' and educational in nature. They were 'usually replete with meaning and message' and imbued with 'national gratitude' and 'patriotism', all of which is evident in the inscriptions on the Dublin monuments. They also sought to 'educate the public and inspire devotion'.[26] However much Dublin's Crimean War memorials may have educated the public in the Victorian and even Edwardian periods, allowing old soldiers to reminisce, stimulating young soldiers and encouraging future generations to emulate the deeds of their fathers, today they educate in a different way. They are now one more asset, along with wills, death notices and gravestones, for the historian and genealogist to use to develop people's knowledge and understanding of their history, heritage and culture.

and the Crimean War', p. 227.   **24** Breathnach & Butler, 'Death notices', p. 257.   **25** Spiers, *Army and society*, p. 97.   **26** Paula Murphy, *Nineteenth-century Irish sculpture: native genius reaffirmed* (New Haven, CT, 2010), p. 32.

A new kind of death: the Niemba funeral and Irish military funerary ceremonial

JAMES McCAFFERTY

And then those men who die bravely on active service,
We shall reckon them as men of gold.
And we shall bury them with special ceremonies,
And for the rest of time treat their tombs with reverence.[1]

Funerals – especially those of patriots or fallen heroes – are inextricably woven into the social and historical fabric of our 'Irish-ness'. The deaths of nine Irish soldiers at Niemba, in Katanga province of the Republic of the Congo, on 8 November 1960 represented a very different kind of dying. This was a new kind of death – death in the service of UN peacekeeping – and their funeral was a new kind of funeral, as in Irish Army tradition there was no precedent for common burials. This 'Niemba funeral' was, perhaps, somewhat of a construct – a construct to enhance the reputation of the Defence Forces. In this context, the positioning of the Irish Defence Forces UN plot at Glasnevin Cemetery is significant. Although a new kind of death, there were similarities between the Niemba funeral and the funeral of Michael Collins. To begin, it might be useful to touch very briefly upon the question of why nine Irish soldiers died at Niemba, in Katanga province, the Republic of the Congo, in 1960.

* * *

On 17 July 1960, the Irish government received a request from the UN to contribute a battalion of Irish infantry to the UN force then being formed to help stabilize the new Republic of the Congo, which was descending into chaos, shortly after achieving its independence from Belgium.[2] The Irish government agreed; on 27 July 1960, the 32nd Irish Infantry Battalion departed for the Congo. Three weeks later – following on a UN request for a further Irish battalion – the 33rd Irish Infantry Battalion also departed for the

1 Plato, *The Republic*, trans. Desmond Lee (2nd ed., London, 1974), p. 256. 2 Memorandum for Cabinet, prepared by Departments of External Affairs & Defence, dated 19 July 1960, NAI, Files of the Department of the Taoiseach, S16137B.

Congo. Now, some 1,300 armed Irish soldiers were, for the very first time since the foundation of the Irish state, serving overseas under UN command.[3] The men who met their deaths at Niemba were from the ranks of 33rd Irish Infantry Battalion. Both 32nd and 33rd Battalions had marched in ceremonial parade down O'Connell Street, Dublin, before leaving for the Congo.[4] At the GPO on O'Connell Street the parades were reviewed by the taoiseach, who was accompanied by the ministers for defence and external affairs. The positioning of the reviewing stand, outside the GPO, resonates with the Easter Rising of 1916 and the first Irish heroes of the twentieth century. This was also the site for reviewing stands for the annual Easter Rising commemorative military parades.[5]

On 8 November 1960, eleven men from 'A' Company, 33rd Infantry Battalion, based at Niemba, Katanga, left their base on a patrol to repair a bridge over the Luweye River, thirty kilometers south of Niemba. The purpose of the bridge repair was to ensure freedom of movement – not only for the UN troops, but also for the population at large. For nine of the men, it would be their last patrol. On the day prior to the ambush, at the Luweye river-crossing, another patrol had found the bridge destroyed; local disputes between tribal factions were probably the reason for its destruction.[6] The dominant local tribe in this part of Katanga was the Baluba. Although the ambush was perpetrated at the Luweye river-crossing, Irish Army vernacular and documentation in Irish Military Archives refer to the occurrence as 'The Niemba Ambush'.[7] Indicative of the place that this had in Irish cultural memory, a new pejorative term, 'Baluba', from the perpetrators – meaning an untrustworthy or despicable individual – entered the Irish vernacular of the day.

* * *

Having briefly shown the historical backdrop to the Niemba funeral, the funeral itself will now be discussed: then, it will be compared to another, earlier Irish military funerary ceremonial and interment – that of General Michael Collins, the first chief of staff of the Irish Army. On 22 November 1960, four months after the departure of 33rd Irish Infantry Battalion, the Niemba funeral took place. This was two weeks after the ambush itself; eight

---

3 General Sean McKeown, 'Congo (ONUC): the military perspective', *Irish Sword*, 20:79 (Summer 1996), pp 43–5. 4 Unit history, 32 IrBatt, Military Archives, Ireland [hereafter MAI], pp 5–6; Unit history, 33 IrBatt., MAI, p. 5. 5 *Irish Independent*, 18 Apr. 1960. 6 Report on Niemba ambush prepared by Colonel Behan, Irish Defence Forces, annex, Library of the Oireachtas – reference no. 54023001093282, pp 3–4. 7 Unit history, 33 IrBatt, MAI, pp 88–104.

bodies were not recovered until two days after the ambush. The body of the ninth soldier who died, Trooper Anthony Browne, was not recovered until two years later. The funeral cortège that passed through Dublin comprised nine coffins: eight of them held the recovered remains of those who had died at Niemba, the additional one held the remains of a soldier who was accidentally shot two days after the ambush.[8]

The funeral cortège and the ceremonial order, including the graveside ceremonies, were based on the then-current procedural orders, written in 1943, for military funerals.[9] The coffins of the fallen had been air-lifted from the Congo, arriving at Baldonnel military airfield on the evening of 20 November, where they lay-in-state on the following day; on the morning of 22 November they were brought to Dublin city, accompanied by a military motorcycle escort, halting at Bachelors Walk where the funeral cortège formed up. The cortège, headed by the Army Number One Band, then marched at slow-time up O'Connell Street – past a reviewing stand at the GPO and via Parnell Square to a further halt at the junction of Dorset Street where they were met by the motorcycle escort, before proceeding to Glasnevin Cemetery. Following the Army band was a colour party of two officers carrying the flags of Ireland and the United Nations; two NCOs carrying rifles with bayonets fixed flanked the colour party. Behind the colour party came an escort party of thirty men, led by an officer, all of whom marched with arms reversed. The marching-order of 'Arms Reversed' traditionally signifies an absence of hostilities while the dead are buried.[10]

Following the escort party came the first of the coffins, that of the patrol commander Lt Kevin Gleeson, carried on what might be termed as a gun carriage – not a true gun carriage – but a trailer towed by a Land Rover vehicle. (A true gun carriage is, in fact, an artillery piece with its barrel removed leaving the wheeled carriage.) The following eight coffins were placed two each on four artillery-towing lorries, AEC Matadors, and positioned on bases traversing the sides of the lorries so that these eight coffins were about two-and-a-half metres above street level. The patrol commander's coffin was somewhat less than one metre above street level. All the coffins were draped with Irish and UN flags, with floral tributes placed about them. Eight officers flanked the first coffin on the gun carriage; the four Matador lorries were each flanked by ten NCOs and men.[11]

---

8 Ibid.   **9** Defence Forces Regulations, A 6, 'Deaths and Funerals', MAI, 1943.   **10** Ibid.; Arlington National Cemetery, arlingtoncemetry.net/customs.htm.   **11** Newsreels, *Amharch Éireann*, Nov. 1960, Irish

12 Large crowds pay their respects as the coffin of patrol commander at Niemba,
Lieutenant Kevin Gleeson, passes the GPO, 22 November 1960
(reproduced courtesy of Pól Ó Duibhir).

As the cortège proceeded along O'Connell Street, the Army Number One
Band played Chopin's solemn *March Funebre*.[12] The use of the Matador lorries
was significant. It may have been the case that as the Army had sent a
considerable number of Land Rovers and their trailers to the Congo, there was
an insufficient number of these vehicles remaining at home; or, perhaps, the
elevated height of the eight coffins was to facilitate the view of the estimated
300,000 people who lined O'Connell Street and Parnell Square, in reverential
silence, during the procession.[13] In the event, such an elevation was, perhaps,
symbolic of 'offering-up' of the dead soldiers in the cause of UN peacekeeping.
The funeral party's last unit was the firing party, marching with arms reversed:

film archives.   **12** Adjutant, Army School of Music & No. 1 Army Band, Cathal Brugha Barracks, Dublin.
13 *Irish Press*, 23 Nov. 1960.

the composition of the firing party, a lieutenant's party of a lieutenant, a sergeant and twelve men was as prescribed in the relevant ceremonial orders.[14] Normally in military funeral ceremonial order the relatives of the deceased would then follow the firing party, but in the case of the Niemba funeral the relatives were not part of the procession but awaited the cortège at Glasnevin Cemetery. The coffins were sealed before leaving the Congo; even when lying-in-state at Baldonnell they remained closed and thus relatives were unable to look upon the remains of their family members.

When the cortège arrived at Glasnevin Cemetery, a further lieutenant's firing party had been formed up there, as it would not have been practicable to await the arrival of the firing party from the O'Connell Street procession. This firing party was in two ranks, facing northwards and standing atop the grave of Michael Collins, the Irish Army's first chief of staff.[15] Collins' grave lies west to east – just outside Glasnevin Cemetery Museum – to the east of it is the grave of soldiers fallen in the Irish Civil War, and then immediately to the east of the Civil War grave lies the Irish UN plot. This UN plot was opened for the first time for the Niemba funerals. To the west of Collins' grave and slightly north of it stands the round tower memorial to Daniel O'Connell; further north lies the grave of Kevin O'Higgins, minister for justice and vice president of the executive council of the Irish Free State, shot in 1927. The Irish soldiers who fell at Niemba lie in distinguished company; their resting place was chosen with the proximity to that of Michael Collins very much in mind. Archbishop John Charles McQuaid, with a retinue of attending priests, received the coffins near the graveside, blessed them and said the Catholic prayers of commitment – while facing the vehicles that still carried the coffins.

As the coffins weighed some 250 kilos each a mobile crane was used to lower them into their graves. This crane was parked behind, and was partly screened by, some cypress trees; however, the crane was visible to those at the graveside, including the relatives of the fallen. When the prayers were concluded, the firing-party discharged the ceremonial three volleys; then Irish Army buglers and drummers sounded the 'Last Post' call and after an interval of a minute, sounded the 'Reveille' call. The firing of the volleys represents the discharging – for the last time – of the weapons of the fallen.[16] 'Last Post' is the final bugle call of the military day, 'Reveille' is the first call of the military

---

14 Defence Forces Regulations, A 6, 'Deaths and Funerals', 1943, MAI, Office of the Adjutant-General, Irish Defence Forces, Ceremonial Order 17/1960.   **15** S.J. Connolly (ed.), *Oxford companion to Irish history* (Oxford, 2002) pp 108–9.   **16** Arlington National Cemetery, arlingtoncemetry.net/customs.htm.

13 Official and family mourners observe the military salute over the graves of the troops killed at Niemba, Glasnevin Cemetery, 22 November 1960 (reproduced courtesy of the Irish Military Archive).

day; these calls signify sleep and awakening, death and resurrection. This was the conclusion of the military ceremonial. Following an interval, the families of the Niemba fallen left the cemetery and the coffins were then lowered into the grave.

The use of a common grave evokes a common sacrifice, and echoes the military cemeteries of the First World War. This was the first occasion on which the Irish Army had conducted a mass burial; there was no precedent. The selection of the route – mirroring the route of the parades prior to departure for the Congo, past the GPO with its links to the Easter Rising of 1916, suggests a careful construct by the Army, as does the positioning of the UN plot. The Irish public, by lining the parade route in such numbers, demonstrated the esteem in which the Army was now held.

* * *

For comparison it is relevant to consider an earlier 'great' military funeral in Ireland – that of Michael Collins, on 28 August 1922. At the Pro-Cathedral, Dublin, the archbishop of Dublin said requiem mass and also gave the graveside blessing.

A large number of priests attended: this was a 'funeral Irish-style', the more priests or clergy in attendance the more important was the dead person. The military ceremonial began outside the Pro-Cathedral, when the coffin was draped with the recently adopted national flag. The gun carriage was drawn by horses, the ceremonial was based on British Army tradition – but the rider-less, caparisoned horse was not used. The escort and firing party, marching with arms reversed, flanked the gun carriage, on the limber of which were seated two soldiers wearing bandoliers. This gun carriage, unlike the one that bore the remains of Lt Gleeson at the Niemba funeral, was a true gun carriage, in use at that time. The officer-pallbearers marched outside the flanking firing party: unlike the officers at the Niemba funeral, they did not wear swords, but wore black armbands on their sleeves. As with the Niemba funeral, thousands of people lined the funeral route, from the Pro-Cathedral to Glasnevin Cemetery.

In Glasnevin Cemetery, Collins, the Niemba fallen and other notable Irish graves 'come together' – their relative positioning is meaningful. The grave of Michael Collins lies inside the south gate of the cemetery, just beside the museum walls; below Collins' grave is the Army pre-truce plot, where lie some of the Free State soldiers who died in the civil war. Immediately south of this is the Army's UN grave, the Niemba fallen were its first occupants. Unlike the Niemba soldiers, the pre-truce plot is not a common grave, in that those reposing there did not fall in a single engagement. The positioning of the Niemba grave, evokes links between Michael Collins, first Irish Army chief of staff, Free State soldiers and Irish UN soldiers. These Niemba dead lie in illustrious company – near O'Connell, Parnell, de Valera and O'Higgins.

* * *

An incident just prior to the Congo mission reflected, perhaps, the common perception of the Irish Army. On 5 November 1958, at Ballina district court the judge, in disposing of a case where a man was charged with theft from a local shop, offered the defendant the option of six months in jail, or, he could join the Army. The defendant, reportedly, chose to join the Army and the case was adjourned for one month.[17] The attitude behind this reported 'jail or join the Army' case contrasts with headlines such as 'many thousands lined the streets of Dublin to see our soldiers depart for UN duty in the Congo', and '300,000 people – some kneeling in prayer – lined the funeral parade route for our Congo dead'.[18] This funerary ceremonial was, and still is, part of our social tradition, our history. But, in some respects there were deliberate constructs in its arrangement: the route past the GPO, the mirroring of the departure parades, the high trucks carrying coffins, the positioning of the UN plot in Glasnevin, the presence of the Dublin archbishop. Why the constructs? Were they to enhance the Army's reputation or to evade broader questions about the military mission?

Entwining the graves of all of these dead – the Niemba dead, Michael Collins, the Irish dead resting in Belgium – are common threads of sacrifice, memorial and symbolism. Yet this was a 'new kind of dying' – Irish soldiers who died not in a national cause or in a foreign war – but with the United Nations force for peace in the Congo. Their shared sacrifice was the price that Ireland paid as a political actor on the world stage.

17 *Irish Times*, 5 Nov. 1958. **18** *Irish Times*, 23 Nov. 1960.

'No hanging here': the persistence of the death penalty in twentieth-century Ireland

IAN MILLER

In September 1975, garda officer Michael Reynolds, while shopping with his wife and 4-year-old daughter in Killester, Dublin, noticed an armed bank robbery taking place. Despite being off-duty, Reynolds pursued the raiders at high speed in his car until they abandoned their vehicle at St Anne's Park, Raheny. Undeterred, he pursued the raiders on foot, dragging one of them to the ground. Within earshot of his family, Reynolds was shot in the head. Two hours later, he died in hospital. In the following year, Noel and Marie Murray – members of the anarchist group Dublin Black Cross – were sentenced to death for Reynolds' murder.[1] Notwithstanding the violent and emotive death of a garda officer, the imposition of the death sentence – the first instance in Ireland since 1954 – caused international outrage. In Bonn, anarchists stormed the Irish Embassy and threw a bleeding sheep's head over the counter at startled staff members.[2] In Munich, anarchists placed sheep heads, dripping with blood, on the counter of an Aer Lingus office alongside a sign that read 'Ireland: A Murder State'. Amnesty International, novelist Heinrich Böll, Lord Longford, and the International Catholic Movement for Peace (among others) publicly objected.[3]

The public scandal occasioned by the Murrays' sentencing raised questions about the function of capital punishment in late-twentieth-century Ireland. By the 1970s, most other European countries had revoked the death penalty. Hanging seemed somewhat anachronistic; a remnant of a more violent, somewhat alien, past that bore little relevance to modern penal contexts. Nonetheless, capital punishment remained on the statute book in Ireland until as late as July 1990. Historians of Ireland have focused primarily on political executions, particularly those performed at Kilmainham Gaol following the Easter Rising. This emphasis conceals a broader historical debate on execution in twentieth-century Ireland. Ian O'Donnell and David M. Doyle have suggested that the ongoing use of execution in post-independence Ireland

---

1 Death sentence on Murray: security aspects, NAI, TAOIS/2007/110/3. 2 Death sentence in Murray case: correspondence, NAI, TAOIS/2009/120/2040. 3 Death sentence on Murray: security aspects.

reflected the fact that hanging was a legacy of 'colonialism' and English tyranny; the use of English, rather than Irish, hangmen representing 'an English solution to an Irish problem'.[4] Yet the authors pay relatively little attention to a broader spectrum of ideas and ideologies that surrounded the issue of hanging in Ireland.

Internationally, historians have focused on investigating nineteenth-century capital punishment debates, as exemplified by Vic Gatrell's *The hanging tree: execution and the English people, 1770–1860*. Recent literature such as Lizzie Seal's *Capital punishment in twentieth-century Britain: audience, justice, memory* has begun to fill a historiographical lacuna by focusing on twentieth-century debates.[5] With the intention of providing the groundwork for a more comprehensive Irish-focused historical inquiry, this essay asks: why did the Murrays' sentencing prove so contentious? For what reasons did public concern over capital punishment peak in Ireland in the 1970s, a decade when national security seemed severely threatened by politically motivated violence? And why did the Irish government hesitate until 1990 to relinquish its prerogative to kill serious offenders? Ultimately, the Murrays' plight in Dublin sparked a heated national and international debate. Even at peaks in paramilitary activity, campaigners for the abolition of the death penalty in Ireland prioritized human rights concerns above the perceived need to punish political subversion. The public outcry against capital punishment was driven by expressions of compassion and emotion that conflicted with a rational political logic intent on safeguarding national security interests.[6]

* * *

Capital punishment was inherited from a pre-modern penal code that relied upon the spectacle of public hanging to enforce public order. In early-nineteenth-century Ireland, hanging for minor offences was gradually abandoned; a development that ran in tandem with the rapid extension of the prison network.[7] Prison sentences became standardized; punishments became more uniform and were more frequently used.[8] Given the existence of

---

4 I. O'Donnell and D.M. Doyle, 'A family affair: English hangmen and a Dublin jail, 1923–54', *New Hibernia Review*, 18:4 (2014), pp 101–18. **5** V.A.C. Gatrell, *The hanging tree: execution and the English people, 1770–1868* (Oxford, 1994); L. Seal, *Capital punishment in twentieth-century Britain: audience, justice, memory* (London, 2014). **6** For an analysis of capital punishment and its emotional aspects, see C. Langhamer, '"The live dynamic whole of feeling and behavior": capital punishment and the politics of emotion, 1945–57', *Journal of British Studies*, 51:2 (2012), pp 416–41. **7** Gatrell, *The hanging tree*, p. 10; M. Ignatieff, *A just measure of pain: the penitentiary in the industrial revolution, 1750–1850* (London, 1978), p. 16. **8** M. Foucault, *Discipline and punish: the birth of the prison* (London, 1991 [1975]), pp 78–82.

imprisonment as an alternative – seemingly more humane – punishment, the excessive use of hanging for trivial offences seemed increasingly unjust. In 1842, controversy emerged when a judge sentenced a man to death for the crime of killing a goat.[9] As part of a reorganization of the penal code, the number of capital offences was drastically reduced, a step with important judicial implications.[10] Between 1823 and 1832, an average of 267 people had been sentenced to death in Ireland each year, although less than 40 (annually) were ultimately executed. In stark contrast, between 1853 and 1862, an average of three executions took place each year.[11] The lord lieutenant commuted a high proportion of death sentences, particularly among female criminals.[12] From the 1860s, executions were no longer performed in public, although the removal of hanging to private institutional spaces such as Mountjoy Prison camouflaged an ongoing propensity to inflict a violent death on serious offenders.[13]

Throughout the mid-nineteenth century, capital punishment evolved into an issue with complex moral, legal and ethical implications. Increased agitation for its abandonment resulted partly from shifting attitudes toward the body as sensitivities grew towards the infliction of pain and physical suffering (mirrored in contemporaneous debates on child welfare and animal cruelty).[14] At the same time, new emotional sensibilities evolved that privileged compassion and sympathy as the bedrock of a modern, civilized, western society.[15] In these contexts, opponents of hanging emphasized its archaic nature. They stressed its origins in an obsolete and barbaric punitive system predicated on vengeance, retribution and violence. In 1935, the Society for the Abolition of the Death Penalty was formed in Dublin, a group which described the death penalty as a 'grisly relic of barbarous times when punishments were brutal and vindictive'.[16] Hanging, opponents suggested, was a stain on modern society.

---

9 'Criminal law: killing of a goat (Ireland)', House of Commons debates, 18 Feb. 1842, vol. 60, cols 635–6. **10** S.J. Connolly, 'Unnatural death in four nations: contrasts and comparisons' in S.J. Connolly (ed.), *Kingdoms united? Great Britain and Ireland since 1500: integration and diversity* (Dublin, 1999), pp 200–14; P.M. Prior, *Madness and murder: gender, crime and mental disorder in nineteenth-century Ireland* (Dublin, 2008), pp 12–13. **11** Report of the Capital Punishment Commission, HC 1866 [3590] xxi, pp 611–12. **12** E. Farrell, 'A most diabolical deed': infanticide and Irish society, 1850–1900* (Manchester, 2013), pp 210–39. **13** Gatrell, *The hanging tree*, p. 590; P. Priestley, *Victorian prison lives: English prison biography, 1830–1914* (London, 1985), p. 234. **14** P. Spierenburg, 'The body and the state: early modern Europe' in N. Morris & D.J. Rothman (eds), *The Oxford history of the prison: the practice of punishment in western society* (Oxford, 1995), pp 44–70 at p. 47. **15** Gatrell, *The hanging tree*, pp 234–5. **16** *Irish Independent*, 2 Nov. 1935; *Irish Independent*, 2 Jan. 1939.

1 Coffins stacked in the crypt of St Michan's on Church Street. Built on the site of an earlier church (1095), the present St Michan's Anglican church was built in the 1680s. The crypts contain bodies that date to the thirteenth century (image taken by kind permission of St Michan's parish).

An open Hearse used at the funerals of the Higher Rank

2 Hugh Douglas Hamilton, funeral of the higher ranks, *c.*1760 (private collection).

Three Papist Criminals going to Execution.

3 Hugh Douglas Hamilton, sketch of 'Papist' (Roman Catholic) prisoners on their way to the gallows, *c.*1760 (private collection).

4 Sir Francis and Lady Cecilia Agard, accompanied by a strategic array of both their families, on the Agard Memorial, Christ Church Cathedral south transept, *c.*1584 (image, Ciarán Wallace).

5 Bust of Sir Toby Butler (d. 1721) in St James' Graveyard, probably the most substantial surviving Jacobite monument in Dublin (image, Sean Murphy).

7 Goldenbridge Cemetery, the first burial ground in Dublin not controlled by the established Anglican Church since the Reformation, was opened in 1829 by the Catholic Association. Its success led to the creation of the much larger Glasnevin Cemetery in 1832 (photo, Ciarán Wallace).

6 (*opposite*) The Huguenot Cemetery, Merrion Row, which dates to 1693, reflects the influx of French Protestants to Ireland in the aftermath of the revocation of the Edict of Nantes in 1685, which drove Protestants out of their home country (photo, Lisa Marie Griffith).

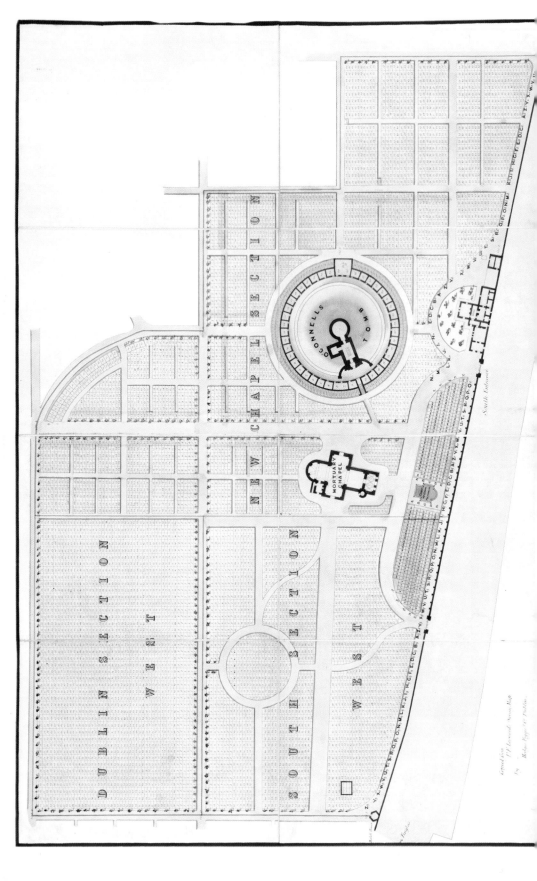

9 Glasnevin Cemetery, an example of a well-preserved garden cemetery with its sombre vertical monuments (photo, Ciarán Wallace).

8 (*opposite*) Late nineteenth-century map of Glasnevin Cemetery's new Finglas Road entrance and the O'Connell tomb, showing the orderly arrangement of the plots and tree-lined avenues characteristic of the garden cemetery movement (reproduced courtesy of Glasnevin Trust).

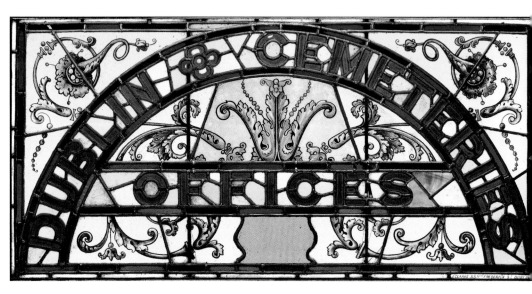

10 Stained glass window of the Dublin Cemeteries Offices
(reproduced courtesy of Glasnevin Trust).

11 (*left*) Memorial window to the officers, NCOs and men of the 18th (Royal Irish) Regiment who died during the Crimean War. Located in the north trancept of St Patrick's Cathedral (photo, Paul Huddie).

12 Brass relief of 'weeper' soldier and militaristic paraphernalia on plaque to Captain Jackson Wray, 88th (Connaught Rangers) Regiment, in St Stephen's Church (photo, Paul Huddie).

13 The Irish UN plot today, situated close to the graves of prominent Irish leaders from before and after 1922, overlooked by the Glasnevin Cemetery Museum building (photo, James McCafferty).

14 Sigerson Memorial in Glasnevin Cemetery honouring those who died in 1916 (photo, Siobhán Doyle).

15 St Kevin's Church (now St Kevin's Park), Camden Row. A popular city burial site from the thirteenth until the early twentieth century, it holds the graves of archbishops, leading rebels and the brewer John D'Arcy, whose controversial funeral indirectly led to the establishment of the Dublin Cemeteries Committee.

16 View of Mount Jerome Cemetery. Opened in 1836, it is a non-denominational cemetery with 250,000 burials.

17 Sheares brothers' crypt in St Michan's. The brothers were executed for their part in the 1798 rebellion and were interred in the crypt. Their coffins were conserved in the 2000s by Nichols' Undertakers (image taken with permission from St Michan's parish).

Campaigners such as Dublin-based social reformer James Haughton buttressed these perspectives with statistical evidence which suggested that hanging failed to deter murderers. In 1850, Haughton lamented that 'the scaffold has reeked with blood in these lands during the last year, and yet we find that murder is rife amongst us notwithstanding'.[17] The inadequacy of hanging as a safeguard against murder continued to underpin debates on capital punishment in the twentieth century. The issue of wrongful conviction also proved controversial. Sensationally, even Albert Pierrepoint – Britain's official executioner who performed executions in Ireland – became opposed to capital punishment (despite having hanged 530 criminals) upon learning that he had hanged an innocent man.[18] In addition, the death penalty raised theological questions about the moral right of man (or the state) to take life.[19] Haughton firmly believed that hanging usurped God's authority to decide when death should occur, adding that 'when rulers make light of human life, the governed do not exhibit a due sense of its sacredness'.[20] Nineteenth-century Irish theologians pondered over questions such as why Cain had not been sentenced to death for murdering his brother Abel and whether the Mosaic Law permitted man to execute.[21] Evidently, capital punishment was imbued with overlapping social, moral and religious intricacies. Yet, as the remainder of this essay demonstrates, twentieth-century Dublin provided a unique and highly problematic context in which these debates were played out.

* * *

At the heart of the Irish capital punishment question rested two contradictory forces: a moral sense that the death sentence was ethically inappropriate and a political imperative to maintain national security. This inherent tension between the humane and political aspects of capital punishment persisted throughout much of the century and was, in many ways, unique to Ireland. The state tended to enforce its right to execute at critical periods when national security seemed threatened by groups such as the Irish Republican Army (IRA). Yet strong public feeling emerged in Dublin even despite the ominous presence of political violence and bombings (from both republicans and loyalists) in the 1970s, as evidenced by the public reaction against the Murrays' death sentence in the city. This scenario is perhaps unexpected given

17 J. Haughton, *On death punishments* (Dublin, 1850), pp 6, 8, 11.   **18** A. Pierrepoint, *Executioner, Pierrepoint* (London, 1974).   **19** *Freeman's Journal*, 21 July 1858.   **20** Ibid., 4 Feb. 1848.   **21** H.J.C., 'The scriptural argument for capital punishment', *Dublin University Magazine*, 75 (1870), pp 414–21.

that one might anticipate greater public tolerance for the death penalty in the context of civilian bombings and high-profile murders.

How had these debates evolved over time? In the revolutionary period, a high number of official and unofficial executions had discouraged support for capital punishment.[22] Between 1922 and 1923, during the Irish Civil War, seventy-seven state-supported executions took place, primarily involving opponents of the newly formed Irish state.[23] The Cosgrave government also made carrying firearms a capital offence – part of a policy directed at defeating anti-treaty IRA agitators.[24] When a Public Safety Bill was put before the Senate in 1923, James Green Douglas made an emotive case for abolishing the death penalty. The discussion that ensued revealed that Senate members mostly agreed upon the moral repugnancy of execution but felt that the tense socio-political climate evident in Ireland meant that 1923 was an inappropriate time to enact legislation, given that the newly formed state was rife with armed opponents.[25]

Yet hanging remained a possibility for most of the century. Moreover, it tended to be murderers and sexual offenders who found themselves hanged, a fact that calls into question contemporary suggestions that Ireland's unique political circumstances necessitated a resort to hanging, as noted by Doyle and O'Donnell.[26] Wartime exigencies provided an exception. The circumstances of the Second World War (or the 'Emergency' in Ireland) fortified opposition to capital punishment. The outbreak of conflict saw the implementation of emergency legislation including the Offences Against the State Act of 1939. This act established special criminal courts and enhanced garda power to prevent seditious activities. Its implementation coincided with a period of sustained republican violence in both Britain and Ireland, marked by bombings and the killing of garda officers. In response, the Emergency Powers Amendment Act of 1940 conferred extra powers to employ the death sentence.[27] During the Emergency, a number of IRA members were executed in Ireland in prisons such as Mountjoy – an act that inflamed nationalist opinion in both parts of Ireland. Large protests took place in Dublin.[28]

---

22 See T.M. Breen, 'The government's executions policy during the Irish Civil War, 1922–1923' (PhD, NUIM, 2010). **23** J. Maguire, *IRA internments and the Irish government: subversives and the state, 1939–1962* (Dublin, 2008), p. 11. **24** E. O'Haplin, *Defending Ireland: the Irish state and its enemies since 1922* (Oxford, 1999), pp 30–3. **25** 'Public Safety (Emergency Powers) Bill 1923', Seanad Éireann debate (30 July 1923), 1:35. **26** D.M. Doyle & I. O'Donnell, 'The death penalty in post-independence Ireland', *Journal of Legal History*, 33:1 (April 2012), pp 65–91. **27** Death sentences: procedure, NAI, TAOIS/S7788B. **28** O'Halpin, *Defending Ireland*, p. 252.

Yet the Emergency proved to be a turning point. Ex-IRA chief of staff and lawyer Seán MacBride represented a considerable number of executed IRA prisoners at inquests. Despite having left the IRA, MacBride forged a legal and political career marked by a determination to draw attention to issues such as prison conditions and the controversial matter of execution. His arguments against capital punishment were steeped in ethical principles and paved the way for a sustained questioning of political responses to subversion.[29] Internationally, the global violence witnessed during the Second World War provided a framework for a concerted international drive towards upholding human rights. Given the strong public reaction to the widespread violence and persecution evident across Europe during the conflict, harsh punitive measures such as capital punishment became increasingly contested. In 1948, when serving as minister for external affairs, MacBride publicly equated executions performed during the Emergency with the brutality of the Nazi concentration camp, a site where, in his view, 'mass extermination [was] done by people who were every much as civilized as we are'. Drawing upon notions of civility and humanity, MacBride asserted that abolishing capital punishment was crucial to the broader project of stopping the human race from pursuing a violent course that might ultimately lead to its destruction.[30] Minister for local government and public health, Seán MacEntee, concurred. In 1948, he wrote to the taoiseach asserting that 'we must start under the premise that no human being has the right to take human life, be it on behalf of the State or on behalf of an individual'.[31] MacBride and MacEntee's statements drew upon by now familiar moral arguments against capital punishment. They were also rooted in evolving ideas on the need to limit state-sanctioned violence and promote human rights interests. MacBride presented Irish state executions as an extension of broader European violence while MacEntee tacitly suggested that state violence set a negative example to political opponents.

The last execution in Ireland was that of Michael Manning, a Limerick carter found guilty of drunkenly murdering 65-year-old nurse Catherine Cooper. Manning was hanged at Mountjoy Prison on 20 April 1954.[32] In the same year, Brendan Behan dramatized *The quare fellow*, a theatrical work in which protagonists in a prison discuss the looming execution of a butcher who murdered and expertly cut up the body of his brother.[33] Throughout the 1950s

---

29 C. Nic Dháibhéid, *Seán MacBride: a republican life, 1904–1946* (Liverpool, 2011), p. 137.   **30** *Irish Times*, 25 Oct. 1948.   **31** 'Letter from Seán MacEntee to the Taoiseach', 24 Nov. 1948, NAI, TAOIS/S7788B.   **32** 'Michael Manning: death sentence', NAI, TAOIS S/15641.   **33** B. Behan, *The quare*

NOEL MURRAY

Noel Murray was 26 when he was sentenced to death by the Special Criminal Court on June 9th 1976. He was a metal fabricator and was employed in C.I.E. for several years. He first became politically involved in 1966 when he joined the Republican Movement. In those days Noel was one of the few people involved in the movement in the Celbridge area but he made up for it with hard work. He is well remembered in the Kildare area for selling Republican literature and later on Socialist and Revolutionary literature. After the Republican Movement split in 1970 Noel went with Official Sinn Fein and worked hard carrying out their policies. In 1971 Noel was arrested on a picket outside the American Embassy which was protesting over American involvement in Vietnam. He was arrested later on that year for occupying Fianna Fail headquarters over their failure to intervene in the Northern crisis at the time. During his time in the Celbridge cumann he covered most of the Kildare area selling the United Irishman and is remembered in places like Naas where he did his regular paper round.

He then moved to Dublin where he met Marie Mac Phillips and later married her. Both of them were in the Connolly Cumann of Official Sinn Fein in the Ballyfermot/ Drimnagh area until 1973. Noel resigned at this stage over disagreement with changes in the policy of the Official Republican Movement.

Since 1973, like Marie, he remained politically active, attending protests about prisoners conditions and repressive legislation continuing to fight for his ideal an independent socialist Ireland.

12 charged with damaging flag at U.S. embassy

Twelve young Dublin people appeared on remand in the Dublin District Court yesterday on a charge that last Saturday they wilfully and maliciously damaged, to an extent of not more than £200, the American flag and the rope attached to it, when it was being flown in the grounds of the American Embassy at Pembroke road, Ballsbridge, Dublin.

The defendants are Peter Kavanagh, of Howth road, Sean O Cionnaith, of Coolock avenue, Mairin de Burca, of Wilfield road, Ballsbridge. Mrs. Nuala Monaghan, of St. Patrick's road, Walkinstown, Martin Gaffney, of Lower Kimmage road, Gorenka Gaffney, of Lower Kimmage road, Fionnuala O'Connor, of Lower Baggot street, Tadek Gaj, of Lower Baggot street, Vladek Gaj, of Lower Baggot street, Marie McMahon, of Pembroke lane, Noel Murray, of Church road, Celbridge and Columba Longmore, of Foyle road, Fairview.

14 Anti-death penalty pamphlet *No hanging here: the case of Marie and Noel Murray* produced by the Murray Defence Committee, 1976 (sourced from the collection in the Left Archive). **15** Profile of Noel Murray, and photograph of him by a prison van from *No hanging here*, 1976 (sourced from the collection in the Left Archive).

Capital punishment had essentially been imposed on two individuals for whom the act had not been intended. Marie Murray was aged 27 when she was sentenced to death. In 1968, she had joined the republican movement and actively promoted Irish-language interests and improved housing in impoverished areas such as Ballyfermot. She resigned from Sinn Féin in 1973 in a disagreement over policy changes. Noel Murray was 26. He had been active in the Celbridge republican movement and campaigned on issues including prisoners' rights. He left the republican movement alongside his wife.

In response to the controversial sentencings, the Murray Defence Committee formed in Dublin in 1976. The committee sought the total abolition of capital punishment in Ireland, the establishment of an independent commission to inquire into the Murrays' sentencing and the reopening of the trial on human rights grounds. In an emotive pamphlet entitled 'No hanging here: the case of Marie and Noel Murray', the committee maintained that solicitors had been denied the right to visit the Murrays following their arrest; Noel Murray had been stripped naked, repeatedly punched in the stomach, dropped head first on to the floor and had his head placed in the toilet by investigating gardaí; the Murrays had been tried in a Special Criminal Court consisting of three judges, designed primarily to deal with IRA crimes; the Murrays had not been permitted to present evidence or be tried by jury; the government had subjected the Murrays to sustained psychological torture by drawing out the reprieve procedure; and members of the Murray Defence Committee had been harassed and intimidated by the gardaí.[36]

The death sentences imposed on Noel and Marie Murray reignited discussion about the function of capital punishment in Ireland and called into question the compromise measures applied in 1964. In July 1976, Trinity College Dublin law lecturer and human rights advocate Kadar Asmal asserted in the *Irish Times* that:

> Capital punishment is the most violent response by a society against those who kill. Execution by the State, with all the macabre trappings that it entails, has neither a reformative nor a deterrent effect on such persons. In the case of murders for a political reason, there is the additional factor that all governments must bear in mind that such executions are counter-productive in political terms.[37]

Asmal was a co-founder of the Irish Council for Civil Liberties (established in the same year as the Murrays' sentencing), a group that held a public meeting on the matter in Dublin in November 1976 and unanimously passed a resolution urging the government to abolish capital punishment.[38] In response to the Murrays' plight, the Irish Commission for Justice and Peace (consisting of five episcopal members) rejected physical retaliation or retribution as a morally defensible justification for judicial execution.[39] Lord Longford, a prominent campaigner for human rights, wrote to the Department of Foreign Affairs declaring that he viewed the Murray sentences with 'absolute horror', adding

---

36 *No hanging here: the case of Marie and Noel Murray* (Celbridge, 1976).   37 *Irish Times*, 31 July 1976.
38 *Irish Independent*, 4 Nov. 1976.   39 Irish Commission for Justice and Peace: a statement on capital punishment, 11 Nov. 1976, NAI, TAOIS/2006/133/702.

that their executions would be 'most shameful' for Ireland.[40] In the Netherlands, the Federation of Free Socialists protested outside the Irish embassy carrying an anarchist flag and waving banners with slogans reading 'Irish Free State = Terror State', 'I Loathe Your Gallows', 'Free the Murrays from the Gallows' and 'No Hanging Here'.[41]

The heated debates that surrounded the Murrays' plight demonstrated a strong, emotionally charged public response to the implementation of capital punishment, which clashed with a rational political logic of retaining the death penalty for national security purposes. Notably, the sentencing coincided with pronounced concern about national security, given that both loyalist and republican groups were involved in bombing campaigns in Dublin and other Irish towns.[42] The government sought to safeguard its citizens and democratic institutions and ensure that Ireland would not be used as a base for mounting attacks on Northern Ireland.[43] At the peak of the Murray debates, British ambassador Christopher Ewart-Biggs was murdered in Sandyford, Dublin, by an IRA landmine. This controversial high-profile death strengthened the political resolve to retain the death penalty to deter political subversion.[44] Minister for Justice Desmond O'Malley publicly stated that 'I don't think one can rule it [the death penalty] out in present circumstances'.[45] Evidently, the issue of capital punishment acquired considerable complexity in twentieth-century Ireland, as those seeking its abolition operated in a socio-political climate that placed value on deterrent legislation.

In republican circles, the retention of capital punishment formed part of a wider debate on excessive political responses to militant republicanism. Discussion of the issue reflected contemporaneous debates on the treatment of IRA prisoners such as the Price sisters and Michael Gaughan – individuals whose health had been compromised in the mid-1970s by harsh regimes of prison punishment that included force-feeding. Committed republicans responded to the Murrays' sentencing by maintaining that the bodies of political dissidents were inappropriate sites for enacting punishment for politically motivated acts. Propaganda produced by the Murray Defence Committee asserted that the economic downturn and Northern Irish instability had encouraged the Irish government to brutally repress anti-establishment groups

40 Letter from Irish Embassy (London) to Department of Foreign Affairs, 19 July 1976, NAI, TAOIS2006/133/700.   **41** Letter from Irish Embassy (Netherlands) to Department of Foreign Affairs, 13 Oct. 1976, NAI, TAOIS/2009/111/69.   **42** For Irish responses, see D. Ferriter, *Ambiguous republic: Ireland in the 1970s* (London, 2011), pp 119–20.   **43** Death sentence in Murray case: correspondence, NAI, TAOIS/2009/120/2040.   **44** *Irish Independent*, 4 Aug. 1976.   **45** *Irish Times*, 26 July 1976.

by 'forging a tyranny ostensibly to deal with terrorists'. The Irish government was propagating a tough counter-terrorist image, the committee claimed, 'whilst its policies are in ruins and Irish society is careering towards dissolution'. In *No hanging here*, the committee contextualized the renewed implementation of the death sentence as one manifestation of a broader attack on republicanism, exemplified by efforts to stifle commemorations of the Easter Rising, the impounding of the body of Frank Stagg (who had died on hunger strike following a fatal bout of force-feeding), an unwillingness to tackle militant loyalism and biased media censorship.[46] Militant republicanism, opponents of the death penalty suggested, was being tackled in a dis-criminatory, unjust manner. Republicans presented the state itself as inherently violent, inverting the logic of policies ostensibly in place to deter violence.

* * *

In May 1977, Marie Murray was granted a retrial and acquitted of the capital murder of Reynolds. Although the jury was satisfied that she had fired the shot that killed Reynolds, it acknowledged that Murray had been unaware that Reynolds was a garda officer.[47] Nonetheless, the initial sentencing had ignited public feeling on the capacity of the Irish state to execute its enemies. Throughout the late 1970s, Amnesty International raised concerns about the ongoing inclusion of the death penalty in Irish legislation, and its potential use against political opponents.[48] The department of justice remained insistent on the need to retain capital punishment given the high number of bombings and murders in Dublin and elsewhere.[49] The debate was renewed in 1980 following the murders of garda officers Henry Byrne and John Morley by alleged members of the Irish National Liberation Army. Although three men were sentenced to death for these murders, their sentences were reduced to life imprisonment. One commentator in the *Irish Times* noted, 'at the same time abortion is forbidden by the government, again acting on behalf of the people, and those who participate in this act are condemned as murderers. Either both of these acts are murder or neither of them is'.[50]

The political imperative to preserve capital punishment legislation found the Irish government swimming against an international tide of public opinion that fed on the emotional and ethical implications of imposing death, even on

46 *No hanging here*, p. 7. **47** Death sentences in the Murray case (correspondence), Mar. 1977, NAI, TAOIS/2009/120/2074. **48** MacBride (ed.), *Crime and punishment* (Dublin, 1982), p. 168. **49** *Irish Times*, 14 Dec. 1977. **50** *Irish Times*, 17 Dec. 1980.

individuals publicly denounced as terrorists. The question of whether or not these individuals deserved punishment was generally not disputed. Yet the sanctioning of executions appeared increasingly unnecessary when alternative and more humane options such as imprisonment were available. In many ways, capital punishment provided an indicator of the moral standing of the nation itself. How could murder be discouraged if the state itself partook in the act? In 1981, in Dublin the National Conference of Priests of Ireland announced their support for the abolition of the death penalty.[51] In the same year, Amnesty International, the Prisoners' Rights Organisation, the Irish Council for Civil Liberties and the Free Legal Advice Centre united to campaign for abolition. Working in unison, these groups held public meetings throughout Ireland and played an important role in the process of bringing the Criminal Justice Bill (1981) before the Dáil.[52]

Nonetheless, political imperatives continued to overrule moral and ethical objections. The issue of protecting garda officers took centre stage in the ongoing public discussion. In the debates that surrounded the 1981 Bill, Fianna Fáil politician, Brian Hillery, declared that capital punishment offered the most emphatic renunciation by the community of its abhorrence for the murder of unarmed gardaí, adding (somewhat unconvincingly) that he had not detected significant public demand for abolishing the death penalty. Adding to Hillery's claims, Brian Mullooly, also of Fianna Fáil, observed that since the implementation of the 1964 Act the country had witnessed an escalation of violence and political subversion which, if anything, seemed likely to worsen. In his view, capital punishment provided the only available protection to unarmed gardaí against the IRA, a group seemingly intent on murdering them.[53] Prison officers and governors also objected to the endangerment of their lives that they feared might result from abolishing hanging.[54] In 1985, when discussing the abolition of the death penalty, Eoin David Ryan of Fianna Fáil asked:

> What we have to consider at present is whether in this country at the moment we have what could be regarded as normal conditions, whether we are a country with normal political conditions, or whether we are in fact more akin to a country which is at war ... it can be argued that at present this country is in a state of almost being at war, very near to a

---

state of war … In these circumstances there would be no question that capital punishment would be tolerated. As much as people disliked it, it would be tolerated and, in these circumstances, this is an inappropriate time to bring in a Bill of this kind.

Ryan conceded that there was a general movement across Europe away from capital punishment but maintained that most other countries had a more favourable climate.[55]

This political rationale sat uneasily within a broader international context in which capital punishment was framed as a gross assault upon the body; an unnecessary remnant of a violent past that needed to be discarded. It was only in 1990 that Fianna Fáil, under pressure from the Progressive Democrats with whom they had formed a coalition government, conceded that the death penalty was potentially counter-productive. 'Experience has shown', explained minister for justice, Raphael P. Burke, 'that the Provisional IRA and their ilk place so little value on human life in pursuit of their misbegotten campaign that even the lives of their own members are considered expendable where it can be turned to their own advantage. Such people would be more likely to welcome the death penalty for the political capital they could make out of martyrdom than to be deterred by it'.[56] Capital punishment was abolished for all criminal acts on 11 July 1990 under the Criminal Justice Act 1990.

* * *

The sentencing of Noel and Marie Murray in a Dublin court provided an important catalyst for public discussion on the ethical and political implications of retaining the death sentence. Yet the issue of capital punishment acquired considerable complexity in twentieth-century Ireland. In Ireland, the evolution of public thought on the death penalty broadly corresponded with developments in most other European countries. Throughout the twentieth century an emotional imagining of the death penalty (now taking place privately behind prison walls) encouraged the public to consider and contest the authority of states to impose death. This development arose from a mixture of concerns, including the evolution of thought on human and prisoner rights. In twentieth-century Ireland, humane perspectives clashed with a political determination to retain the death penalty

55 Criminal Justice (Abolition of Death Penalty) Bill, 1984, Seanad Éireann debate (13 Feb. 1985), 107:3.
56 Criminal Justice (No. 2) Bill, 1990, Seanad Éireann debate (21 June 1990), 125:11.

in certain circumstances, particularly in relation to politically motivated violence. The death sentences imposed on the Murrays – two Dublin-based individuals not actively engaged in republican activity at the time of their arrest – encapsulated this contradiction between political and moral imperatives, serving as a microcosm for a much broader human rights debate that remained unresolved in Ireland until 1990.

The death, burial and commemoration of the Agard family in sixteenth-century Ireland

EAMON DARCY

Sir Francis Agard's career, and the complex story of his family's memorial, illustrate how fortune-seeking English Protestant settlers could quickly climb the social ladder and amass considerable political influence. Having settled permanently in Ireland in 1551, he was named constable of Ferns Castle and was appointed to the Irish colonial council within two years. Agard took this latter commitment seriously, for he attended more council meetings than anyone else. In recent times he has been dubbed the 'most reliable councillor of the entire period' and his influence is reflected in the fact that he served as the *de facto* military advisor to four chief governors of Ireland, most notably, Sir Henry Sidney, the lord deputy in the years 1565–7, 1568–71, and 1575–8.[1] Not only was Agard a competent administrator but he was also an astute soldier as, by the 1560s, he had facilitated the expansion of Tudor rule by breaking the hold of the O'Tooles and the O'Byrnes in Wicklow. This prompted Sidney to deem Agard 'the most sufficient servant to the queen'. The chronicler Raphael Hollinshed praised Agard highly, claiming he was 'a very wise man and of a deep judgement and experience in all matters of policies'.[2] Agard's increasing influence and loyal service to the English crown meant that he was granted considerable landholdings in Co. Wicklow and Grangegorman in Dublin.[3] He was, in short, an upstart English soldier of relatively humble origins who carved a respectable living and political niche

1 Jon G. Crawford, *Anglicizing the government of Ireland: the Irish Privy Council and the expansion of Tudor rule, 1556–1578* (Dublin, 1993), pp 163–9, 441–2 at p. 166; Ciaran Brady, 'Sidney, Sir Henry' in *Dictionary of Irish biography (DIB)*, consulted online 18 Sept. 2014. **2** Colm Lennon, *Sixteenth-century Ireland: the incomplete conquest* (Dublin, 2005), p. 201; *Calendar of state papers of Ireland (CSPI), 1509–1573*, p. 296; Raphael Hollinshed, *The second volume of chronicles: conteining the description, conquest, inhabitation, and troblesome estate of Ireland; first collected by Raphaell Holinshed; and now newlie recognised, augmented, and continued from the death of king Henrie the eight vntill this present time of sir Iohn Perot knight, lord deputie* (London, 1586), p. 152. **3** On Agard's Wicklow landholdings please see: *Calendar of patent and close rolls of the Chancery of Ireland, 1514–1575*, pp 300–1, 302; on Dublin landholdings please see: *CSPI, 1509–1573*, p. 274; RCBL, MS C6/1.26/1, f. 6 is a lease of fee farm to Francis Agard of lands in Cabra dated 1560. RCBL, MS C6/1.26/1, f. 7 is a fee farm lease to Agard for the manor of Grangegorman and nearby meadows. RCBL, MS C6/1.26/1, f. 10 is a letter from Queen Elizabeth, dated 14 Jan. 1560, ordering the lord deputy and council to grant a fee farm lease to Francis and his heirs and successors of the manor and farm at Grangegorman.

for himself in sixteenth-century Ireland. Upon his death in 1577, he was afforded a heraldic funeral and was buried beside his wife and son. Agard's close family relationship is reflected in the fact that years later his friend and son-in-law, Sir Henry Harrington (who also served in Wicklow with Agard), erected a monument to Agard's memory that still survives in Christ Church Cathedral in Dublin. The purpose of this essay is to understand what the death, burial and commemoration of the Agard family can tell us about early modern Ireland.

* * *

Sir Francis Agard died a widower on 11 October 1577 and was buried the next day. The Ulster king at arms, or herald, recorded the funeral procession. This reflected Agard's political importance to the colonial administration in Ireland and the centrality of funerals as expressions of political power in the early modern period. The herald recorded the order of the procession and named the chief mourners, many of whom were deeply involved in Irish colonial politics. Aside from politics, Agard's burial and commemoration also reveals much about the early modern family in the following ways.[4] First, it is clear that Agard wished to be interred alongside his family in Christ Church Cathedral. This was made possible by the reburial of his only son, Thomas (and potential heir to all his landed property and title), who had died twelve years previously and was originally buried in St Michan's Church. Second, the herald later recorded that Agard's daughter, Cecilia, was buried beside her family of origin upon her own death in 1584 despite the fact that she died a married woman, having become Sir Henry Harrington's wife seven years previously. What made this even more unusual was she and Henry had two sons together. Normally, once a woman had provided her husband with a male heir, she would then be buried with her husband's family upon her death.[5] Finally, the Agard monument that survives in Christ Church reveals much about contemporary concerns about the afterlife and the need to commemorate the dead adequately. The memorial was (in terms of fashion) ahead of its time and was not planned by Agard, as one would expect, but was

---

4 For further information about the Ulster king at arms please see: John Barry, 'Guide to records of the Genealogical Office, Dublin, with a commentary on heraldry in Ireland and on the history of the office', *Analecta Hibernica*, 26:1 (1970), pp 3–43, especially pp 27–8 regarding the survival of this manuscript; Edmund Curtis, 'Extracts out of heralds' book in Trinity College Dublin, relating to Ireland in the sixteenth century', *JRSAI*, 62 (1932), pp 28–49.   5 Clodagh Tait, *Death, burial and commemoration in Ireland, 1550–1650* (Gordonsville, VA, 2003), pp 67–8.

built by his son-in-law, Harrington.[6] So, how did the Agard family come to be buried in Christ Church Cathedral?

We do not know when Agard's wife, Jacoba de la Brett, died, but it is clear that it was after her son's death in 1565 and before Sir Francis' death in 1577. Her funeral, however, provided an opportunity to offer her son a heraldic burial, one befitting his father's social standing. After Jacoba was buried in Christ Church Cathedral all the mourners left the church and returned to Agard's house in Grangegorman where his son's corpse (having been removed from its original tomb in St Michan's) was laid out. From there, Thomas' body was carried in procession to Christ Church Cathedral.[7] At the head of the procession the Ulster king of arms and fourteen men in black robes marched in front of the boy's corpse, 'borne by four yeomen in black coats and four other yeomen bearing black appointed to assist the bearers of the corpse'. Agard's sisters then marched behind him (presumably as Thomas had never married and Jacoba had just died), accompanied by a Mr Alcoth who witnessed one of their marriages (it is not specified which). There were also 'diverse other women in black gowns and hats and also diverse maidens in black gowns & other clothes'. Most importantly, and this proved the crux of the visual spectacle aside from all the mourners in black, Thomas Agard's corpse was accompanied by 'diverse of the council of Ireland and others of the council of Dublin [and] the baron of the exchequer of Ireland' all of whom wore 'black gowns' and waited in the church with Thomas' body until he was laid to rest. They then accompanied Sir Francis Agard back to Grangegorman, and concluded by having a 'sumptuous dinner'.[8] Despite his early death and lack of an honorific title, some time after his death Thomas Agard was afforded a funeral procession that was fit for a member of the elite.

* * *

Upon the death of Sir Francis Agard in 1577 the Ulster king of arms again documented the forms and procedures to be followed by the nobility of Ireland and the citizens of Dublin in laying the deceased to rest. Agard was

---

6 For example, see the first earl of Cork who ordered the construction of no less than five funerary monuments in honour of his family before his death: Clodagh Tait, 'Colonizing memory: manipulations of death, burial and commemoration in the career of Richard Boyle, first earl of Cork (1566–1643)', *PRIA*, 101C:4 (2001), pp 107–34. The seventeenth-century travel writer, Thomas Dingley, argued that the nobility were very concerned with how they would be commemorated and thus hoped to complete funerary sculptures before their deaths. Thomas Dingley, 'Tour of Ireland, c.1680' (NLI, MS 392, f. 141). 7 Christopher Ussher, the Ulster king at arms, referred to the boy as John, yet he is named Thomas on the funerary memorial in Christ Church. 8 Collections related to Irish heraldry in the sixteenth and

buried on 12 October 1577 in Christ Church Cathedral. The outer rails of the church were all covered with black cloth. The hearse that bore Agard's corpse was also covered with black cloth and decorated with the coat of arms of the Agard and de la Brett families. The Agard cross was born by the constable of Agard's castle in Newcastle, in Co. Wicklow. After the procession of the corpse and the coat of arms, there followed 'a fair company of gentlemen in black clothes', accompanied by the Ulster king of arms (also bearing Agard's coat of arms). The corpse was borne by four gentlemen who were assisted by eight women. The sheet that covered Agard's corpse was also decorated with his coat of arms, as well as the family arms of his wife, his father and his mother. Agard's privileged position and prominent location within Irish politics is reflected in the fact that Lucas Dillon, the baron of the exchequer, was the chief mourner.[9] These were followed by a 'good company of gentlemen in black gowns', a number of soliders and by Sir Henry Sidney, Agard's closest political ally, who also happened to be the lord deputy of Ireland at this time. Not only was Sidney paying respects to a trusted advisor, but also a close friend whom he referred to as '*fidus Achates*', a term of considerable affection in the early modern period, signifying a trusted companion.[10] These two men had both suffered the loss of a child in the 1560s; Sidney's daughter died in 1567 and was also buried in Christ Church Cathedral, two years after Thomas' death. The last people to enter the church, aside from the mourners, were seven poor men. The prayers of the poor were deemed particularly valuable and also they reflected the extent of Agard's social power in his locality.[11] They then listened to a 'godly sermon' and Agard was buried alongside his wife and son with a 'fair tomb' erected over them.[12] Traditionally, at this moment in funerals for the elites, the herald symbolically revealed the transfer of power, land and title from father to son.[13] In this instance, however, Agard died without a male heir; thus, his funeral did not include this act.[14]

seventeenth centuries (TCD, MS 663, f. 17).   **9** Dillon became a close and trusted advisor to Sir Henry Sidney upon the latter's arrival in Ireland. His steadfast loyalty to Sidney alienated many of his family in the controversy that surrounded Sidney's removal in 1578. See Terry Clavin, 'Dillon, Sir Lucas' in *DIB*, consulted online 9 Sept. 2014.   **10** Raphael Hollinshed, *The second volume of chronicles: conteining the description, conquest, inhabitation, and troblesome estate of Ireland; first collected by Raphaell Holinshed; and now newlie recognised, augmented, and continued from the death of king Henrie the eight vntill this present time of sir Iohn Perot knight, lord deputie modernize* (London, 1586), p. 152; John Finlayson, *Inscriptions on the monuments, mural tablets, &c, at present existing in Christ Church Cathedral Dublin* (Dublin, 1878), p. 13.   **11** Raymond Gillespie, 'Funerals and society in early seventeenth-century Ireland', *JRSAI*, 115 (1985), pp 86–91 at p. 89.   **12** Collections related to Irish heraldry in the sixteenth and seventeenth centuries (TCD, MS 663, f. 18).   **13** Gillespie, 'Funerals and society', p. 86; Tait, *Death, burial and commemoration*, p. 43.   **14** Gillespie, 'Funerals and society', p. 88; Tait, *Death, burial and commemoration*, p. 43.

The same year that Agard died, one of his daughters, Cecilia, married Sir Henry Harrington and within seven years had borne him two sons. Their marriage was short-lived as Cecilia tragically died on 9 September 1584. Wives were traditionally buried with their husbands; in fact, sometimes husbands were buried with all their wives. One James Keally, for example, was buried in 1646 with his two wives while his epitaph read: 'Both wives at once he could not have/Both to enjoy at once he made this grave.'[15] In an unusual step, however, Cecilia's husband ordered that she be buried in the same tomb as her family of origin as opposed to a dedicated Harrington family crypt. Furthermore, the order of her funeral procession has survived (whereas details of her mother's funeral procession were not recorded or do not survive). Cecilia's hearse was covered in black cloth and adorned with the coat of arms of Sir Henry Harrington. The rails in the cathedral were once more draped with black cloth and Lady Harrington's body was conveyed from the former Agard (and now the Harrington) family home in Grangegorman to the cathedral. Some of Sir Henry Harrington's men, followed by Henry Ussher, the archdeacon of Saint Patrick's Cathedral and later archbishop of Armagh, and the Ulster king of arms, accompanied Cecilia's corpse. She was then brought into the church, being carried by 'six mourners being gentlemen & six more to assist them'. The chief mourners, members of the wider Agard and Harrington families, marched behind them and they then sat and listened to a 'notable sermon' by Ussher, after which Cecilia's corpse was laid to rest.[16] There was no mention of the attendance of key figures from the colonial administration, as happened at her brother and father's burials in Christ Church. Cecilia's burial beside her family is particularly thought provoking. Furthermore, her widower, Sir Henry Harrington, later commissioned an ornate funeral monument to his wife and the Agard family (see plate 4). The inscription below the monument underlined Sir Francis Agard's importance to the colonial government, for he was praised as a 'most sagacious councilor of Ireland' and noted his close friendship with Sir Henry Sidney, who was lord deputy of Ireland at the time of his death. The Agards are depicted as pious Protestants and this portrayal captures how Harrington wanted them to be commemorated. A kneeling Lady Cecilia deep in prayer (and her two children kneeling in prayer behind her) faces her family of origin, including her two sisters, her parents and her deceased brother, all of whom are also depicted in

15 Tait, *Death, burial and commemoration*, p. 115.   **16** Collections related to Irish heraldry in the sixteenth and seventeenth centuries (TCD, MS 663, f. 19).

prayer. These postures were unusual for the 1580s and did not become popular until the seventeenth century.[17] Sir Francis Agard is depicted wearing full military armour, underlining his career path and his role as a soldier under the Tudor monarchs, while his sword remains in its scabbard.[18] His wife and daughters are all depicted as pious, upright women in full noble garb, while Thomas Agard and his nephews all wear clothes traditionally associated with noble children. Furthermore, Thomas carries a skull as a symbol of his mortality and early death.[19] The inscription below the sculptures reveals that Cecilia was a 'dear and loving wife' and that her 'loving husband' erected this monument to her memory and to the memory of her father, 'at his own charges'. Even a contemporary stranger to Irish politics would recognize the political power and Protestant piety of the Agard family upon viewing the memorial.[20]

* * *

This contribution posed a key question: what does the death, burial and commemoation of the Agard family reveal about early modern Ireland? From this study it is clear that death can be used as a keyhole through which we can view early modern society. Funerals and funerary monuments were, after all, spectacles that reveal as much about the living as they do the dead.[21] The heraldic funeral processions for Cecilia, Francis and Thomas Agard indicate Sir Francis Agard's political influence.[22] The burial of the Agard family together, and steps taken to ensure that Thomas was buried with his parents, illustrate the wider trend of ensuring the common familial burial, particularly when it concerned honorific burial.[23] Harrington's memorial to the Agards, depicting the reunion of spouses and families in the afterlife, further reflected the wider concerns of the plight of the extended family after death and pertains to the age-old question of 'shall we know one another in heaven?'[24]

---

17 Rolf Loeber, 'Sculptured memorials to the dead in early seventeenth-century Ireland: a survey from "Monumenta Eblanae" and other sources', *PRIA*, 81C (1981), pp 267–93, 272–5. **18** Normally, the family patriarch was depicted with insignia that indicated what office he held during his career, Raymond Gillespie, 'Irish funeral monuments and social change, 1500–1700: perceptions of death' in Raymond Gillespie & Brian P. Kennedy (eds), *Ireland: art into history* (Dublin, 1994), pp 155–68 at pp 157, 163. **19** Tait, *Death, burial and commemoration*, p. 116. **20** Thomas Dingley noted this in his tour of Ireland, which included a detailed discussion of funerary monuments of note. See NLI, MS 392. **21** Raymond Gillespie, 'Irish funeral monuments and social change, 1500–1700', pp 155–68 at p. 158; Tait, *Death, burial and commemoration*, p. 30. **22** For a further discussion on this see: Tait, *Death, burial and commemoration*, p. 40. For a similar discussion of the funeral of Viscount Hugh Montgomery, see Gillespie, 'Funerals and society', pp 86–91. **23** Tait, *Death, burial and commemoration*, p. 85. **24** Peter Marshall, 'The company of heaven: identity and sociability in the English Protestant afterlife', *Historical Reflections*, 26:2 (2000), pp

The burial and commemoration of the Agards provides a rare, yet valuable insight into familial relationships, the close bond between parents and children, and among friends. Harrington's memorial reconstitutes the Agard family and presents them as united in death. Cecilia Harrington faces her parents and her brother who all predeceased her. The inclusion of her two sisters and two sons revealed the key blood relationships for Cecilia – her family of origin and her two children. Harrington's decision not to bury Cecilia in a Harrington family plot perhaps illustrates his respect for the wishes of Sir Francis Agard who made sure that his deceased son would be buried with Jacoba in Christ Church. One could view Harrington's memorial to his deceased friend (and his in-laws) as a cynical attempt to link his own political star with that of Sir Francis Agard, yet it also reveals a considerable degree of affection for his lost friend and (perhaps from Harrington's perspective) more importantly, his 'loving wife'.[25] Here Cecilia is presented as a beloved spouse and a loyal daughter. Yes, the Agards' burials reveal much about Irish social and political hierarchies, but they also reveal a commensurate amount about familial relationships and personal friendships that is often overlooked in studies of early modern Ireland.

311–33; Peter Marshall, 'After purgatory: death and remembrance in the Reformation world' (forthcoming). I am very grateful to Prof. Marhsall for providing me with a copy of this text in advance of publication. **25** For further comments on this see: Tait, *Death, burial and commemoration*, p. 115.

Politics, patriotism and posterity: the funeral of William Conolly in 1729

PATRICK WALSH

Public performance and display mattered in eighteenth-century politics. Few Irish politicians understood this better than speaker William Conolly. His remarkable contributions to Ireland's built heritage, whether at Castletown or at College Green, are testament to this. Castletown, Conolly's great country house, epitomized his great political power and accumulation of personal wealth. Intended as a venue for convivial politicking, its design and interior decoration emphasized both the power of display and the speaker's promotion of native industry and craftsmen. Castletown was also about posterity and securing Conolly's legacy for future generations. This chapter is concerned with a more ephemeral expression of Conolly's concerns for display, patriotism and posterity – his remarkable public funeral of 4 November 1729. Described by one Dublin newspaper as the 'finest funeral that has been seen in this kingdom these many years' it was both an exercise in political pageantry and a very public attempt by the parvenu Conolly to secure posthumous entry into the 'quality'.[1] As will become clear, Conolly in death as in life trod a fine line between the limits of what was publicly acceptable and what contemporaries saw as the final vulgar excesses of the self-made man and his devoted and socially ambitious widow. The manipulation of funerary rites to benefit the living has a long tradition in Irish history and this chapter locates Conolly's extravagant final journey within the contexts of both the early modern tradition of the heraldic funeral and the processional culture of eighteenth-century Ireland. In doing so, it explores both the eye-catching funeral procession itself and the various ways in which Katherine Conolly sought to memorialize her husband. These included ostentatious public displays of mourning, the purchase and distribution of expensive mourning rings and, most importantly, the commissioning of an elaborate funerary monument. This chapter argues that these various mourning and memorializing activities were cumulatively designed to secure the speaker's personal and political legacies.

* * *

---

1 *Dublin Gazette*, 8 Nov. 1729.

William Conolly died at his home on Dublin's Capel Street on 30 October 1729 at the age of 67. His death came one month after he had collapsed on the floor of the House of Commons, almost certainly from a stroke.[2] His reputation as a wily politician was such that one hostile observer was convinced that this was merely an exercise in political distraction, describing Conolly as a 'complete fox'.[3] Whatever about 'political fainting', the commons chamber was an appropriate location for Conolly's last meaningful public appearance. It was in this arena that he had made his political reputation over an almost forty-year period beginning with his entry as MP for Donegal borough in 1692 and culminating in his highly influential fourteen-year tenure as speaker of the House. During this period he established himself as the dominant figure in Irish politics, becoming in effect Ireland's 'prime minister'.[4] His political power owed much to his parliamentary abilities, but also to his unrivalled control of revenue patronage as 'first commissioner' of the revenue board and his great electoral interest in north-west Ulster. Conolly's political and electoral power also reflected his great wealth. His landed estates, containing over 150,000 acres in total, were spread across ten Irish counties and yielded an annual rental income of almost £16,000. Remarkably, he had amassed all of this great landed portfolio and huge fortune within his own lifetime, thanks in part to the opportunities provided by the wholesale confiscation of Jacobite property in the aftermath of the Williamite War. Through a combination of a good marriage, legal skulduggery and sharp practice he had emerged from a position of pre-war obscurity and his reputed birth in a Donegal alehouse to become Ireland's wealthiest commoner.[5]

This meteoric ascent to riches did not always endear him to the more established members of the Irish political elite, even if many of their fortunes, titles and estates were themselves products of earlier conquests and confiscations. In 1717, when Conolly was first appointed a lord justice, Sir John

---

2 Marmaduke Coghill to Edward Southwell, 27 Sept., 14 Oct. 1729 in David Hayton (ed.), *Letters of Marmaduke Coghill, 1722–1738* (Dublin, 2005), pp 73–4; Hugh Boulter to the Duke of Newcastle, 23 Oct. 1729 in Hugh Boulter, *Letters to several ministers of state in England and some others: containing an account of the most interesting transactions which passed in Ireland from 1724–38* (Dublin, 1770), p. 248.   **3** Sylvester Lloyd to Daniel O'Brien, 25 Sept. 1729 in Patrick Fagan, *Ireland in the Stuart papers, 1719–42* (2 vols, Dublin, 1995), i, p. 153. For the immediate jostling for position to succeed Conolly as speaker see James Tynte to Henry Boyle, 1 Oct. 1729; Thomas Carter to Boyle, 4 Oct. 1729 (PRONI, Shannon Papers, D2707/A/1/2/49-50).   **4** Timothy Godwin to William Wake, 16 Jan. 1723, quoted in Patrick McNally, 'William Conolly, 1662–1729' in *ODNB*, described Conolly as 'prime minister'. For a detailed account of Conolly's life see Patrick Walsh, *The making of the Irish Protestant ascendancy: the life of William Conolly, 1662–1729* (Woodbridge, 2010).   **5** For the importance of Conolly's marriage to Katherine Conyngham in 1694 see Toby Barnard, 'A tale of three sisters: Katherine Conolly of Castletown' in T.C. Barnard (ed.),

St Leger, the descendant of a Tudor settler, complained that it would offend 'our quality and old gentry', while Lord Midleton, the son of a Cromwellian officer, was appalled at rumours circulating in 1716 that Conolly was to be raised to the peerage, considering his lowly origins.[6] Conolly's rise through the ranks of Irish society, while spectacular, was not, however, unprecedented. There were other so-called 'mushrooms' in early eighteenth-century Ireland, to borrow a term employed by the Queen's County diarist Pole Crosby to describe his neighbour, the banker Ephraim Dawson, whose father was reputed to have kept an alehouse.[7] The series of conflicts that characterized seventeenth-century Ireland had provided opportunities for dramatic social mobility, of which the most remarkable example was Richard Boyle, first earl of Cork.[8] Boyle had a keen eye for posterity, evident not just in his amassment of titles and, through his children's marriages, connections to longer established aristocratic dynasties, but also in the spectacular funerary monuments he commissioned, notably in Dublin's St Patrick's Cathedral. Clodagh Tait's work on the Boyle monuments and on the funerary and commemorative practices of the Irish elite has demonstrated that where Boyle went others followed.[9] Elaborate monuments and carefully choreographed heraldic funerals, she argues, were used by 'those whose social position was recently acquired to demonstrate their new place in a mobile social order and shake off all vestiges of their origins'.[10]

* * *

Organized by the state's chief heraldic official, the Ulster king at arms, elements of Conolly's funeral conformed to this established pattern, but it also incorporated further political and patriotic elements that, together with its great scale, marked it out as distinctive and worthy of notice by contemporary commentators. Conolly's own vision for his funeral was clearly laid out in his

Irish Protestant ascents and descents, 1641–1770 (Dublin, 2004), pp 271–2.   **6** Sir John St Leger to Chief Justice Parker, 21 Feb. 1717, and Alan Brodrick, Lord Midleton, to Thomas Brodrick, 21 Mar. 1717, both quoted in Walsh, *Making the Irish Protestant ascendancy*, pp 14, 24.   **7** Walter FitzGerald, 'Autobiography of Pole Cosby of Stradbally, Queens County, 1703–1737', *Journal of the Kildare Archaeological Society*, 5 (1906–08), p. 14.   **8** Nicholas Canny, *The upstart earl, a study of the social and mental world of Richard Boyle, first earl of Cork, 1566–1643* (Cambridge, 1982).   **9** Clodagh Tait, 'Colonizing memory: manipulations of death, burial and commemoration in the career of Richard Boyle, first earl of Cork (1566–1643)', *PRIA*, 110C (2001), pp 107–34.   **10** Clodagh Tait, *Death, burial and commemoration in Ireland, 1550–1650* (Basingstoke, 2002), pp 43–4. On heraldic funerals see R.G. Gillespie, 'Funerals and society in early seventeenth-century Ireland', *JRSAI*, 115 (1985), pp 86–91; and more generally Jennifer Woodward, *The theatre of death: the ritual management of royal funerals in renaissance England, 1570–1625* (Woodbridge, 1997), pp 15–36.

will, wherein he allocated £1,000 to cover its expense.[11] Added to this princely sum were various bequests to friends and relations to purchase mourning dress so that they could commemorate Conolly in private as well as public. These bequests amounted to £480 in total and individually ranged from £100 for his brother-in-law Thomas Pearson to a more modest £20 for his vicar at Celbridge.[12] Here, as elsewhere, Conolly's generosity, or conspicuous display, stands out. The wearing of mourning dress was expected within eighteenth-century society, and there seems to have been some expectation that the costs would partly, at least, be borne by the deceased or their executors, and those who failed to provide for this expenditure were on occasion criticized.[13] The speaker's generosity, although exceptional in monetary terms, was not, however, entirely unique within the wider Conolly social circle. In 1732, for instance, the speaker's widow Katherine was left £100 by a Donegal relation to purchase a mourning ring, leading her to enquire of her sister 'whether diamonds be now reasonable for as Colonel Montgomery left me £100 to buy a ring, I think I ought to do it soon but I would have it cheap? And good.'[14] It is unknown whether the beneficiaries of Conolly's own will were tempted by diamonds, but the expenditure allocated in his will for mourning dress and other 'emotional objects' gives some indication of his own pretensions.

Conolly's funeral itself, carried off with 'great pomp', did justice to these pretensions.[15] Directed by William Hawkins, the Ulster king at arms, it elaborated on existing traditions of the heraldic funeral to include elements of state pageantry. Mourners gathered at Conolly's townhouse on Capel Street, where his widow, Katherine, had draped the main staircase and principal reception rooms in black cloth in an ostentatious public display of her grief.[16] Outside the formal funeral procession took shape.[17] At its head was one of seven specially employed funeral managers accompanied by six city constables,

11 'Will of William Conolly', 18 Oct. 1729 (NAI, T.92). For a useful discussion of the costs of eighteenth-century Irish funerals see Toby Barnard, *Making the grand figure: lives and possessions in Ireland, 1641–1770* (London, 2004), pp 267–9.   12 'Will of William Conolly'.   13 On expectations regarding the costs of mourning dress see, Sir John Peyton to Kean O'Hara, 1 Jan. 1704 (PRONI, O'Hara Papers, T2812/5/129). More generally see Lou Taylor, *Mourning dress, costume and social history* (London, 1983).   14 Katherine Conolly to Jane Bonnell, 27 Nov. 1732 (NLI, Smyth of Barbavilla Papers, MS 41,578/6). On mourning rings see Barnard, *Making the grand figure*, p. 270. See also Diana Scarisbrick, *Rings: miniature monuments to love, power and devotion* (London, 2014). I am indebted to Sally Holloway for this reference.   15 Coghill to Southwell, 8 Nov. 1729, in Hayton (ed.), *Coghill letters*, p. 77.   16 Barnard, *Making the grand figure*, p. 265.   17 The following account is based on newspaper reports and the official printed 'order of funeral'. See W. Hawkins, *The order of proceeding to the funeral of the Rt. Hon. William Conolly esq.* (Dublin, 1729); *Faulkner's Dublin Journal*, 5 Nov. 1729; *Dublin Gazette*, 8 Nov. 1729, *British Journal*, 15 Nov. 1729; and

who were charged with keeping the anticipated crowds at bay. Behind them sixty-seven poor men all dressed in black lined up, each one signifying a year in Conolly's life. They were followed by dignitaries including the lord lieutenant, Lord Carteret, the lord mayor, members of parliament marching two by two, as well as other representatives of the nobility and gentry. Finally, came the coffin carried by pall bearers drawn from among Conolly's fellow privy councillors, and the family mourners led by Conolly's nephew and heir, William James Conolly. In total over 700 mourners gathered to pay their final respects to the late speaker. Each one was presented with an Irish linen scarf, popularizing a recent initiative, started at the funeral of another Ulster landlord, Colonel George Groves, to encourage the use of Irish cloth rather than foreign silks as appropriate mourning dress.[18]

This last element emphasized Conolly's credentials as a defender of Irish trading interests, an economic patriotism that was given its greatest expression in the building of Sir Edward Lovett Pearce's new parliament building at College Green, a project initiated by Conolly in his capacity as speaker of the House of Commons.[19] Conolly's funeral procession did not pass through College Green, but it did pass other sites rich with personal and political symbolism. Departing his townhouse, the scene both of his happy domestic life and of various political cabals and convivial dinners, it continued down Capel Street to Essex Bridge, where it passed the equestrian statue of George I, whom Conolly had served with distinction as a lord justice and parliamentary manager for thirteen years. Crossing the river the cortège passed on the left Thomas Burgh's custom house, where Conolly had been in almost daily attendance overseeing the expanding revenue service for fifteen years. Straight ahead was Dublin Castle, where Conolly had been a regular presence whether as a lord justice, privy councillor or trusted guest of successive lords lieutenant. There would, however, be no last trip to the castle. Instead the funeral procession turned right down the Liffey quays heading towards the Royal Barracks on the opposite side, the physical emblem of the Irish fiscal-military state that Conolly had done so much to create. Having reached the outer limits of the city, the formal procession dispersed and Conolly's body was

Monthly Chronicle, Nov. 1729.   **18** Groves, like Conolly, was resident in Dublin's St Mary's parish, *Faulkner's Dublin Journal*, 18 Oct. 1729. See also Martyn Powell, *The politics of consumption in eighteenth-century Ireland* (Basingstoke, 2005), p. 182. For similar contemporary North American concerns about the importation of foreign luxuries for funeral wear see Kathleen A. Staples & Madelyn Shaw, *Clothing through American history: the British colonial era* (Westport, CT, 2013), pp 63–4. I am indebted to Carly Fisher for the latter reference.   **19** Walsh, *Making of the Irish Protestant ascendancy*, pp 156–7.

taken to its final resting place at Celbridge, near his great country house at Castletown – as we shall see, a significant choice.

Conolly's funeral procession attracted attention. This was perhaps inevitable, its scale and the very public involvement of the leading officers of state ensured that it was reported upon in the Dublin and London press, with special attention given to the provision of linen scarves to the mourners, something that was seen as endorsing the precedent recently established by Col. Groves.[20] If this was generally regarded as a laudable, even patriotic, gesture other aspects of the funeral were derided for their extravagance. Katherine Conolly drew opprobrium for dressing her staircase and drawing rooms in black cloth, with some contemporaries suggesting that she had outdone the official vice-regal mourning for George I two years earlier.[21] Explicit in such criticisms was the assertion that Conolly was not of the 'first quality', and that they were acting above their social position. Some even maintained that she had gone beyond what was acceptable of a duchess.[22] Such critiques could have been extended to include the whole carefully choreographed funeral procession, and it is instructive to compare it with the final journeys of some of Conolly's peers. Archbishop William King, Conolly's long-time colleague as a lord justice, predeceased the speaker by only a few months, but he was buried with much less pomp and ceremony.[23] Conolly's successor as speaker, Sir Ralph Gore, was buried in Christ Church Cathedral after a midnight service in 1733, while Lord Midleton, Conolly's great political rival, made a similarly quiet exit upon his death in 1728.[24] Midleton was, of course, by the time of his death out of office, having resigned the lord chancellorship in 1725, but the contrast with Conolly, like that explored by David Hayton between their respective country houses, reveals their very different political styles.[25]

The elaborate procession on foot through Dublin's cold November streets was only the first part of Conolly's funeral.[26] His body was transferred from the city quays to the parish church at Celbridge, approximately a mile from the newly completed Castletown, for burial. The choice of Celbridge as his final

---

20 Coghill to Southwell, 8 Nov. 1729 in Hayton (ed.), *Coghill letters*, p. 77.   **21** Francis Burton to Jane Bonnell, 9 Dec. 1729 (NLI MS 41,579/9); Burton to Bonnell, 26 Jan. 17230 (NLI MS 41,579/10). **22** Owen Gallagher to Oliver St George, 4 Nov. 1729 (TNA, C110/46/773).   **23** *Dublin Gazette*, 10 May 1729; Philip O'Regan, *Archbishop William King of Dublin (1650–1729) and the constitution of church and state* (Dublin, 2000), p. 332.   **24** *Faulkner's Dublin Journal*, 23 Feb. 1733; *Daily Courant*, 9 Mar. 1733; *Daily Journal*, 10 Mar. 1733.   **25** D.W. Hayton, *The Anglo-Irish experience, 1680–1730: religion, identity and patriotism* (Woodbridge, 2012), pp 79–82.   **26** A newspaper advertisement had advised that, weather permitting, the procession would be on foot, *Faulkner's Dublin Journal*, 4 Nov. 1729.

resting place was significant, and again carried echoes of the seventeenth-century tradition of the heraldic funeral as a form of social mobility, whereby the socially ascendant chose to associate themselves in death not with their place of birth but with their recently acquired landed estates.[27] Burial in the local churchyard could also act as a powerful symbol of the intended permanence of a new proprietor, and the final stage in the replacement of the previously dominant local interest. In Conolly's case he was interred in the traditional burial place of the Dongan family, the previous Jacobite lords of Castletown, who had forfeited their estates in 1691. Incidentally, the last member of the family to be buried at Castletown was the young William Dongan, Viscount Clane, who was killed at the Battle of the Boyne.[28] Conolly's choice of Celbridge as his final resting place, together with his acquisition in the 1720s of other previously Jacobite estates in the Castletown hinterland, symbolized the final stage of his reorientation of the local political landscape towards the post-revolutionary Whig ascendancy he had done so much to establish.[29]

The speaker's choice of burial place was important, but more permanent was the funerary monument erected by his widow to commemorate his achievements. James Arbuckle, the Dublin political writer, in an essay published in his periodical the *Tribune* to coincide with Conolly's funeral, had argued, drawing inspiration from classical Roman republicanism, that the late speaker having 'eminently served the commonwealth' deserved a public monument.[30] In an age where the few statues that were erected in Dublin commemorated the monarchy rather than local political figures, such a commemorative gesture was unlikely. In any case, as another anonymous contemporary suggested, Conolly's qualities – 'his public and private virtues' – would 'outlive any marble bust'.[31] This latter view proved to be rather optimistic. Instead, the responsibility for commemorating Conolly passed into the private realm, where his widow took it up with enthusiasm.

* * *

27 Tait, *Death, burial and commemoration*, p. 71.   **28** Lena Boylan, *Castletown and its owners* (Castletown 1970), p. 11.   **29** These included the purchase of Lord Louth's estate at Killadoon in 1725 and the Whyte family's holding at Leixlip in 1728. See Patrick Walsh, 'Biography and the meaning of an Irish country house: William Conolly and Castletown' in Terence Dooley & Christopher Ridgway (eds), *The Irish country house: past, present and future* (Dublin, 2011), esp. p. 39.   **30** James Arbuckle, *The Tribune no. 8* (Dublin, 1729). **31** James Sterling, *A funeral poem on the death of the right honourable William Conolly esq.* (Dublin, 1729).

Widows, unsurprisingly, often played a key role in maintaining their husband's posthumous reputation. Toby Barnard has described how Katherine Conolly, ably assisted by her nephews, turned Castletown into a rival political centre in opposition to the official court at Dublin Castle in the 1730s, building on the late speaker's vision for his great house. She also intervened in electoral contests, maintaining his west Ulster parliamentary interest, while those expectant of promotion in the revenue service or the Church of Ireland continued to pay court in her Capel Street parlour.[32] As time went on, the speaker's residual political influence waned and Katherine began to look to other avenues to perpetuate his memory. These included circulating engraved copies of his portrait to friends and relations, including new marriage connections in England acquired through the union of the speaker's nephew and the earl of Strafford's daughter.[33]

Most importantly Katherine took on the task of overseeing the construction of her husband's funerary monument at Celbridge. These acts of commemoration were motivated both by a desire to publicly remember her husband, but also by a very real emotional bond. She expressed this enduring love for her late husband in a letter to her sister where she described her plan to commission a mourning ring containing a lock of her husband's hair inscribed with the motto 'we part no more'.[34] This motto would eventually be metaphorically realized in white marble as part of the monument she commissioned for him. Katherine's role in managing her husband's memory mirrored that of her widowed sister Jane Bonnell a generation earlier. Following the death of her husband, the Irish accountant general, in 1699, Jane first oversaw the publication of his spiritual biography – which ran through a number of editions – and then the erection of a commemorative monument in the Church of St John the Evangelist in Dublin.[35] She not only oversaw its construction but also managed its maintenance over succeeding decades remotely from London, where she spent her long widowhood.

Katherine's role in managing the Conolly monument was more 'hands on', and reflected the greater scale of the project. Funerary monuments had, since at least the seventeenth century, become another important way for newly established dynasties to lay down a physical marker of their pretensions. The

---

32 Barnard, 'A tale of three sisters', pp 278–83.   **33** Lady Anne Conolly to Thomas Wentworth, 3rd earl of Strafford, 29 Jan. 1734; William J. Conolly to Strafford, 26 Feb. 1734 (BL, Strafford Papers, Add. MS 22,228, ff 102, 110).   **34** Katherine Conolly to Jane Bonnell, 26 Aug. 1731 (NLI MS 41,578/6).   **35** William Hamilton, *The exemplary life and character of James Bonnell* (Dublin, 1704). Later editions appeared in 1707 and 1718. On the Bonnell monument see Mary Jones to Jane Bonnell, 25 Jan., 9 Aug. 1737 (NLI MS 41,577/1).

16 The Conolly monument in its original setting in Tea Lane Church, Celbridge.
(reproduced courtesy of National Library of Ireland).

Conollys conformed to this practice but perhaps inevitably the speaker's monument, if not on the same scale as the sumptuous Boyle monument in St Patrick's Cathedral, was on a greater scale than many of its contemporaries. Its scale was reflected in the sums of money that Katherine expended on it. In 1732 she described the various costs in a letter that is wonderfully rich in its description of such important, but rarely recorded, details:

> I have great occasion for money now in London and must draw next post for £150 on Gould and Nisbet for marble I cannot get here for the monument I am making for my dear Mr Conolly which will cost me above £600 and I have this summer built an aisle to our church that has cost me above £300 for the church was by much too little for the people and though many people said they would contribute towards rebuilding the old church I found so many objections and so little money like to come in that I have done all at my own expense – and it's larger and ten times handsomer than the old church.[36]

This is the earliest mention of the monument in her surviving correspondence, and it reveals much about its construction, the costs of the marble, the expected costs of the carving, and her relationship with the other parishioners in Celbridge. Each of these is worth considering in more detail. First, it is noteworthy that Katherine did not follow her husband's preference for utilizing Irish material and craftsmanship. The focal point of the monument, life-sized effigies of both the speaker and his widow, was carved from English marble by a London sculptor, Thomas Carter.[37] The surrounding pediment was, however, made in Dublin. It would take four years to complete this work, and the final statues, magnificent examples of their kind, arrived in Ireland only in 1736. In the meantime Katherine had, in typical Conolly fashion, run over budget, with the total cost of the monument amounting to the colossal sum of £2,000.[38] Much of this extra cost was related to the second element mentioned in the earlier quotation from her 1732 letter, negotiating a suitable space for the monument in what she termed 'my church in the country'. Put simply, the existing church was too small. Katherine, as this letter makes clear, had paid for the enlargement of the church, having failed to persuade her neighbours to contribute to the project. However, the final monument still did not fit. She was obliged to pay for a further purpose-built extension to the

---

36 Katherine Conolly to Bonnell, 27 Nov. 1732 (NLI MS 41,578/6). **37** Rupert Gunnis, 'Some Irish memorials', *Bulletin of the Irish Georgian Society*, 4 (1961), pp 1–15. **38** Conolly to Bonnell, 14 May 1736

church, known as the death house, within which the monument was eventually installed.

Aside from featuring superbly carved marble figures of the speaker and his still-living widow (the sculptor signified this by leaving her eyes open), the Conolly monument included a large stone plaque with a Latin inscription detailing Conolly's achievements as well as his public offices.[39] These included the 'modest though splendid use of the great riches he had acquired'. Any eighteenth-century, or indeed modern, visitor to either Castletown or his mausoleum might dispute the word 'modest', while even during his own lifetime the 'honest' nature of his fortune was hotly contested.[40] The inscribed text also drew attention to Conolly's philanthropic activities, notably the bequest made in his will to establish a charity school upon his Castletown estate. Conolly as benevolent landlord, not calculating politician, was the image being constructed for posterity. The Irish poet Henry Jones, who visited the monument in the 1740s, drew out the links between it and the nearby charity school in the following lines:

> No Pride but Piety there strikes our eyes,
> And Meekness lifts yon Pillar to the skies,
> Why smokes at Dawn that hospitable dome
> To feed the fatherless, the orphans home …[41]

Jones' poem suggests that while the Conolly monument was situated outside the capital in a country church, it was still accessible to the curious visitor. The early eighteenth century had seen a shift away from the metropolitan monuments erected in the Dublin cathedrals by members of newly arrived families like the Boyles and the Jones. Eighteenth-century monuments were instead found in picturesque churches associated with the builder or their social aspirations. Thus the elaborate funerary monument erected in honour of Conolly's parliamentary lieutenant Marmaduke Coghill was erected near his new house at Drumcondra, even though Coghill died elsewhere. Incidentally, his monument also ended up larger than was initially anticipated, leading his sister to fund the remodelling of the church to

(NLI MS 41578/9); *Daily Gazeteer*, 21 Sept. 1736. **39** C.I. Graham, 'The Right Hon. William Conolly, speaker of the Irish house of commons', *Journal of the Co. Kildare Archaeological Society*, 3 (1899), pp 115–16. **40** Walsh, *Making of the Irish Protestant ascendancy*, pp 14–15, 51–4. **41** Henry Jones, 'On viewing the monument of the Right Hon. William Conolly' in Jones, *Poems on several occasions* (London, 1749), p. 201. On Jones, a protégé of Lord Chesterfield, see his entry in the *DIB*.

accommodate it.[42] Later in the century the Latouche banking dynasty signified their migration from the city to suburban county Wicklow by building a mausoleum on their newly acquired Delgany estate. The Conolly, Coghill and Latouche monuments are also significant because, as this chapter has suggested, they helped legitimize new fortunes and recent acquisitions of status. Furthermore, in the Conolly and Coghill cases, their failure to produce a direct heir played an important role in both their own and their wives' and sisters' 'family strategies'. As Tait has argued in relation to similar instances in the previous century, 'the monuments, chapels and vaults they created to subvert this outcome would have continued to be used by the extended family, thereby at the very least ensuring the symbolic creation of closer relationships between the benefactors and their heirs in death than in life'.[43]

In the Conolly case this was particularly true. His principal heir was his nephew William James Conolly who spent most of his life, both before and after his inheritance, in England. His personal connection with the speaker was not a particularly close one; indeed he was plucked from Nottinghamshire obscurity to become heir to Ireland's largest fortune. Yet upon his death in 1754 he was interred in the Conolly death house following a much lower-key funeral in Celbridge, as were subsequent generations of the Conolly family.[44] This continued even after the destruction of the adjoining church during the 1798 Rebellion. The mausoleum also survived the transfer of the Conolly name to even more distant relations in 1821 when Edward Michael Pakenham inherited the estates and name of his granduncle Thomas Conolly. Again the continued use of the family vault helped legitimize the inheritance by a junior branch of the family. The family continued to use the mausoleum right through the nineteenth century despite attempts by the local Church of Ireland vicar to remove the monument to the new parish church in 1884, although some members of the Conolly family were buried in the new church's grounds from this time.[45] It was only in the early twenty-first century that Carter's carved figures, of the speaker and his formidable widow, were removed from the death house to nearby Castletown for safekeeping, where they remain today.

* * *

42 Hayton (ed.), *Coghill letters*, p. xxii; Homan Potterton, *Irish church monuments, 1570–1880* (Belfast, 1975), pp 76–7.   **43** Tait, *Death, burial and commemoration*, pp 106–7.   **44** Samuel Shepherd, *A sermon preached in the parish church of Celbridge, January 13th 1754: being the Sunday next after the funeral of William Conolly esq.* (Dublin, 1754).   **45** C.I. Graham, 'Celbridge: some notes on its past history', *Journal of the County Kildare Archaeological Society*, 2 (1899), p. 204; Desmond J. O'Dowd, *Changing times: the story of religion in 19th century Celbridge* (Dublin, 1997), p. 37.

William Conolly's mausoleum was erected to commemorate both the public and the private man. Its execution and planning reflected his widow's devotion to her husband's memory, as well as the Conollys' desire to establish themselves as country gentry at Castletown. The elaborate carved figures of the speaker and his widow were the physical manifestation not just of their enormous fortune, but also of their marriage – a union described by Anthony Malcomson as a 'love match' – and of Katherine's desire that they should 'part no more'.[46] The scale of the monument, with its classical pediment and entablature, and the lengthy celebratory Latin inscription indicate that it was also intended as a site for public veneration and commemoration. Together with the nearby charter school and the famous Conolly Folly, erected in 1741 to designs by Richard Castle supposedly intended both as a form of famine relief and as a monument to the speaker, it reinforced an image of Conolly as a public-spirited patriot. The speaker had cultivated this image during his lifetime, whether through the employment of Irish craftsmen, through his promotion of native economic interests, or through his active leadership of charitable efforts during the crisis years of the late 1720s.[47] The widely reported distribution of Irish linen scarves at his funeral was but the last of such grand political statements in defence of local economic interests. Combined with the very visible participation of the leading state officers in his funeral procession, this gesture elevated it beyond the private and into the public sphere. While it was also, of course, an occasion of private mourning, it is hard not to read it as a carefully orchestrated attempt to secure post-humous entry into the ranks of the quality through the time honoured tradition of the heraldic funeral. The processing privy councillors, MPs and civic officers were however more redolent of the loyal political processions that would become a feature of eighteenth-century Dublin from the 1730s onwards. Serendipitously, Conolly's funeral took place on what was already emerging as key date in the 'Protestant calendar', King William III's birthday, a coincidence noted, and approved of, by Arbuckle in the *Tribune*.[48] In death, as in life, Conolly was indelibly linked to the revolutionary monarch whose actions had done so much to alter both his own personal circumstances and those of the kingdom he had helped to shape over the course of his forty-year public career.

46 A.P.W. Malcomson, *The pursuit of the heiress: aristocratic marriage in Ireland, 1740–1840* (Belfast, 2006), p. 116.   **47** Walsh, *Making of the Irish Protestant ascendancy*, pp 184–5, 196–8.   **48** Arbuckle, *The Tribune*, pp 56–7. On the 'Protestant calendar' see James Kelly, '"Glorious and immortal memory": commemoration and Protestant identity in Ireland 1660–1800', *PRIA*, 94C (1994), pp 25–52, esp. p. 32.

Burial in eighteenth-century Dublin city
and its hinterland

FIONNUALA PARNELL

John Speed's map of Dublin shows the city in 1610. Depicted on it are twelve churches and associated burial grounds that would have catered for a population of some 10,000 people.[1] Six decades later Bernard de Gomme's map shows a much expanded city.[2] By the time John Rocque drew his map of the city of Dublin in 1756, the population had reached an estimated 150,000.[3] By then the city burial grounds were under pressure from over-use and encroaching development, which may partly explain why we find that burials of city dwellers began to take place in the outer suburbs and further afield throughout county Dublin and even beyond the county boundary. Examination of parish burial records for the eighteenth century give an indication of the mortality rate and thus the demand for burial space. The surviving historic graveyards of Dublin city are now few. Sadly, many have disappeared altogether and, at others, their headstones are either lost or stacked in inaccessible tiers against boundary walls.[4] Fortunately the sterling work of the Society for the Preservations of the Memorials of the Dead, which recorded headstone inscriptions in the late nineteenth and early twentieth centuries, and Egan and Flatman's *Memorials of the dead* compiled in the 1970s, have preserved the texts of many headstones that no longer survive or are now illegible.[5]

* * *

Few seventeenth-century headstones survive in Ireland. Examples in Dublin date to the later part of the century. It is probable that wooden grave markers were used more frequently than headstones and these would not have survived weather damage and reuse of grave plots. Well-carved stone grave markers dating to the early years of the eighteenth century are not uncommon and an

---

1 John Speed, *Dubline* (London, 1611), reproduced in Colm Lennon, *Dublin part 2, 1610 to 1756* (Irish historic towns atlas, no. 19, Dublin, 2008), p. 2. **2** Bernard de Gomme, *The city and suburbs of Dublin* (London, 1673), reproduced in Lennon, *Dublin part 2*. **3** John Rocque, *A plan of the city of Dublin* (Dublin 1756), reproduced in Lennon, *Dublin part 2*, p. 2. **4** Michael Egan & Richard Flatman, *Memorials of the dead: Dublin city and county*, vols 1–3 (Dublin, 1988–1990). **5** *Association for the Preservation of the Memorials of the Dead* (Dublin, 1888–1916); Egan & Flatman, *Memorials of the dead:*

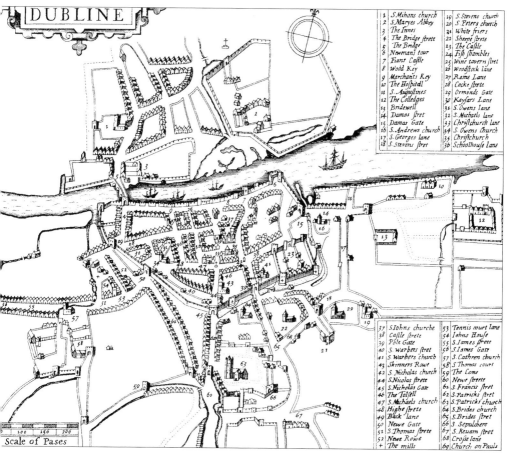

1	S.Mihans church	19	S.Stevens church
2	S.Maryes Abbey	20	S.Peters church
3	The Innes	21	White friers
4	The Bridge ftrete	22	Sheepe ftrete
5	The Bridge	23	The Caftle
6	Newmans tour	24	Fifh fhambles
7	Fiant Caftle	25	Wine tavern ftret
8	Wodd Key	26	Woodftock lane
9	Marchants Key	27	Rame Lane
10	The Hofpitall	28	Cocke ftrete
11	S.Auguftines	29	Ormonds Gate
12	The Colledges	30	Kayfars Lane
13	Bridewell	31	S.Owens lane
14	Damas ftret	32	S.Michaels lane
15	Damas Gate	33	Chriftchurch lane
16	S.Andrews church	34	S.Owens Church
17	S.Georges lane	35	Chriftchurch
18	S.Stevens ftret	36	Schoolhoufe lane

37	S.Iohns churche	53	Tennis court lane
38	Caftle ftrete	54	Iohns Houfe
39	Pole Gate	55	S.Iames ftrete
40	S.Warbers ftret	56	S.Iames Gate
41	S.Warbers church	57	S.Cathren church
42	Skinners Rowe	58	S.Thomas court
43	S.Nicholas church	59	The Cons
44	S.Nicolas ftrete	60	News ftrete
45	S.Nicholas Gate	61	S.Francis ftret
46	The Tolfell	62	S.Patricks ftret
47	S.Michaels church	63	S.Patricks church
48	Highe ftrete	64	S.Brides church
49	Back lane	65	S.Brides ftret
50	Newe Gate	66	S.Sepulchers
51	S.Thomas ftrete	67	S.Keuarn ftret
52	Newe Rowe	68	Croffe lane
+	The mills	69	Church on Pauls

17 John Speed's map of the city, *c.*1610, shows twelve city churches and associated graveyards (reproduced courtesy of Joe Brady).

increase in the numbers of headstones is evident throughout the century. This rise in the popularity of the headstone in the eighteenth century has been attributed to the growing consumer society, which placed emphasis on the ownership of goods. This would have extended to burial plots.[6] The focus of this essay is on the socio-cultural significance of headstone inscriptions in Dublin, an area explored in the British and Irish context by Harold Mytum.[7]

Dublin city and county (Dublin, 1991–7).   **6** Harold Mytum, 'Popular attitudes to memory, the body, and social identity: the rise of external commemoration in Britain, Ireland and New England', *Post-Medieval Archaeology*, 40:1 (2006), p. 106.   **7** Harold Mytum, 'Artefact biography as an approach to material culture: Irish gravestones as a material form of genealogy', *Journal of Irish Archaeology* (2004), pp 111–27; Harold

Headstones, he points out, tell us about hopes and fears, social strategies and ambitions, occupations and personal tragedies; they are a direct link to a significant proportion of the past population, allowing us to learn about their lives and deaths.[8] Memorials self-evidently make claims about the identity of the deceased. However, as every individual has many types of identity, those referred to sometimes reflect the wishes of the surviving family rather than the deceased.

Mytum highlights that when dealing with inscribed stones literacy among the larger population is assumed. The shift from initials, which might be seen on very early headstones, to full texts reflects increasing literacy on the part of those commissioning the monument and those who subsequently viewed it in the graveyard.[9] Headstones could now actively define and promote social identities with longer inscriptions that could be read and understood by a significant proportion of the population. Headstones serve a variety of functions. Primarily, they mark the grave of a family member and identify a location where the deceased can be remembered and prayed for. The text on a headstone gives a synopsis of a life, some with more, some with less detail. Social relationships are indicated by reference to family, to address and to occupation. But far from being mere factual statements of death and commemoration, headstones may reveal socio-economic status, individual and family identity, values regarding death, concern with ownership of the grave-plot and attachment to community.

* * *

Throughout the eighteenth century, ownership of the grave plot is indicated by two textual formulae: 'This stone and burial place belongs to/is the property of ...' and 'Erected by/This stone erected by ...' Following this text, many headstones also bear the additional inscription 'for him and his posterity', a clear statement that the family use of the plot is intended for generations to come. Two headstones are known that proclaim a more overt message of ownership.[10] Both state that 'This ground was purchased by ...' It is notable that many of the headstones bearing ownership inscriptions do not

Mytum, 'A long and complex plot: patterns of family burial in Irish graveyards from the 18th century', *Church Archaeology* (2004), pp 31–41; Harold Mytum, 'Local traditions in early eighteenth-century commemoration: the headstone memorials from Balrothery, Co. Dublin and their place in the evolution of Irish and British commemorative practice', *PRIA*, 104C (2004), pp 1–35. **8** Harold Mytum, 'Recording and analysing graveyards', *Council for British Archaeology Handbook*, vol. 15 (York, 2000), p. 51. **9** Mytum, 'Popular attitudes', p. 106. **10** St Douglah's and Balrothery cemeteries.

actually refer to burial although it is assumed that burials did take place in the plot but personal details were not added to the headstone. Two unusual headstone inscriptions make very definite statements regarding plot ownership. These are quoted in full below, including original spellings, as inscribed on the headstones.

This stone and burial place
belongeth to Michael Stott and
Elinor Larking daughter to Chr[i]
Larking and Betty Cane and we
do intend to be buried here
when the Almighty God is
pleased to call us and now we
are in the 68 year of our age
December 1786

This stone and burial place
Belongeth to the Warren,s of
Cillock and his postererity,
this three hundred years and
White hath no right to this
burial place only by marriage
And Barthw Warren has caused
this stone to be erected for
the use of him and his family

The first inscription, from St Mary's Abbey, Howth, is an example of ownership of a burial plot being proclaimed without further information as to whether either person was interred or when. The second inscription, from St Margaret's in north county Dublin, seems to indicate a family feud. Although undated, the font and language indicate it is an eighteenth-century headstone. Whatever occurred between the Warrens and the Whites will probably never be known but it was important enough for Bartholomew Warren to have it inscribed in stone. As with the Howth headstone, there is no further inscription to tell us if any Warrens were buried there. Interestingly, there is an eighteenth-century headstone to the White family directly behind the Warrens' plot. This is the only headstone found that gives a glimpse of daily life in rural Dublin. Inscriptions remembering the deceased are more commonly seen on headstones than inscriptions proclaiming ownership. 'Here lyeth the body of ... who died' appears most often on headstones dating from the earlier decades of the eighteenth century. This formula emphasizes the presence of the corpse and acknowledges that the body is in the process of decay.[11] Concern with the decaying body was replaced in the latter half of the century with remembrance of the living person as indicated in the increased usage of the phrase 'in memory of'.

* * *

11 Mytum, 'Recording and analysing graveyards', p. 51.

Many inscriptions mention those who commissioned the headstone and their relationship to the deceased, thus providing an identity structured through kinship.[12] The normal pattern of inscription on memorials where there is not a long-term use of a monument is that of the married couple, possibly followed by some of their children who die in the parent's lifetime.[13] In my study of eighteenth-century headstones in the Fingal area, approximately half of the headstones commemorated more than one person.[14] In the majority of cases the person in the primary position on the headstone was male. The relationships of the other persons, including children, commemorated are recorded in reference to that person whether male or female. Inscriptions on Irish headstones typically describe women in terms of kinship relations such as wife and mother more often than men are described as husbands. My research has shown that only 25 per cent of headstones in the Dublin area mention women. The majority of these headstones record the full married name of the woman with a lesser number adding her maiden name. Few married women are commemorated by their full maiden name alone and these fall in the earlier decades of the century. One headstone from St Mary's Abbey in Howth is a good example of this with the following inscription: 'This stone and burial place belongeth to Michael Stott and Elinor Larking daughter to Chri [Christopher] Larking and Betty Cane'. It not only links Elinor Larking back to her parents but also gives her mother's maiden name. Few examples of a woman being described as a widow are seen and those that do most commonly date from the 1770s to 1790. In the later part of the century, headstones erected by women to their deceased husbands are to be seen. This would indicate the financial stability of the woman in question along with a desire not only to commemorate her husband but to ensure her own identity in the community.

The majority of eighteenth-century Dublin headstones refer to children in terms of their parents and most often in terms of their father. The most common inscription is 'his children' while 'their children' and 'her children' occur less frequently and usually towards the end of the century. It is not common to find the children named. The majority of these headstones do not record the number of children buried or commemorated. The inscriptions simply say 'children', 'several children' or 'some children'. The age of death of children is rarely inscribed, while 'died young' is commonly used. There are,

---

12 Harold Mytum, *Mortuary monuments and burial grounds of the historic period* (New York, 2004), p. 34.
13 Ibid., p. 127.   14 Fionnuala Parnell, 'Death and remembrance in eighteenth-century Fingal' (MA,

however, some rare exceptions. In St Margaret's graveyard, mentioned above, one infant is recorded as having died at ten days old. There are very few examples of children being accorded their own headstone. However, there is one very interesting headstone in Kinsealy. On this stone five unnamed children, whose ages are not given, are recorded as having died on 27 October 1754. In addition, a daughter who died five days later is named and her age, 3 years, is inscribed. A further headstone recording the deaths of children who died within days of each other is also found in Kinsealy. Twin daughters aged 5 months died on 9 November 1789 and a 4-year-old daughter died ten days later.

One cannot help speculating that an outbreak of fever in the later part of those years led to the deaths of so many children in each household. The greatest number of children recorded on a single headstone appears in St Margaret's, Co. Dublin. These consist of two named adult daughters, fourteen 'more' children and thirteen grandchildren and were the family of James Casey, a victualler of the city of Dublin.

* * *

Place, according to Harold Mytum, can indicate much to contemporaries about a person. A street in a town may carry a particular level of social standing and a farm would be known for its scale and relative worth. Place can be defined in inscriptions at a number of levels. Many people are defined by parish or region. Place of birth can be stated, showing an identity with another region, and, where place of death is some distance away, this may imply a different form of relationship to the community within which the memorial is erected.[15] In the case of the Dublin, approximately 25 per cent of headstones record an address within the city – a parish, townland or locality. Of these, most specifically mention street names. In the Dublin area, the association with place is linked to men with only a few headstones noting the addresses of women, perhaps reflecting the male role as property-holder in eighteenth-century society.

While headstones describe women in terms of kinship relations such as wife and mother, men are often described by their occupation. The range of trades and occupations inscribed on eighteenth-century headstones is a fascinating part of the story of Dublin's graveyards. It has been noted that those commissioning headstones in Dublin considered that their trades, or those of

UCD, 2009).   **15** Mytum, *Mortuary monuments*, p. 153.

their kin, were an important aspect of the person who owned or was buried in the grave plot. Such headstones are reasonably numerous in Dublin but only isolated instances of trade symbols, and fewer mentions of trades and occupations, are to be found in other parts of the country. Similar instance of such trade inscriptions have been noted only in Belfast and some coastal towns in Northern Ireland and Wales. Eighteenth-century Scottish headstones display a wealth of trade symbols and inscriptions.

In my research of approximately 2,500 eighteenth-century headstones in Dublin city and county, and counties Kildare and Wicklow, a total of 560 headstones bearing trade inscriptions have been found. On these 125 different trades are recorded. With only 40 exceptions, all of the inscriptions also mentioned an address, whether broadly giving 'City of Dublin' or specifying a street in the city or a locality. There is a spread of trade inscriptions throughout the city and county graveyards but the graveyards in which trade inscriptions are most frequently found are Mulhuddart with 73 examples, St James with 65 and Drumcondra with 43. St Mobhi's, Crumlin, St Catherine's, Bluebell and Merrion Road are also noteworthy for the number and range of trades mentioned.

In looking at the trades mentioned on the Dublin headstones, we find that the most numerous are those described generally as merchants although the type of business is not specified. Fifty-eight merchants' headstones are known, along with 7 'dealers'. Grocers, referred to on 33 headstones, indicate the importance of provisioning and feeding the city. In this they are joined by 11 victuallers, 21 bakers and assorted dairymen, poulterers and corn chandlers. Nineteen farmers who provided meat and grain to the city are to be found in graveyards outside the city boundary. Gardeners, surprisingly, had 14 headstones. While the growing city certainly had houses with gardens requiring care, a return to Rocque's map shows us large areas of market gardens that are mainly concentrated in the northern outskirts of the city. It is likely that the gardeners referred to on headstones were operators of these large undertakings.

Adjunct trades to the supply of meat are those of skinner, tanner and currier. Skinners and tanners are mentioned on 27 headstones. In looking at the addresses on the headstones we see that the skinners are centred on Watling Street and the tanners close by. As a point of interest, the majority of these two trades are buried in the northern outskirts of the city. Skinners, tanners and curriers were mentioned on later headstones and I would suggest

of Hearse or Sedan used at Cork for people of middling Station.

18 Funeral of the middle rank sketched by Hugh Douglas Hamilton, *c.*1760 (private collection).

that the nearby urban graveyards were full at that stage and burials took place in the closest rural graveyards. The provisioning of the city would not be complete without the brewers, distillers and vintners. Predictably, there are a large number of brewers. The twenty headstones mainly give the general address 'City of Dublin'. Those few that do specify a street name are centred around St James Street. This reflects Dublin's diverse and vibrant brewing trade before the rise of the Guinness brewery and its dominance of the market from the mid-nineteenth century. Coopers are commemorated on nine headstones and are similarly described as being of the 'City of Dublin'. Those with addresses are, again, in the St James Street area. Distillers are few, only four are named. Vintners, found mainly on later headstones, number five. Four publicans and five inn-keepers also served the needs of the population.

The eighteenth century was a booming time economically in Dublin which led to an expansion in the trade of luxury goods. The city's many new Georgian squares and terraces needed to be decorated and furnished, a fact reflected in memorial inscriptions. The builders of the city are well represented. Four land surveyors and measurers would have been responsible for mapping the city. Three architects and 6 stone cutters are joined by bricklayers, masons, slaters, 5 timber merchants and 13 carpenters. A pavior (someone who makes and installs paving stones), glassmaker, locksmiths and plasterer add to the story of the expansion of the city. The importance of trade into Dublin is attested to by the three revenue officers, a ballast master and a toll master. Two anchor smiths, two rope makers and a shipwright reflect an active Dublin port. The largest trade group referred to on headstones are those in the silk, wool, linen and cotton businesses. The importance of cloth manufacturing in Dublin is evident from my research and the range of specialist crafts and trades illustrates a thriving textile industry, and suggests the prosperity of Dublin's economy more generally. The weavers, although not specified in what medium they worked, account for 14 of the 49 headstones that fall into this category. Their headstones date to the 1760s with addresses in the Patrick Street/Coombe area. The majority of the weavers are buried in Bluebell graveyard. The silk trade is represented by, among others, two silk weavers, a silk thrower, a silk and ribbon manufacturer and a silk dresser. A cotton dyer and five cotton manufacturers outnumber one linen weaver and two linen manufacturers. A hemp and flax manufacturer completes this sector. Wool, although it was a home-produced and plentiful material, only has three manufacturers and three wool combers. Probably the most unusual trade, to our eyes, is the mohair throwser and twister. Four bleachers and four dyers could have worked with any of the four cloth materials. Indeed, Rocque's map shows a number of tenterfields in the Weaver Square/Marrowbone Lane area and a bleaching green just north of the Linen Hall, in what is now Kings Inn Park. Eight linen drapers and two woollen drapers bought raw linen or wool for bleaching and finishing before selling it wholesale or to the public. Moving on from the raw material to a finished product, we find evidence of Dublin's busy retail fashion trade in the headstones to 3 master tailors, 4 merchant tailors and 7 tailors. Clothiers, who could be either manufacturers or retailers of cloth and clothing, and number sixteen in the headstone record, confuse the list slightly. Fourteen shoemakers bridge the gap between the tanners and the public. The two glovers would have catered to the gentry and obtained their raw goods from the silk merchants or the currier who produced fine leather. Four hatters, a britches maker, two embroiderers (appropriately named Lacoste) and two collar makers complete the clothing sector.

As well as a wide range of merchants in the city's cemeteries, we also find the craftsmen who made domestic goods. Cabinetmakers, cutlers and upholsterers are to be found. Cultural life is echoed in the headstones of two harpsichord makers. An unexpected herald painter also appears. In such an intellectual era it is no surprise to find a parchment maker, paper maker and merchant and three printers. Two booksellers, three tobacconists and two apothecaries are the only specialized shopkeepers mentioned. Two tallow chandlers would have supplied candles and oils to provide lighting in the house. Travel around the city is represented in eight coachmakers although only one coach owner is noted. A saddler, a smith and farrier are also recorded. One of the interesting headstones, now being eroded by pedestrian wear at St Mary's, is one dated 1735 to Thomas Leister, Farrier to His Majesty in Dublin. Industry in the form of an iron founder, a pumpmaker and turner, edge-tool maker and a tin plate worker belong to the later decades of the century. Of the five headstones to servants, three are effusive in their praises of the men but it is made quite clear that the headstones were erected by their masters. An inscription in Ballyboghil states that the headstone was erected by the master who gave his place of business, Capel Street in the City of Dublin, and mentioned the humble station of the servant who died in 1747 at the age of 27. This is a clear case of the master using the headstone as a means of proclaiming his own status. It is of interest that these five servants noted on nineteenth-century headstones all died young. Another such example is the memorial to Alexander McGee in St Patrick's Cathedral. He died in 1722 at the age of 29; he was servant to Dean Swift.

It is noteworthy that only five women are shown as having trades. A baker, confectioner, pastry cook and grocer are not unusual occupations for an eighteenth-century woman but the trade of hemp and flax manufacturer would not be one we would associate with a woman of the time and it is interesting to find it represented on her headstone. Trades commonly associated with women in the eighteenth century, such as the seamstresses and milliners who would have clothed the ladies of the city, are absent. Despite the paucity of evidence from gravestones of women's involvement in trades it should be noted that *Wilson's directory* of 1783 mentions quite a number of women involved in a wide variety of trades. This would lead one to suppose that they are carrying on the trade of deceased husbands but undoubtedly many may have been trading in their own right.[16]

Consideration of the trades and professions leads us to think about the occupations that are absent from the headstone record. The professions are notably scarce. Two attorneys, two bachelors of law, one physician and a number of clergymen account for the upper middle class. While we did come across the builders of the Georgian city, the stuccodores who embellished the homes and public buildings of the city are represented only by Michael Stapleton who worked on the Trinity College plasterwork. Georgian silversmiths are also absent and only one goldsmith is to be found.

* * *

The latter part of the eighteenth century saw a shift in tone of headstone inscriptions towards a focus on remembrance of the living person. This trend is emphasized as we move forward into the nineteenth century when remembrance of the dead and expressions of sorrow and mourning commonly appear on headstone inscriptions. The great cemeteries of Glasnevin (1832), Mount Jerome (1836) and Deansgrange (1865) opened to provide much needed burial ground, and also as places in which to display class and social standing. The Victorian cemetery is laid out as a park with paths, planting and vistas and the monumental headstones, tombs and vaults are testimony to success in life. In contrast to the tradesmen of the eighteenth century we now find the professions and gentry commemorated with considerable emphasis on status and achievement. These headstones provide insights into family relationships and emerging concerns on the part of a growing artisan and middle class with social status. In pointing to the growth in disposable income of this class, the headstones show that Dubliners were becoming more concerned with creating memorials to themselves and their families.

---

16 Dublin City Merchants and Traders in *The Gentleman's and Citizen's Almanac compiled by Samuel Watson Bookseller for the Year of our Lord 1783*, www.swilson.info/wat1783.php, accessed 17 Sept. 2014.

Burying poor and gentry: St James' Church and Graveyard, Dublin

SEAN J. MURPHY

St James' Church of Ireland Church and Graveyard are located at the western end of James' Street, adjacent to the Guinness brewery. The Roman Catholic St James' Church is nearby, reflecting the fact that since the Reformation in the sixteenth century there has been a duality of Protestant and Catholic churches in Dublin city, dedicated to the same saint in many cases. To the rear of the Church of Ireland church there is a 1.5-acre graveyard, the largest burial place in the inner city and one that remained in use longer than most urban cemeteries. St James' Church is of medieval creation and a copy of the foundation charter has survived fortuitously in the register of the abbey of St Thomas. In the charter, which is dated between 1189 and 1192, Henry Tyrrell granted land to the clergy of St Thomas' Abbey for the creation of a church and cemetery (*ecclesiam et cimiterium*) dedicated to St James the Apostle.[1] In a separate document from the same period, John Comyn, archbishop of Dublin, confirmed the grant of St James' Church to the abbey of St Thomas and also set out the boundaries of the parish, running from Newgate in the east to the lands of Kilmainham in the west.[2] St James the Apostle or 'Santiago' is the patron saint of Spain who, legend has it, was buried at Santiago de Compostela, which as a result became a famous pilgrimage centre. While a medieval link between St James' Church in Dublin and the pilgrimage to Santiago de Compostela has not been documented, it is an entirely plausible one given the popularity of the pilgrimage in Ireland.[3]

* * *

The new church of St James does not appear to have thrived in its early years; in about 1294 it was found to have insufficient revenue to pay ecclesiastical taxation, a situation in which other city churches, such as St Catherine's, also

---

1 J.T. Gilbert (ed.), *Register of the abbey of St Thomas, Dublin* (London, 1889), p. 383; Revd Aubrey Gwynn, 'The early history of St Thomas' Abbey, Dublin', *JRSAI*, 84 (1954), p. 16. **2** Ibid., pp 284–5. **3** Richard Hayes, 'Ireland's links with Compostella', *Studies*, 37 (1948), pp 326–32. Reflecting the revival of a perceived tradition, St James' Catholic church in James' Street is currently involved in the issuing of camino 'passports', being one of a European network of starting points for modern pilgrims to Santiago.

found themselves.[4] The earliest account we have of a burial in St James' is that of Walter Soggyn, a merchant of Dublin, whose will dated 1495 stated that he was to be 'buried in the church of St James without the city'.[5] Burial within the walls of churches was reserved for notables and the wealthy. The majority of parishioners would have been interred in the adjoining churchyards. The density of burials in medieval and early modern cemeteries was high and these could be 'rather unsavoury sites'. Graveyards could also be employed for grazing animals and as dumping grounds.[6]

A feature of the Reformation was the dissolution of the great monasteries such as St Thomas' Abbey. In 1544, the abbey and its possessions were granted to Sir William Brabazon,[7] whose descendants, the earls of Meath, held a right of appointing ministers to St James' and St Catherine's churches from 1660 until the disestablishment of the Church of Ireland in 1869.[8] In 1545 St James' Church was united with the churches of St Catherine and St John in Kilmainham.[9] In 1630 it seems St James' was under repair as it was described by one contemporary as being 'new covered but not glassed, the chancel down'.[10] St James' and St Catherine's again became separate parishes by act of parliament in 1707, while in 1761 St James' collapsed and was rebuilt. The present church was constructed to the design of Joseph Welland during the years 1859–60 and in the 1940s its spire had to be removed when found to be in a dangerous condition.[11]

Although St James' Church was controlled by the Church of Ireland since the Reformation, Roman Catholics were also interred there. In the Reformation and penal eras, Catholics in Dublin city had to worship in out-of-the-way and often temporary locations. Even when permanent structures were permitted from the later eighteenth century onwards, the Catholic churches of the city, including St James' Church, were notable for the fact that they did not have burial grounds attached. Replicating the experience of its Protestant counterpart, Catholic St James' parish was detached from St Catherine's in 1724 and having occupied places of worship in various locations, came to rest in a chapel at James' Gate, which was in use until 1854.

---

4 M.J. McEnery & Raymond Refaussé (eds), *Christ Church deeds* (Dublin, 2001), p. 61.   5 H.F. Twiss (ed.), 'Some ancient deeds of the parishes of St Catherine and St James, Dublin', *PRIA*, 35:C (1919), pp 274–5.   6 Clodagh Tait, *Death, burial and commemoration in Ireland, 1150–1650* (Basingstoke, 2002), pp 64–5.   7 Ibid., p. 61.   8 Revd John Crawford, *Around the churches: the stories of the churches in the St Patrick's Cathedral group of parishes, Dublin* (Naas, 1988), pp 17, 22.   9 John D'Alton, *The memoirs of the Archbishops of Dublin* (Dublin, 1888), p. 230.   10 Revd Myles Ronan (ed.), 'Archbishop Bulkeley's visitation of Dublin 1630', *Archivium Hibernicum*, 8 (1941), p. 62.   11 Crawford, *Around the churches*, p. 20.

In that year the present church building in James' Street was opened, having been designed by Patrick Byrne. Its foundation stone was laid in 1844 by Daniel O'Connell.[12]

Catholic links to the Protestant graveyard were underlined in 1612, when the executed Catholic bishop of Down and Connor, Conor O'Devany, and a priest, Patrick O'Loghran, were buried there. Both men were considered martyrs by the Catholic Church and this would have made the graveyard a site of pilgrimage.[13] Furthermore, in the seventeenth and eighteenth centuries St James' had the status of a 'great Catholic burial-place' and was the 'chief burial ground of the Catholic aristocracy of Ireland'.[14] Notables buried there include Dr Thady Fitzpatrick of the Ossory family of that name, in 1674, and Sir Stephen Rice, a supporter of the deposed King James II, in 1714.[15] Some mystery surrounds the circumstances of the death of another Catholic aristocrat interred in St James' Graveyard, namely, Thomas Preston, 3rd Viscount Tara, who was killed in July 1674 by Sir Francis Blundell and his brothers William and Winwood. The Blundell brothers were acquitted of murder and furthermore received a royal pardon, which might indicate that the killing was an affair of honour.[16] While no trace of Lord Tara's tomb survives in the graveyard, an illustration of it is included in Thomas Dineley's journal.[17]

Arguably the most notable individual buried in St James' Graveyard is Sir Theobald (Toby) Butler (b.1650, d.1721), whose tomb is also the most striking in the cemetery. Sir Toby, who belonged to the Boytonrath branch of the Butlers, was a contemporary of the aforementioned Sir Stephen Rice, and served as solicitor-general under King James II in 1689–90. After the victory of the forces of King William III, Butler was closely involved in the drafting of the Treaty of Limerick in 1691, whose terms were not ungenerous to the defeated Irish Catholics but which would not be implemented in full. In succeeding years, when Catholics laboured under increasingly discriminatory laws, Butler was able to continue practicing as a solicitor and in 1704 he famously pleaded in the Irish House of Commons against the severity of anti-Catholic penal legislation.[18] Sir Toby's tomb, probably the most substantial

12 Revd Nicholas Donnelly, *Short histories of some of Dublin parishes*, part 9 (Dublin, 1910 [1979]), pp 229–33. **13** Tait, *Death, burial and commemoration in Ireland*, pp 18, 54.   **14** John D'Alton, *Illustrations historical and genealogical of King James' Irish army list, 1689* (Dublin, 1855), pp 104, 236.   **15** Ibid., pp 184, 507. **16** Sir Bernard Burke, *A genealogical history of the dormant, abeyant, forfeited and extinct peerages of the British Empire* (London, 1866), p. 445.   **17** F. Elrington Ball (ed.), 'Extracts from the journal of Thomas Dineley', *JRSAI*, 43 (1913), p. 293. The illustration of Lord Tara's tomb gives the date of death as 6 July 1678. **18** George Butler, 'Sir Toby Butler, solicitor-general in Ireland, 1689–90', *Dublin Historical Record*, 23

surviving Jacobite monument in Dublin, was repaired by a member of the Butler family in the late nineteenth century and, having once more fallen into disrepair, has recently been restored alongside other monuments in the graveyard, by a stonework expert commissioned by Dublin City Council.[19]

* * *

The feast day of St James, 25 July, was the occasion of ceremonies in the graveyard and a fair in the street outside. Richard Stanihurst gave an account of festivities at St James' fair in a work published in 1577, while in 1610 Barnaby Rich noted the 'multitude of rascal people' spending their time drinking ale sold at the fair.[20] In the early decades of the nineteenth century it was observed that during the fair-time festivities it was the custom to 'deck the graves with garlands and ornaments, made of white paper, disposed into very extraordinary forms'.[21] Another source described these decorations as forming 'effigies or images of all the persons who have been buried in the same grave', and that 'a mother is frequently seen sitting on a grave surrounded by the rude figures of her deceased children, with whom she is holding a communication'. It was further recorded in the same source that St James' was 'the general cemetery of the lower classes', who were 'persuaded that prayers are offered up on that [St James'] day by his holiness the pope, for the souls of all those who were there buried'.[22] A notable obelisk fountain stands opposite St James' church, reputed to mark the site of the holy well dedicated to the saint, which was designed by the architect Francis Sandys, erected in 1790 and restored in the 1990s. An interesting funeral custom, which is still well-remembered locally, consisted of carrying the coffin three times around the fountain before burial in the graveyard.[23]

The burial, baptism and marriage registers of St James' Church of Ireland parish are extant from 1742 and can now be searched online to the year 1883, while the originals from their commencement until 1989 are held in the Church of Ireland archives.[24] It is likely that a number of pre-1742 St James' burials are included in the registers of St Catherine's parish.[25] The baptism and

(1970), pp 113–26. **19** Veronika Zemska, 'Stone art restoration', http://www.stoneartrestoration.ie/gallery/3-tombstones, accessed 9 Oct. 2014. **20** Patrick Lynch & John Vaizey, *Guinness' brewery in the Irish economy, 1750–1876* (Cambridge, 1960), p. 74, n. 1. **21** G.N. Wright, *An historical guide to ancient and modern Dublin* (London, 1821), p. 164. **22** John Warburton, James Whitelaw & Robert Walsh, *History of the city of Dublin*, vol. 2 (London, 1818), pp 1, 175. **23** D.G. Hiney, 'Only drink and horses: the story of St James' street fountain', *Dublin Historical Record*, 50 (1997), pp 198–9. **24** St James' Church of Ireland registers of baptism, marriage and burial, 1742–1883, Irish Genealogy, http://churchrecords.irishgenealogy.ie/, accessed 10 Oct. 2014, original registers 1742–1989 held in RCBL. **25** St Catherine's

marriage registers of St James' Catholic parish commence in 1752 and there are no burial registers for the reasons already explained.[26] Vestry or parish council records survive for St James' Church of Ireland parish for the mid- to late seventeenth century and from the mid-nineteenth to mid-twentieth centuries.[27] Completing the substantial range of surviving primary source materials, transcriptions of the inscriptions on memorials in St James' Graveyard have been published together with a plot map.[28]

* * *

It can be seen from the appended table that the registered burials in St James' Graveyard increased steadily in the late eighteenth century but fell from about 500 per annum in the 1780s to about 300 per annum in the 1820s. A spike of 503 in 1798 in the otherwise declining trend of burials may reflect mortality during the United Irish Rebellion of that year. In the year before the rebellion, 1797, funerals of two United Irishmen proceeded to St James' Graveyard with thousands in attendance,[29] showing the association of the place with political dissent and indeed that the mass political funeral was a phenomenon predating the nineteenth century. While the drop in registered burials to about 100 per annum in the 1830s may be due partly to gaps in the records, the principal explanation was probably the opening of Goldenbridge Cemetery in 1829 and Glasnevin Cemetery in 1832 (see below). Examination of the entries for the years 1858–71 indicates that there may have been significant under-registration in St James' during these years and that most of the unrecorded burials were likely to have been Catholic.

Just over 700 tombstones survive in St James' Graveyard, of which about 530 have legible inscriptions ranging in date from the early seventeenth to the late twentieth century.[30] The earliest surviving gravestone located in St James' is dated 1627 but unfortunately does not contain names, only the initials

Church of Ireland registers of baptism, marriage and burial, 1699–1966, partly online at http://churchrecords.irishgenealogy.ie/ and original registers held in RCBL. See also Herbert Wood (ed.), *Registers of the parish of St Catherine, Dublin, 1636–1715* (Dublin, 1908, repr. by RCBL, 2003). **26** St James' Roman Catholic registers of baptism and marriage, 1752–1896, http://churchrecords.irishgenealogy.ie/, accessed 10 Oct. 2014, and originals held by parish. **27** Raymond Gillespie (ed.), *The vestry records of the parishes of St Catherine and St James, Dublin, 1657–1692* (Dublin, 2004); St James', Dublin, vestry minute books, 4 vols, 1845–1963, RCBL. **28** St James' Graveyard project, *Memorial inscriptions from St James' Graveyard, Dublin* (Dublin, 1988), http://homepage.eircom.net/~seanjmurphy/epubs/stjames%27sinscriptions.pdf, accessed 10 Oct. 2014. **29** James Smyth, 'Dublin's political underground in the 1790s' in Gerard O'Brien (ed.), *Parliament, politics and people* (Dublin, 1989), p. 143. **30** St James' Graveyard project, *St James' Graveyard, Dublin: history and associations* (Dublin, 1988), p. 16, http://homepage.eircom.net/~seanjmurphy/epubs/stjames%27sgraveyard.pdf, accessed 10 Oct. 2014.

'D K A N', which appear from the text of the inscription to refer to at least two individuals.[31] As is the case in most graveyards before the twentieth century, only the wealthier deceased are commemorated with permanent memorials, and the vast majority of those buried there would have been too poor to afford anything other than impermanent grave markers. The theft of bodies for medical dissection by 'resurrectionists' or 'sack-em-up men' posed a problem in many cemeteries, and the presence of a permanent sexton did not always provide protection. In December 1742 the sexton of St James', Thomas Owen, removed the body of a Mrs Murphy from her vault and sold it.[32]

Certainly in the later period of its use, most of the memorials to Protestants buried in St James' Graveyard are located closer to the church building, while those for Catholics are further away. The Protestant memorials tend to contain less decoration and, from the later nineteenth century onwards, frequently conclude with pious verse or a biblical quotation. In contrast, the Catholic memorials are found to be more freely decorated, including crucifixes and other religious objects, while many feature the letters 'IHS' (an abbreviation for Jesus, although other meanings have been suggested), which was rarely used by Protestants. In the eighteenth and early nineteenth centuries in particular, memorial inscriptions frequently contain addresses and occupations as well as names and dates of death. Thus the tombstone of Patrick Byrne, with an inscription for his daughter dated 1786, describes him as a linen and cotton manufacturer resident in Rainsford Street, while the 1767 inscription on the stone of Terence Duffy lists his address as Watling Street and his trade as parchment maker.[33] The memorial inscription to Mary and Laurence Murphy, died 1790 and 1805 respectively, contains a verse often encountered in graveyards which warns passers-by of their mortality:

> Stay passenger, see where I lie
> As you are now, so once was I
> Now as I am, so must you be
> Prepare for death, and follow me.[34]

The only memorial plaque surviving within the church itself is to city alderman and brewer Mark Rainsford (Ranford) who died in 1693 and was buried apparently in a then extant church vault. In 1759 Rainsford's grandson

---

31 Ibid., p. 17. 32 Ibid., pp 26–7. 33 *Memorial inscriptions from St James' Graveyard*, pp 11, 30. 34 Ibid., p. 72.

and namesake signed the famous 9,000-year lease of the core property on which the Guinness brewery stands.[35] One of St James' Graveyard's most striking and armorially decorated tombs is that of the brewer William Espinasse, who died in 1740 and whose firm passed via the Rainsfords to Arthur Guinness.[36] At the rear of the graveyard stands the tomb of Sylvester Costigan, died 1817, a distiller who resided in Thomas Street and was an activist for Catholic relief from the penal laws.[37] Other notable memorials include one to William Limerick Martin, a district inspector of the Royal Irish Constabulary who was killed in 1889 in Gweedore, Co. Donegal,[38] and another to John J. O'Grady, Dublin Brigade, Irish Volunteers, who was killed in action during the 1916 Rising.[39] Military burials include Lieutenant Lewis D.M. Beard, Machine Gun Corps, died 19 October 1916, and Christopher Dolan, Royal Air Force, died 18 January 1920.[40] Church of Ireland clergymen buried in St James' Graveyard include Revd William Tisdall (1755), Revd John Ellis (1764) and Revd Richard Connolly (1848), while Catholic religious interred there include Fr Redmond McCarron (1666), Revd Dr William Gahan (1804), Mother Mary Bellew (1726) and other nuns of the Dominican convent of Channel Row (now North Brunswick Street).[41] St James' Graveyard is also the last resting place of brothel madam and memoirist Margaret (Peg) Leeson, who died in 1797 in reduced circumstances and for whom no memorial survives.[42]

The proportion of Catholics buried in St James' Graveyard grew over the eighteenth century reflecting a shift in the city's population at large. By the nineteenth century, the Church of Ireland baptism registers contain substantially fewer entries than the burial registers. In the 1820s official refusal to countenance non-Church of Ireland graveyards, together with occasional prevention of graveside prayers conducted by Catholic clergy in Protestant churchyards, constituted unacceptable humiliations which spurred Daniel O'Connell and his supporters to found cemeteries first at Goldenbridge and then at Glasnevin.[43] Addressing a meeting of the Catholic Committee in Dublin on 3 November 1823, O'Connell observed to general laughter that he

35 Ibid., p. 82; D.F. Moore, 'The Guinness saga', *Dublin Historical Record*, 16 (1960), p. 53. **36** *Memorial inscriptions from St James' Graveyard*, p. 33. **37** Ibid., p. 20. While the tombstone, with the name spelt 'Costigin', gives the date of death as 4 Feb. 1816, the burial entry for Sylvester Costigan is dated 7 Feb. 1817. St James' Graveyard burial register, RCBL. **38** Memorial inscriptions from St James' Graveyard, p. 65. **39** Ibid., p.76. **40** Ibid., pp 3, 26; Commonwealth War Graves Commission, http://www. cwgc.org/media/122171/2013_07_04_website_notice.pdf, accessed 13 Oct. 2014. **41** *St James' Graveyard: history and associations*, p. 16. **42** Mary Lyons (ed.), *The memoirs of Mrs Leeson* (Dublin, 1995), p. 251. **43** W.J. Fitzpatrick, *History of the Dublin Catholic cemeteries* (Dublin, 1900), pp 16, 18–19.

doubted if 'sowing turnips or other vegetable' in St James' Graveyard 'would be as productive as sowing Papists', going on to state that he was informed that 'the freehold of St James' … produced the minister near a couple thousand a year'. The latter claim may have been an exaggeration, but having regard to their limited means, the rate for poor burial in Goldenbridge and Glasnevin was set first at 2*s*. 6*d*. 'per head', reduced later in 1846 to 1*s*. 6*d*.[44] It would appear from entries in the registers of St James' Graveyard that in 1882 burial charges ranged from 4*s*. to 10*s*.[45] Yet the parish's concern for the less well-off is shown by the fact that in 1848 the sum of £50 was charged to its accounts in respect of 'coffins for the poor'.[46]

St James' Graveyard is located not far from the site of the old Dublin workhouse for the destitute, founded in the eighteenth century and later called the South Dublin Union when the poor law system was established in the nineteenth century, being now the campus of the modernized St James' Hospital. In 1861 it was observed that 'when a Roman Catholic pauper dies, his remains are carried to the Glasnevin Cemetery, and when a Protestant pauper dies, to St James' Churchyard, and the [workhouse] guardians defray the expenses.'[47] In preceding years it is likely that Catholic as well as Protestant paupers would have been buried in St James', indicating that, as Ciarán Mac Murchaidh's article highlights, death was a great equalizer.

* * *

As the twentieth century commenced, the addresses of those buried in St James' included the South Dublin Union and hospitals mostly in the south of Dublin city, with residents of James' Street and the immediate district also figuring prominently, followed by inhabitants of the Liberties to the east, Kilmainham and Inchicore to the west, and some others from further afield. Given the progressive closure of most other inner-city Dublin church graveyards and the availability of the larger commercial cemeteries, it is perhaps surprising that the number of burials in St James' Graveyard had begun to rise again in the late nineteenth century, reaching an average of nearly 200 per annum by the 1890s. Indeed, in 1899 Sir Charles Cameron, Dublin's medical officer, brought the condition of St James' Graveyard to the attention of the parish vestry, which resolved to put it in order.[48] There was

---

44 Ibid., p. 21.   **45** St James' Graveyard burial register, RCBL, 1882.   **46** 25 Apr. 1848, St James' vestry minute books, 1, RCBL.   **47** *Report of the select committee on poor relief (Ireland)*, 6 (1861), p. 185. **48** 1 Mar., 6 July 1899, St James' vestry minute books, 2, RCBL.

then a fall back to about 130 burials per annum in the 1910s. No significant increase in burials is evident during the year of the Easter Rising in 1916 (see reference to the casualty John J. O'Grady above), but, interestingly, two blank pages are to be found in the register for this year, perhaps an indication of an expectation of mass burials, which did not materialize due to adequate capacity being available in the larger cemeteries.[49] In contrast, there was an increase in burials in 1918 and 1919, 212 and 230 respectively as against the aforementioned average of 130, most likely a result of the influenza epidemic of those years.[50]

After the achievement of Irish independence from Britain in 1922 the average numbers of registered burials in St James' Graveyard fell progressively, declining to less than thirty per annum in the 1940s. In its final years of use St James' retained its connection with the more affluent, as shown by the interment there on 15 September 1944 of Sir William Haldane Porter CB.[51] The appropriately surnamed Porter was managing director of the Guinness brewery and was buried from his residence at 98 James' Street nearby, in a grave with his wife Sybil Osborne, who had predeceased him in 1941.[52] Porter was born in Ulster in 1867 and before his career in Guinness had worked for the Home Office.[53] St James' Graveyard was closed to further burials by government order in 1955, with the exception of families who held burial rights in existing graves.[54] Since then there have only been four burials in St James' – in 1958, 1966, 1976 and 1989 – the final two being appropriately of a Protestant and a Catholic respectively.[55] In 1956, the Church of Ireland St James' Church was closed and the parish reunited with St Catherine's.[56] The church building was eventually turned over to commercial use, being occupied by Lighting World until that firm's closure in 2009.

Having fallen into a condition of considerable neglect, St James' Graveyard was the subject of a community restoration project in 1987–8, with support from the then-state training and employment agency, Foras Áiseanna Saothair

---

49 Of the recorded 1916 Rising fatalities, 250 were buried in Glasnevin Cemetery, 24 in Mount Jerome and 49 in Dean's Grange (*1916 Rebellion handbook* (Dublin, 1916 [1998]), pp 56–8). 50 Caitriona Foley, *The last Irish plague: the great flu epidemic in Ireland, 1918–19* (Dublin, 2011). 51 (Sir) Haldane Porter CB, 98 James' Street, aged 70 [*sic*], buried 15 Sept. 1944 (St James' Graveyard burial register, 1884–1989). 52 *Memorial inscriptions from St James' Graveyard, Dublin*, p. 80; the Porter gravestone, located to the rear of the church, is here mis-numbered 535 rather than 553. 53 *Irish Times*, 13 Sept. 1944, 16 Sept. 1944. 54 Crawford, *Around the churches*, p. 21; 20 June 1954, St James' vestry minute books, 4, RCBL. 55 Ann Boyd, St James' Hospital, aged 87, buried 9 Mar. 1976, minister G. Linney, Vicar; Elizabeth Hardiman, Royal Hospital Donnybrook, late of 49 James' Street, aged 90, buried 11 Sept. 1989, minister Fr James Carroll (St James' Graveyard burial register, 1884–1989). 56 Crawford, *Around the churches*, p. 21.

(FÁS), and the late Canon John Crawford and his Catholic parochial counterparts. The project team of young trainees tidied up the graveyard, researched its history and transcribed legible memorial inscriptions, publishing an historical booklet with the transcriptions.[57] Unfortunately, with the passing of time the condition of St James' Graveyard deteriorated again, until in 2010 it was acquired from the Church of Ireland by Dublin City Council. Once more the graveyard was tidied up, an access path commenced and a number of memorials repaired, including that to Sir Toby Butler. Dublin City Council has now commissioned a feasibility study concerning the future of the graveyard, with the aim of facilitating visitor access to a park environment where monuments and historical features will be protected.[58]

In 2014, St James' Church was acquired by Dr Pearse Lyons, president and founder of Alltech, the Kentucky-headquartered international animal nutrition and health company, whose grandfather John Hubert Lyons lies buried in the graveyard.[59] Work is now in progress to convert the church building into a craft distillery and visitor centre, taking due account for the protection of archaeological and architectural features and endeavouring to match any new building work to the historic streetscape.[60] It is noted that efforts are also being made to harmonize the St James' Graveyard and Church project plans, and both are flagged as key attractions on the developing 'Dubline' heritage trail.[61]

* * *

From the time of their foundation in the twelfth century, St James' Church and Graveyard have been focal points in parochial life, witnessing religious, demographic and political change. Although it was a Protestant possession after the Reformation, the graveyard retained a special significance for Catholics of all classes, not only as a place of burial but also of celebration associated with St James' feast day every July. While other city churchyards were closed to burials in the nineteenth century, St James' Graveyard remained in regular use until the mid-twentieth century. In short, it can be said that

---

57 St James' Graveyard project, 'St James' Graveyard, Dublin: history and associations'; ibid., 'inscriptions from St James' Graveyard, Dublin'.   58 'St James' Graveyard feasibility study', http://archiseek.com/2011/st-james-graveyard-feasibility-study/#.VDk_-vldWSo, accessed 11 Oct. 2014.   59 John H. Lyons, 28 South Earl Street, 58, buried 1 Oct. 1948, St James' Graveyard burial register, 1884–1989.   60 Aisling Collins, *Archaeological assessment of St James' Church, James' Street* (2014), http://www.dublincity.ie/AnitePublicDocs/00467625.pdf, accessed 26 Sept. 2014.   61 'The Dubline, Dublin discovery trail', http://dubline.failteireland.ie/, accessed 10 Oct. 2014.

Dublin's St James' Church and Graveyard have had a remarkable 800-year history, encompassing the stories of Catholics and Protestants, laymen and clerics, rebels and soldiers, the poor and the gentry, the ordinary and the notable.

TABLE 1 St James' Graveyard, average yearly burials registered 1742–1989

1742–60	310	
1761–80	510	
1781–1800	490	Gap 1788–91, 1798 503 burials
1801–20	380	
1821–40	250	Gap 1836–40, average 100 per annum 1830s
1841–60	100	Gap 1841–9
1861–80	130	Registration may be understated 1856–71
1881–1900	190	Burials above 200 per annum 1885–99
1901–20	130	1916 135 burials, 1918 212, 1919 230
1921–40	90	
1941–54	20	1954 9 burials, graveyard closed 1955
1958–89	4	Total number of final burials

Taking account of gaps, the estimated total of burials 1742–1989 is 51,600, of which *c.*5,000 would be unregistered (source: St James' Church of Ireland registers of burials, 1742–1989).

Funerary traditions and commemorative practices in Glasnevin Cemetery and Museum

SIOBHÁN DOYLE

Since its gates opened in the early nineteenth century, many aspects of Glasnevin Cemetery have evolved to coincide with the funerary and commemorative needs of succeeding generations. The 1800s saw a change in funerary landscapes that was part of the evolution in customs of tending to, and burying, the dead. The establishment of the cemetery followed Catholic emancipation in Ireland and the removal of restrictions on Catholic burial rights. In sixteenth-century Ireland, Catholic churches and burial spaces became the property of the established Protestant church. Catholics had to pay funeral charges and Catholic funeral prayers could not be said at the grave. Following the Easement of Burials Act (1824),[1] and the securing of Catholic emancipation by Daniel O'Connell in 1829, the Dublin Cemeteries Committee found a site for a Catholic cemetery in Goldenbridge, with a second site at Prospect in Glasnevin. It was O'Connell's wish that the cemetery in Glasnevin would welcome those of all religions and none.

The new ground of nine acres at Glasnevin was blessed on 29 September 1831 and Michael Carey, a young boy from Francis Street, became the first person to be interred in 1832 in Prospect Cemetery, as it was originally known. Since then, over one million people have been buried in Glasnevin Cemetery, including many famous figures in Ireland's history such as Charles Stewart Parnell, leader of the Irish Parliamentary Party, Michael Collins, Irish revolutionary leader, Sir Roger Casement, human rights activist and revolutionary, Gerard Manley Hopkins, Victorian poet, Countess Markievicz, republican and labour activist, first woman elected to Westminster, and Luke Kelly, Irish folk singer with the Dubliners. Some of the funerals that took place at Glasnevin have had huge significance in the course of Irish history. One such example is the funeral of Terence Bellew MacManus in 1861, which was seen as a propaganda coup for the Fenian movement as the remains of MacManus were transported across the United States and at each stop great

---

1 *An act to repeal so much of an act passed in the ninth year of the reign of King William the Third, as relates to burials in suppressed monasteries, abbeys or convents in Ireland; and to make further provision with respect to burial, in Ireland, of persons dissenting from the established church* (5 Geo. 4 c. 25).

rallies were held to publicize the nationalist cause in Ireland and to raise funds. It would take nearly eleven months before the coffin bearing Terence Bellew MacManus would arrive in Ireland. The internment of Bellew MacManus was the first of several in the Young Ireland plot and established Glasnevin Cemetery as the chosen resting place for radical nationalists.

The most significant change seen in Glasnevin Cemetery has been the opening of the museum in 2010. The establishment of the museum has encouraged visitors to connect with the stories and legacies of the deceased interred within the grounds by embarking on a guided tour of the cemetery and interacting with the museum's multiple techniques of engagement and representation. The integration of a visitor attraction within a working cemetery was a challenge for Glasnevin Trust. The museum must provide historical information in an interactive and entertaining way while still maintaining the dignified atmosphere within the grounds for mourners attending funerals at Ireland's busiest operational cemetery. The success of the museum has been reflected in its increasing visitor figures and several notable awards that it has achieved, including the European Museum of the Year Award in 2012.[2] However, the function of Glasnevin Museum is a very complex one as it must continually prolong the memory and the stories of those interred within the grounds in a dignified manner, not just for tourists but also for regular visitors to the cemetery.

* * *

Glasnevin Museum, located on the grounds of the cemetery, uses the stories of those who are buried in the cemetery to trace the social, historical, political and artistic development of Ireland. Visitors are provided with an opportunity to connect with those buried in the cemetery through the museum exhibits but also through guided tours of the grounds provided by the museum. The various interactive features, representational strategies and memorial events within the museum establish Glasnevin Museum as a modern, innovative space in which visitors can experience a connection that outlasts the visit itself. Glasnevin has the ability to humanize all those interred in the cemetery, not just the heroes or certain political groups. The modes of representation and memorial in Glasnevin Cemetery and Museum aim to keep both domestic

2 Other awards include Museum & Heritage Award – Best International Museum DMA Grand Prix, The Award for Outstanding Achievement in Themed Entertainment, IDI Best Exhibition Design, Kenneth Hudson Award at European Museum Awards 2012 and Best Cultural Experience 2015/16 at the Irish Tourism Industry Awards.

and international visitors satisfied as the museum includes several different historical narratives on its guided tours and guides are instructed to maintain a factual and politically neutral stance when giving tours. Glasnevin Cemetery is an authentic site as it is a working cemetery which is managed and maintained through its restoration programme. The aim of the programme is to restore the great necropolis of Glasnevin Cemetery to the pristine glory of the early 1900s by improving the drainage system, maintaining the trees and grass, replacing decayed railings with replicas and restoring the gravestone monuments in a style that honours the commitment to conservation.

A memorial unveiled on the centenary of the 1916 Rising has the names of 488 men, women and children killed during, or as a direct result of, the rebellion engraved on it. Projects undertaken as part of the restoration programme include the replacement of railings, the resurfacing of footpaths and, also, the installation of a winding wooden staircase to the top of the O'Connell Tower leading to a viewing platform, which will offer visitors panoramic views of Dublin from 168ft high. All of these projects aim to involve Glasnevin Cemetery and Museum not just in the Decade of Centenaries but also in the construction of national identity in Ireland. Forms of commemoration in Glasnevin Cemetery and Museum include celebration of anniversaries, re-enactments of famous speeches and orations, celebratory events (Bloomsday, Christmas tree lighting, Heritage Week, Poetry Week) and wreath laying ceremonies. Military History Museum Curator Andrew Whitmarsh has pointed out how state commemoration of war dead tends to deprive individual soldiers of their individuality.[3] However, Glasnevin Cemetery and Museum counteract this by commemorating and remembering individual anniversaries, birthdays and significant events connected to these people (mainly through social media). This enhances, embraces and emphasizes individuality in a way that the state cannot.

* * *

War commemorations, in particular, are always subject to shifts in accordance with generational distance, political ideas and the need to express and resolve emotional traumas caused by war. A well-known example of a shift in commemoration of the war dead in Ireland is the repatriation in 2001 of a group of ten members of the Irish Republican Army who are known as the

---

3 Andrew Whitmarsh, '"We will remember them": memory and commemoration in war museums', *Journal of Conservation and Museum Studies*, 7 (2001), p. 6.

19 The graves of the Forgotten Ten, executed during the Irish War of Independence, reburied in this prominent position at the main entrance to Glasnevin Cemetery in 2001 (photo Siobhán Doyle).

Forgotten Ten. Between 1920 and 1921, during Ireland's War of Independence, the British government executed ten young republican prisoners in Dublin's Mountjoy Prison. Charged as criminals, they were buried in prison soil, where their bodies lay for eighty years in unconsecrated ground. In 1995, the National Graves Association (NGA) erected a monument to the Forgotten Ten at a plot in Glasnevin Cemetery in the hope that their bodies would soon follow.

This brought a heightened awareness of the Forgotten Ten to the cemetery, even though their remains still lay in Mountjoy Prison, a few kilometres away. The monument served as a place where relatives and the public could show their respect for the deceased without restricted access and marked a progression in the campaign to have their bodies laid to rest with the reverence that their families believed they deserved.[4] In a television documentary about the struggle the families underwent in order for the men's bodies to be buried in consecrated ground, Frank Flood – a nephew and namesake of one of the executed prisoners, Frank Flood – described how the families had to make an

4 *An Deichniúr Dearmadta (The Forgotten Ten)*, aired on TG4 on 28 Mar. 2002, directed by Rosie Nic Cionnaith.

appointment each time they wished to visit the graves in Mountjoy Prison, present identification to the prison governor and be supervised during the visit. In 2001, after a prolonged campaign to have their bodies released, they were finally exhumed and returned to their families. The men were given a state funeral that attracted a huge attendance from the general public who lined the processional route waving tricolours and applauding. In his graveside oration, Taoiseach Bertie Ahern described the event as the Irish state 'discharging a debt of honour that stretches back 80 years'.[5] Nine of the bodies were buried in Glasnevin Cemetery with the remains of the tenth – Patrick Maher – being reburied in Ballylanders, Co. Limerick, in accordance with his wishes and those of his family. This event was broadcast live on television. The Forgotten Ten plot is located at the front entrance to Glasnevin Cemetery in a prominent position and is marked by a plaque that tells the story and gives a brief background to Ireland's political struggle in the early 1900s (fig. 19).

As visitors enter the cemetery by the main gates, one of the most striking sculptures is the Sigerson Memorial – a memorial to the rebel dead of 1916, which was designed by the distinguished Irish poet, Dora Sigerson-Shorter. The sculpture consists of Mother Ireland etched in white Carrera marble, as she sits with a warrior draped across her lap. Political and religious imagery are combined in the design, heavily based on Michelangelo's *Pieta*. It was Sigerson-Shorter's desire, seconded very warmly by General Michael Collins and Arthur Griffith, that the memorial should be erected in Dublin. The actual figures were carved in Italy with the cost being paid out of the bequest left by Sigerson-Shorter. She bequeathed a sum of £1,000 for the purpose of providing the memorial and for its erection.[6] By 1927, the memorial had been finished but the sensitivities of memorialization at the time meant that there was no official unveiling ceremony. The monument was originally placed behind the chapel in Glasnevin Cemetery in an inconspicuous location, but in 2007 it was relocated to its current prominent position beside the front entrance of the cemetery where it is also visible from the main road. Each year on Easter Sunday, a commemoration ceremony is held at the Sigerson Memorial to remember those who died in 1916, establishing the monument as the principal historical symbol in Glasnevin Cemetery during Easter Rising

5 'Bertie honours Barry', *History Journal*, n.d. (http://www.historyjournal.ie/the-war-of-independence/52-war-of-independance-topics/83-bertie-ahern-honours-barry.html, accessed 30 Sept. 2014).   6 Dáil Éireann, vol. 14 – 24 February 1926, Supplementary and additional estimates – vote 11 – Public Works and Buildings (http://historical-debates.oireachtas.ie/D/0014/D.0014.192602240015.html, accessed 30 Sept. 2014).

commemorations. Glasnevin Cemetery is the first site in the country to have Easter Rising commemoration events as the ceremonies begin at 10 a.m. with the laying of a wreath at the Sigerson monument and the raising of the tricolour.

The return of the remains of executed Irish rebel Roger Casement to Ireland in 1965 marked another shift in the commemoration of the 1916 Rising at Glasnevin. The reinterment of Casement's remains was by no means straightforward with vacillations of British prime ministers, difficulties in Northern Ireland and controversy over Casement's personal diary all contributing to the delay in the return of his remains to Irish soil. Casement's wish was to be buried near the family home in Murlough Bay, Co. Antrim, but the hostility of the Northern Irish government made his reburial in the Republic a more practical option. Casement's sister chose a plot in Glasnevin Cemetery, which was subsequently purchased. Although Casement's wish to be laid rest in the North was not fulfilled, the returning of his body to the island of Ireland was a significant event in a lengthy struggle. In 1961, Sean Lemass noted that the transfer of Casement's remains would be 'entirely in line with the better spirit' that characterized improved relations between Britain and Ireland. Casement's exhumation from Pentonville Prison in London was a low-key affair with the work carried out after dark because of the risk that it might be seen by prisoners. Irish officials insisted on being present at all stages of the exhumation in case they 'may be called upon to testify certain facts' and the largest crowd at the grave observing at any one time was fifteen. The coffin was placed overnight in the prison chapel and the following afternoon, 23 February 1965 at 2.30 p.m., six prison officers carried the coffin shoulder high through the corridors of the prison 'with great reverence'. The coffin was placed in a van which was driven to Northolt Military Airport and flown to Dublin on a specially chartered Aer Lingus flight.[7] The process of exhumation was an understated affair in comparison to that of the Forgotten Ten but Casement was also given a state funeral which was attended by thousands, with a graveside oration given by President Eamon de Valera.

* * *

Funerary traditions also contribute to the commemorative process in Glasnevin as the events of the funerals are celebrated as well as the life of the

---

7 Deirdre McMahon, 'Roger Casement: an account from the archives of his re-interment in Ireland,' *Irish Archives* (Spring 1996), pp 3–9.

deceased. The funeral of Charles Stewart Parnell, which took place on 6 October 1891, is commemorated as Ivy Day because of the spontaneous actions of the Dublin artisans at the funeral who took ivy leaves from the cemetery walls to wear as buttonholes as a mark of respect. In February and March 2014, Glasnevin Museum ran a lecture series that analysed and interrogated those funerals which have helped to shape collective memory in Ireland. From the annual gathering at Wolfe Tone's grave in Bodenstown, to the theatrical mourning for Michael Collins, historians and scholars discussed the funerals that have defined Irish political culture. The lecture series was held on a weekly basis and underlined the importance of Irish funerary traditions as a means to understand society's relationship to death, funerals and commemoration at a particular point in history.

The cemetery is a key component in funerary traditions as it is what Doris Francis calls 'an appropriate sacred space where the living and the dead are separated and symbolically joined as one people through the performance of transition and memorial rites'.[8] Ken Worpole has written extensively on the investigation into the way in which places and practices of death and burial reconfigure not just the landscape, but our orientation to space and time, place and history.[9] Worpole explores the cult and celebration of death, traces the history and design of burial places and also investigates how modes of disposal – burial, cremation, inhumation in mausoleums and wall tombs – vary across Europe and North America, according to religious and other cultural influences.[10] In pre-Christian times, families buried their dead wherever they wished to do so, on a mountain or in a bog, while the early Christian people buried their dead outside the walls of their villages in places set aside specifically for that purpose, but these places were not connected with churches.[11] The arrival of Christianity into Ireland created graveyards that grew up around the first timber churches. It was not until the final decades of the seventeenth century that wealthy people began to mark their graves with an inscribed headstone. During the eighteenth and nineteenth centuries in Ireland, headstones became a popular memorial with the burgeoning middle classes and the historic graveyard started to take on the appearance that is so familiar today. Not all graves were commemorated with a headstone and many small and unmarked stones barely protruding above the surface of the

---

8 Doris Francis, 'Cemeteries as cultural landscapes', *Mortality*, 8:2 (2003), p. 223.   **9** Ken Worpole, *Last landscapes: the architecture of the cemetery in the west* (London, 2003), p. 18.   **10** Ibid., p. 1.   **11** Vivien Igoe, *Dublin burial grounds and graveyards* (Dublin 2001), p. 17.

graveyard are, in fact, grave markers.[12] According to Worpole, the twentieth century, particularly the second half, brought a rise in cremation, sometimes chosen because it is cheaper than burial.[13] Worpole also chronicles how in modern times, particularly in northern Europe, there is now a growing preference for what is generally termed 'natural burial', defined as the burial of a body within a bio-degradable coffin or shroud in a naturalistic setting, with grave markings, if any, designed to return to nature.[14] All of these shifts in burial practices and their spaces give us the necessary information to interpret the way society viewed death at a particular point in time. Worpole describes how, while these burial practices have evolved and advanced throughout history, a respect for collective burial spaces, along with the individual grave plots, seems to be one of the continuities of human landscape and culture.[15] In 1982, Glasnevin Crematorium was the first to be established in the Republic of Ireland and the popularity of cremations has increased steadily since then.

* * *

Every commemoration event has its own validity and is a challenge and an opportunity to re-evaluate the particular past which is being remembered.[16] Ireland is currently in the middle of the 'Decade of Centenaries', which is an opportunity to focus on the development of access to historical records and primary sources from the time period of 1912–22 and an opportunity for local and national cultural bodies to bring forward a series of exhibitions and public discussions in order to reconsider and enhance understanding of the events. The only aspect of funerals and burial practices that remains unchanged is the death itself. People do not simply remember, they remember because someone is constantly reminding them and this underlines the importance of the commemorative tradition, both within history and in constructing a national identity, a significant example being the Forgotten Ten.

Attitudes to funerals, burial practices, commemorative traditions, memory and, indeed, the academic study of history, all develop over time as they are re-evaluated, interpreted or contested in new ways. The spaces where these practices are carried out also continue to shift and evolve with Glasnevin Cemetery and Museum being a contemporary Irish example of this. Glasnevin

<hr />

12 *Ireland's historic churches and graveyards*, The Heritage Council of Ireland (2006). **13** Worpole, *Last landscapes*, p. 8. **14** Ibid., p. 10. **15** Ibid., p. 18. **16** Edward Madigan, 'Introduction' in J. Horne & E. Madigan (eds), *Towards commemoration: Ireland in war and revolution, 1912–1923* (Dublin, 2013), p. 7.

'You may be young enough to live, but you are old enough to die': life and death in the sermons of James Gallagher, William Gahan and Silvester Goonan

CIARÁN MAC MURCHAIDH

James Gallagher, William Gahan and Silvester Goonan were noted Catholic preachers in eighteenth-century Ireland. Gallagher's *Sixteen Irish sermons in an easy and familiar stile* first appeared in Irish in 1736;[1] Goonan's *Sermons on various religious subjects* was published in 1798,[2] and Gahan's *Sermons and moral discourses* followed in 1799.[3] Gallagher was bishop of the diocese of Raphoe between 1725 and 1737, when he was translated as bishop to the diocese of Kildare and Leighlin, where he remained until his death in 1751. William Gahan was a priest of the Augustinian Order who was born in Dublin in 1732 and spent most of his life ministering there until his death in 1804.[4] Biographical details for Silvester Goonan are slim, in part because of his death in middle age and possibly also because, unlike Gallagher and Gahan, his sermons were not published during his lifetime.[5] Goonan was ordained in Paris in 1778 and thereafter was based in the city of Limerick[6] where he died unexpectedly in his sleep at the age of 46 in 1796.[7] Goonan's sermons were published posthumously by Patrick Wogan in Dublin in 1798 and were described as 'discourses [of] his own composition … faithfully printed from his manuscripts'.[8] They were edited by an unnamed individual 'at the desire of his friends and numerous acquaintances and this may be considered as an evident proof of their merit', according to the preface.[9] The author of a very short biographical note that appeared as part of a series of biographical

1 The English Short Title Catalogue (ESTC) lists only two copies of this edition, one in Ireland and one in England. James Gallagher, *Sixteen Irish sermons* (Dublin, 1736).   2 The ESTC lists six copies of this edition in Ireland, two in England and one in Australia. Silvester Goonan, *Sermons on various religious subjects for different Sundays and festivals of the year* (Dublin, 1798).   3 The edition used here is William Gahan, *Sermons for every Sunday in the year and for the leading holidays of obligation*, ed. by James O'Leary (New York, 1880). The ESTC lists four copies of the 1799 edition, three in Ireland and one in Australia. William Gahan, *Sermons and moral discourses* (Dublin, 1799).   4 'William Gahan', *DIB*, s.v., pp 4–5.   5 Goonan is not the subject of an entry in the *DIB*, for example.   6 Michael Tynan, 'Silvester Goonan's sermons', *North Munster Antiquarian Journal*, 26 (1984), p. 100.   7 Ibid.   8 Goonan, *Sermons on various religious subjects*, 'Advertisement', p. i.   9 Ibid.

sketches in the *Irish Monthly*[10] of December 1887 drew on the scant information in the published volume and observed that he had included Goonan in the series because 'he is completely forgotten among his own people and priests, although in his day was so distinguished a preacher that two years after his death a costly volume of five hundred pages was devoted to the preservation of his sermons.'[11] Although Goonan ministered in Limerick, the 1798 edition of his sermons was published in Dublin. That first edition contained a list of subscribers, which shows the extent to which the volume was of interest to Dublin-based readers and, indeed, to clergy and laity across the country. Of the 268 subscribers listed whose addresses were given, at least 22 were Dublin-based. One of those, Hugh Fitzpatrick, the noted Catholic bookseller who operated from premises in Capel Street, ordered twenty-five copies of the volume. Other subscribers listed included the Dublin-based priest, William Gahan, whose work is also examined in this essay. Printed sermons were of interest to a wide section of Irish society at the time and through an examination of the location, by county, of subscribers to sermon-books, the historian, David Ryan, has shown how popular this type of religious literature was among the reading public, both lay and clerical.[12] Ryan's study indicates the spread of printed volumes of sermons across the island and the figures he has collated clearly demonstrate that Dublin tops the list, by a significant margin, among clerical and lay subscribers to the published sermons of Joseph Morony (1796), Silvester Goonan (1798), Matthew O'Brien (1798), William Gahan (1799) and Barnaby Murphy (1808).[13] The three preachers with whom this essay is concerned included sermons specifically addressing the theme of death in their respective publications. Gallagher included two sermons on death; Gahan and Goonan one each. However, many of the issues addressed in sermons explicitly treating of the theme of death are also referred to in other sermons in the published volumes of all three priests. These include sermons dealing with penance, confession, morality, Christian vigilance, the last or general judgement, the rigour and duration of the pains of hell and other matters relating to that which the church taught would be faced by the faithful in the afterlife. It is

---

10 The *Irish Monthly* was an Irish Catholic magazine founded by Jesuit priest, Matthew Russell, in Dublin in July 1873. Until 1920, it had the sub-title 'A magazine of general literature' and Russell acted as its editor until his death in 1912. Publication of the magazine ceased in 1954. **11** 'Nutshell biograms', *Irish Monthly*, 15:174 (Dec. 1887), p. 705. **12** David Ryan, 'Catholic preaching in Ireland, 1760–1840' in Raymond Gillespie (ed.), *The remaking of modern Ireland, 1750–1950: Beckett prize essays in Irish history* (Dublin, 2004), pp 77–82. **13** See Tables 1 and 2 in Ryan, 'Catholic preaching in Ireland', pp 79–80.

SERMONS

ON VARIOUS

RELIGIOUS SUBJECTS,

FOR DIFFERENT

SUNDAYS AND FESTIVALS

OF

THE YEAR.

By the late Reverend SILVESTER GOONAN, of the *City*
of *Limerick.*

DUBLIN:
PRINTED BY PAT. WOGAN, NO. 23, OLD BRIDGE.

1798.

PERMISSU SUPERIORUM.

20 The title page of Silvester Goonan's *Sermons on various religious subjects*
(Dublin, 1798) (image courtesy of Ciarán Mac Murchaidh).

proposed to examine in this paper the four sermons written on the theme of death. In each case, the preacher addressed various aspects of the basic tension between life and death. This tension is represented in the context of Catholic doctrine and tradition in respect of dying and the afterlife. At the heart of the sermons lies a concern for the concepts of 'dying well' or 'good death' (*bona mors*) and 'dying badly' or 'bad death' (*mors mala*). To die well was to have followed the precepts laid down by the Catholic Church and to have lived in a manner that prepared the individual for the true purpose of existence – eternal life with the creator of all humankind. The good death, therefore, was generally understood as 'one in the course of which the loose ends of life, spiritual and social, had all been tied up'.[14] To die badly, on the other hand, was to have lived a life that put one's own interests and pleasures at its core – to the exclusion of interest in one's neighbour, one's Christian duty and one's own final salvation.

* * *

In the medieval and early modern periods, 'there was a commonplace perception that people could "learn to die", and manuals of the "art of dying" (*ars moriendi*) expounded at length the requirements necessary for a "good" death'.[15] Father Vincent Caraffa, the seventh superior general of the Jesuit Order, with papal approval, founded the Bona Mors Confraternity in October 1648, the primary aim of which was to prepare its members by a well-regulated life to die at peace with the Lord. The confraternity produced a manual that included instructions and devotions aimed at teaching the faithful how to live and die well, an edition of which was published in Dublin in 1754.[16] The corollary of the '*bona mors*' was the '*mors mala*' or 'bad death'. These might be classed as 'sudden, difficult or uncontrollable departures that inspired fears for the soul of the deceased and that were often seized upon for didactic purposes'.[17] In the Catholic tradition, such departures from this life encompassed what was usually described as a 'sudden and unprovided death', which meant a death that deprived an individual of a chance to ensure that their soul was in a state of grace and that they went properly prepared to meet

---

14 Peter Marshall, *Mother Leakey and the bishop: a ghost story* (Oxford, 2007), p. 48.   **15** Clodagh Tait, *Death, burial and commemoration in Ireland, 1550–1650* (Basingstoke, 2002), p. 7. See also Philippe Ariès, *The hour of our death* (2nd ed., London, 1987), pp 106–23; Tadhg Ó Dúshláine, *An Eoraip agus litríocht na Gaeilge, 1600–1650* (Dublin, 1987), pp 19–22.   **16** Anonymous, *Bona mors or the art of dying happily in the congregation of Jesus Christ crucify'd and of his condoling mother* (n.p., 1706). A later edition may have been published in London in 1709 (see the British Library catalogue.)   **17** Tait, *Death, burial and*

their judgment. Such an end was feared from early modern times because 'it always raised the spectre of possible insufficient preparation; sins unrepented, wrongs not redressed, affairs not settled, prayers not said and faith not proved'.[18] The concept of dying and death, therefore, was of significant concern not only to the church and the individual, but also to the community at large. When the church sought to use death as a means to exhort the faithful to live a good life, the potential influence such exhortation had in relation to assisting in the regulation of normal social behaviour was considerable.

For various reasons, death in the eighteenth century occupied a much more prominent role in the preaching and inner life of the church and of the community than is arguably the case in modern times. Sin, penance, contrition, forgiveness and salvation all featured regularly in the lives of the people and of the clergy who ministered to them. A study of the range of homiletic approaches employed by these three eighteenth-century preachers provides a better understanding of the role preaching played in exhorting the Catholic population to pursue the art of dying well, as opposed to that of dying badly.

It may be argued that the foundation of Christianity rests on preparation for death and a clear understanding of the nature of the afterlife. In the Christian tradition, death is viewed as the gateway out of the limited and time-bound earthly existence into an unlimited and eternal heavenly life with the creator of all existence, or an unlimited and eternal state of punishment. Which fate awaited the individual rested largely on the way in which they lived their life and whether or not they died in a state of proper spiritual readiness.[19] In that respect death was seen as the one event that levelled the existence of all human beings: rich and poor, men and women, paupers and princes. Silvester Goonan expressed this sentiment rather starkly at the beginning of his sermon: 'Do you not see the dreadful havock which death makes every day among the human race? ... Do you not see the young and the old, the rich and the poor, fall a prey to this common leveller of all?'[20] The church, therefore, had a proprietorial interest in providing a commentary on the concept of dying which had its context in the business of living. William Gahan described the Christian as one who 'looks upon himself here on earth as an exile, solicitous to return to his native country, as a traveller hastening to

---

commemoration, p. 7.   **18** Tait, *Death, burial and commemoration*, pp 22–3.   **19** Aodh Mac Aingil warned of the dangers of postponing repentance for one's misdeeds until one's deathbed. See *Scáthán Shacramuinte na hAithridhe* (Louvain, 1618), ed. by Cainneach Ó Maonaigh (Dublin, 1952), pp 31–4.   **20** Goonan, *Sermons on various religious subjects*, p. 471.

21 The opening pages of Silvester Goonan's sermon, 'On Death', the last of thirty-one sermons in his *Sermons on various religious subjects*, which was published in Dublin in 1798 (image courtesy of Ciarán Mac Murchaidh).

the end of his journey, as a captive impatient to be freed from his chains, and to be released from his bondage'.[21] The image of the believer as a traveller was a common one and was included in an early eighteenth-century text on the *bona mors*: 'They are advised to imitate prudent travellers, whose intense thoughts turn towards the journey's end; not to slip a fair tide and favourable gale, lest they sink into the deepest abyss, there to lament too late.'[22] Goonan also adverted to the theme of journeying and used the notion of the probation of this life in his sermon on death:

21 Gahan, *Sermons for every Sunday*, p. 488.   **22** Anon., *Bona mors or the art of dying happily*, p. 12.

For when we reflect that we are here in a state of probation, that we have no lasting dwelling place on earth, that we are hastening to our true home as fast as the winds of time can carry us, reason tells us that we ought not to further our affections to be engrossed by the things of this world; that we ought to raise our hearts above all transitory scenes, and fix them on those solid and everlasting goods, which are prepared for us in our heavenly country.[23]

Peter Bayley has noted that preachers tended to devote more attention to generating a sense of fear and uncertainty about death than to expanding on the 'solid and everlasting goods' that await the faithful 'in the heavenly country'. There are obvious reasons for such an approach. In the first instance, there is no shortage of biblical and classical material associated with death and judgment, 'which is not only at the preachers' immediate disposal but has the advantage of increasing the authority and strengthening the emotional impact of their remarks by allusion to memorable passages familiar to most hearers. Second, the need to denounce the wiles of the world must have a clear priority, if only because their attraction for people is so strong and so constant'.[24] Such worldly temptations are difficult to resist, and the church and scripture would argue that while 'the spirit is indeed willing, the flesh is weak'. (Matthew 26:41).

* * *

A principal feature of the four sermons being considered here is that each of the preachers emphasized the transitory nature of all earthly glory and here three basic motifs may be distinguished. The first may be expressed by the question: where now are all those who once filled the world with their splendour? The second motif dwells on the frightful spectacle of human beauty gone to decay. The third is what the noted cultural historian, Johan Huizinga (1872–1945), has described as the death-dance: death dragging along with it people of all conditions and ages.[25]

Huizinga also noted that while it reminded the spectators of the frailty and the vanity of earthly things, the death-dance at the same time preached social equality as that concept was understood in the Middle Ages – death levelling

---

23 Goonan, *Sermons on various religious subjects*, p. 479.   **24** Bayley was referring to seventeenth-century preaching but the same principle applies to the approach of eighteenth-century homilists. Peter Bayley, *French pulpit oratory, 1598–1650* (Cambridge, 1980), pp 123–4.   **25** Johan Huizinga, *The waning of the Middle Ages* (Middlesex, 1919, [1985]), p. 134; Ariès, *The hour of our death*, pp 116–18.

the various ranks and professions.[26] This was a theme developed by Goonan in many of his sermons and enunciated very bluntly in his sermon on death:

> You must die; to prove the certainty of death would be an insult to your understanding. You must then bid adieu to the world for ever. Your riches you must leave behind you, you cannot carry them to the grave. How soon this may happen, you cannot tell. You may be young enough to live, but you are old enough to die.[27]

The opening of Gallagher's first sermon on death strikes a comparable note: death is a constant in life, a grim reaper almost, stalking among us from house to house, visiting when least expected, seizing both young and old, sick and healthy, rich and poor alike. In fact the verb Gallagher used in the original Irish is *fuadaigh*, which literally means to seize, abduct or kidnap.

> Cia nach b*h*fuil ni ar bith ansa tsaoghal so is coitchiona no an bas, do bhrigh go siubhlann go laitheamhail eidrinn o thigh go tigh, go b*h*fuadaighionn ris an t-og mar an arsuidh agus go dtairnionn iad 'an na huaighe an uair is lugh do shilid, maise, 'na dhiadh so agus uile, nil ni ar bith is eusguidheacha da ndeantar dearmud no don mbas.[28]

> (Although there is nothing in this world more common than death, since it goes daily among us from house to house, seizing the young as well as the old, dragging them to the grave at a time they least expect; for all that, there is nothing more easily forgotten than death.)

Gallagher goes on to point out that there is no object we look upon that does not remind us of death: the earth – we think of ashes; the sky – we remember that life is as a gust of wind. Time passes over us like the waters of a brook. Despite all these constant reminders, there is nothing so readily ignored by us as death. These images all find echoes in the sermons of Gahan and Goonan.[29]

> Ma dhearcamuid fuinn air an talamh, deirfe an talamh linn nach b*h*fuil ionainn acht cre agus luathramhan. Ma fheachamuid suas air an aidhir,

26 Huizinga, *The waning of the Middle Ages*, pp 140–1.   **27** Goonan, *Sermons on various religious subjects*, p. 474.   **28** Quotations throughout this essay are from the original 1736 text, translations are the author's own. This volume and several editions thereafter were published in Roman typeface but without the inclusion of *síneadh fada* accents. Gallagher, *Sixteen Irish sermons*, p. 175.   **29** Gahan, *Sermons for every*

dearbhoidh an t-aidhir dhuinn nach b*h*fuil do bhuanthus annar mbeatha acht urad le siodan guithe. Ma dhearcamuid uainn air an fhairge agus air na srothana, cuirfid a n-amhail dhuinn go n-imidheann ar n-aimsir agus ar saoghal tharainn gan mhothugh air aiste an tsrotha. Anna bhfocal, nil taobh da dtionntomuid nach b*h*fuil iomhaigh an bhais as ar gcomhair. Maise, 'n-aimhdheoin gach oiduis agus gach rabha dhiobh so, ata daille na ndaoine cho mor agus sin, nach b*h*fuil ni ar bith is luaithche da ndeinid dearmud no don mbas.[30]

(If we look beneath us at the earth, it reminds us that we are but dust and ashes. If we look above us into the air, it confirms for us that our lives are no more fleeting than the breeze. If we gaze upon the sea and on the rivers, they show us that our time and our life pass us by unawares, like the passage of a stream. In a word, there is no direction in which we look that the image of death does not appear before us. But yet, in spite of each of these proofs and warnings, the people's blindness is so great that there is nothing they more swiftly forget than death itself.)

The consideration of the constancy of death was a primary message for Goonan in particular. In his sermon, he addressed his audience in a forthright manner asserting:

You study to banish it from your thoughts; all your diversions and amusements are calculated to make you forget it, and to lull you asleep on the very brink of destruction.[31]

Because his listeners neglected to reflect regularly on these matters, Goonan reminded them that death 'is rapidly advancing towards you and you are totally unprepared to receive it and you expose yourselves to the dreadful consequences of an unhappy death. Never to reflect on what deserves the most serious reflections, and must unavoidably take place', he stated, 'is the pitiful resource of a weak and giddy mind.'[32]

As the leaves fall from the trees at the approach of winter, as one wave passes on another, so one generation of men is succeeded by another, which disappears in its turn. We are all borne down by the rapid stream

Sunday, pp 483, 485, 487; Goonan, *Sermons on various religious subjects*, pp 471, 479. **30** Gallagher, *Sixteen Irish sermons*, p. 176. **31** Goonan, *Sermons on various religious subjects*, p. 470. **32** Ibid., pp 470–1.

of time towards the vast ocean of eternity. You live as if this life was never to have an end; as if the next was never to have a beginning.[33]

Goonan reduced what he had to say on the matter to this single proposition: 'the frequent and serious consideration of death is a most powerful motive to engage us to avoid evil and to do good'. He made this statement in the introduction to his sermon and repeated it again later in the text to reinforce the import of the message he sought to relay to his audience.[34]

Gallagher also worked on this theme and reminded his hearers that all of us hasten towards eternity. *Mihi hodie; tibi cras*,[35] he stated repeatedly, and assured them that this simple message applied to all who drew breath, no matter what their station or privilege in life. By way of affirming such truth for people of all ranks and none, Gahan introduced his audience to a Vatican tradition:

> It is still usual at the coronation of a new pope to burn a little stubble or flax to ashes in his presence, one of the attendants saying at the same time: *Thus, Holy Father, the glory of the world passes away*; in order to remind him that the papal dignity does not exempt him from being tributary to death.[36]

Goonan pointedly reminded his listeners that 'Death strips the world of its bloated charms, exposes the emptiness and vanity of its riches, honours and pleasures.'[37] For these three preachers, then, death becomes the leveller; the one that treats all fairly and respects none above the other. Nothing will preserve humankind from death's killing arrow.

* * *

Huizinga observed that from the early fifteenth century onwards 'the conception of death in both art and literature took on a spectral and fantastic shape as a new and vivid shudder was added to the great primitive horror of death'. This development evolved over the course of the centuries that followed and, Huizinga maintained, the macabre vision arose from deep psychological strata of fear. 'Religious thought at once reduced it to a great means of moral exhortation.'[38] It is easy to see why. Many of the examples

---

33 Ibid. **34** Goonan, *Sermons on various religious subjects*, pp 472, 479. **35** 'Me today, you tomorrow', drawing on Sirach 38:22. **36** Gahan, *Sermons for every Sunday*, p. 486. **37** Goonan, *Sermons on various religious subjects*, p. 473. **38** Huizinga, *The waning of the Middle Ages*, p. 140.

cited in the sermons of Gallagher, Goonan and Gahan play on a fear of the unknown, and on the uncertainty of our existence, among their audience.

In an age when mortality rates were higher, diseases more fatal, religious and general superstition more widespread than in our time, such an approach was an effective way of instilling a degree of loyalty to the church and its ministrations. It was a means of encouraging the Christian believer to equate the good life with a need to frequent the sacraments of confession and eucharist in order to keep belief refreshed and the soul cleansed and in a constant state of readiness for its meeting with death. It is, perhaps, the use of fear as a means of spiritual and moral motivation that best characterizes the approach of these three homilists in their preaching about death. There is no doubt but that their primary concern was genuinely for the spiritual welfare of the flock to whom they ministered and preached. However, the power that became associated with a body of men who could style themselves almost as gatekeepers at the juncture of life and death was not insignificant in societal terms. Portraying themselves as spiritual guides to the faithful as they journeyed through life ensured that their influence went much further than the religious sphere. The fact that a consequence of living a good life was behaviour that supported the civil law and the fabric of social order was, no doubt, an added bonus. Good living in the spiritual and moral sense was also part of being a good citizen and it followed quite naturally that the 'just man' (as Gahan referred to all preparing for a good death) would be a better member of society than the 'dying worldling' (that is, the one who lived as if he or she would never die).[39] The creation by the clergy among the faithful of a sense of anxiety about the dangers of having to face death in a state of unpreparedness was a highly effective preaching tool. The notion that individuals could find themselves facing the gaping abyss of eternity, in the realization that this lack of preparation had consigned them to the torments of hell, motivated many people to strive to live a better life. James Kelly has shown how such considerations affected those who were found guilty of serious crimes and were sentenced to die on the gallows as a result. In his study of sixty-two eighteenth-century gallows speeches, all but two of which were published in Dublin, he observed that:

> The primary requirement was that offenders conducted themselves with 'contrition and resignation'. To this end, they were expected to 'behave

---

39 Gahan, *Sermons for every Sunday*, p. 484.

… in a penitential manner'; to make 'ample confession' of the crimes for which they were to die and any others they might have committed; to 'acknowledge the justice of their sentence'; to appeal to onlookers not to emulate their misconduct; and to be seen to wish to make 'peace with God' by praying publicly for mercy.[40]

Not to follow such a pattern was to 'die hard', which may be understood as a variation of the *mors mala* or dying badly.[41] Those criminals who declined to conduct themselves with contrition and resignation were 'regarded with stern disapproval by most commentators'.[42] Part of the irony here was that for those who did display contrition, while they had committed heinous crimes, they also had an opportunity denied to many others – that of making their peace with God. For that reason, not all Catholic commentators were in agreement with the spiritual supports afforded such criminals by comparison with the ordinary citizen:

> In the ordinary providence, 'tis unreasonable to expect these miraculous helps, for it would be of dangerous consequence to the sinful world if notorious offenders went to heaven convoyed by a final sigh, when weeping penitents purchase pardon at a far dearer rate.[43]

Indeed, it is also the case that the civil authorities, on occasion, 'sought to demonstrate their stern disapproval of particularly odious crimes by denying offenders the chance of a "good death"'.[44] However, Kelly also noted, the above notwithstanding, that clergymen of all denominations willingly assisted at capital sentences because they, and society at large, 'acceded to the convention that a "good death" was, if not a demonstration of the redemptive power of Christianity, then a manifestation of its likelihood'.[45] The minister was there to provide spiritual succour, and to help the criminal make a 'good end'.[46] Even outside of the rather drastic situation of the convicted criminal facing the prospect of eternity as a result of the sentence of death, Gahan's synopsis of the natural order of things concurs with the notion of the redemptive power of the Catholic world view as also illustrated in the writings of Gallagher and Goonan: 'If we die well, our happiness is secured for the whole length of

---

40 James Kelly, *Gallows speeches from eighteenth-century Ireland* (Dublin, 2001), p. 36.   **41** Ibid.   **42** Ibid.
43 Anon., *Bona mors or the art of dying happily*, p. 8.   **44** Kelly, *Gallows speeches*, p. 42.   **45** Ibid., p. 43.
46 Marshall, *Mother Leakey*, p. 56.

eternity; if we die ill, we shall be miserable and unhappy without end, as long as God will be God.'[47]

* * *

Irish devotional and spiritual heritage in the eighteenth century represents a continuation of a broader European understanding of life and death. Drawing on an essay by Cathal Ó Háinle, Clodagh Tait suggests that there was a re-emergence of the themes touched upon in the course of this essay in seventeenth-century Irish poetry and literature; themes such as the vanity of life and the corruption of the earthly body in comparison with the beauty and permanence of the soul.[48] This conclusion may be reinforced by reference to works by writers such as Geoffrey Keating (Séathrún Céitinn), Bonaventura Ó hEódhasa and Aodh Mac Aingil, who all drew on an older European devotional tradition including works such as the *Magnum speculum exemplorum* or *Scáthán na samplaí*, as Keating referred to it.[49] Bernadette Cunningham has shown that the *Magnum speculum* was the source for at least nineteen of the moral tales Keating referenced in his famous text on the mass, *Eochair-sgiath an Aifrinn*.[50] Tadhg Ó Dúshláine has also completed a thorough assessment of the various sources used by Irish writers and preachers and how *exempla* were borrowed from such sources for use in preaching.[51]

The Franciscan priests at Louvain, through their translations of and engagement with a wide range of texts in the seventeenth century, were also responsible for introducing much of the mainstream European devotional and theological tradition into Ireland and provided material in Irish for generations of preachers and writers concerning a wide range of pastoral issues, including sin, forgiveness, life, death and final judgement. In that way, the work of

---

47 Gahan, *Sermons for every Sunday*, p. 485. Other Christian denominations in eighteenth-century Ireland also had traditions about dying well, though perhaps not so well developed as Catholic rituals. See, for example, Andrew R. Holmes, *The shaping of Ulster Presbyterian belief and practice, 1770–1840* (Oxford, 2006), pp 238–51, for a discussion of Ulster Presbyterian practices. **48** Tait, *Death, burial and commemoration*, p. 8. Poems by Giolla Brighde Ó hEódhusa, 'A dhuine chuireas an crann' and 'A fhir léaghtha an leabhráin bhig'; by Séathrún Céitinn, 'Caoin tú féin, a dhuine bhoicht'; and by Froinsias Ó Maolmhuaidh, 'Triúr atá ag brath ar mo bhás', are indicative of such trends. For the text and a translation of these poems, see Ciarán Mac Murchaidh (ed.), *Lón anama: poems for prayer from the Irish tradition* (Dublin 2005). See also Ó Dúshláine, *An Eoraip agus litríocht na Gaeilge*, pp 139–51. **49** The *Magnum speculum exemplorum* was a collection of religious moral tales usually referred to as *exempla*. Religious writers and preachers frequently drew on the volume to provide them with short stories to support a moral point being made by them. The title literally means the 'Great mirror of exempla'. **50** Bernadette Cunningham, *The world of Geoffrey Keating* (Dublin, 2000), p. 35. **51** Ó Dúshláine, *An Eoraip agus litríocht na Gaeilge*, pp 22–43, 85–98, 136–51.

Gallagher, Gahan and Goonan in the eighteenth century adapted and used earlier material in a new context, although much of the basic theological message was the same, constant and unchanging truth of earlier ages. Their intention was to present old truths in newer ways to fresh audiences and to encourage a community of beleaguered believers to adhere to venerable, long-established religious principles and traditions. In so doing, the church and its clergy continued to emphasize the importance of living a good life and preparing for death through being in a constant state of spiritual readiness. The presentation in quite a blunt manner of the choice between eternal happiness and eternal suffering was readily appealed to by preachers to convince people of the need to live well in order to die well.

The message may have been stark but the church held out the best reward of all for adherence to the principles it encouraged people to espouse, that of a well-lived passage through this life leading to eternal bliss in heaven. In Gahan's words: 'As we came into the world for nothing else but to provide for a happy eternity by loving and serving the Lord our God, should we not conclude that we came into the world for nothing else but to learn to die well, a good and happy death being the way to a happy eternity?'[52] 'Loving and serving the Lord our God' could also be understood as loving and serving one's fellow human beings, and the implications of such behaviour are clear for the proper conduct of one's life in civil society. Goonan echoed this sentiment towards the end of his sermon and stated: 'Happy the man who has learned to die before death seizes upon him; who has done the business for which he was sent into the world.'[53] That 'business', in Goonan's view, was right and just behaviour in one's own life and in dealings with one's neighbour. In similar vein, Gallagher observed in his second sermon on death:

> Gidheadh, go coitchionna (beir grim air so, a Chriosdaigh) agus go formhor, beidh an bas mur an mbeatha. *Qualis vita, finis ita.* Agus go tuige? Ata, go bhfuil an bas agus an bheatha cho gaolmhur sin, go bhfreugruid a cheile, ar mhodh, ma bhionn an bheatha go maith, beidh an bas go maith agus ma bhionn an bheatha go holc, beidh an bas go holc. Da bhrigh sin, cia be re ar mian fios a bheth aige god e an bas gheabhus se, nil aige acht dearcamh air a bheatha agus biadh se cinnte go formhor go mbeidh a bhas mur a bheatha.[54]

52 Gahan, *Sermons for every Sunday*, p. 483.   53 Goonan, *Sermons on various religious subjects*, p. 483.
54 Gallagher, *Sixteen Irish sermons*, p. 199.

(Therefore, (mark this well, O Christian), generally and for the most part, one's death will be as one's life. *As the life, so the end.* And why? Simply that death and life are so inter-related that they reflect one another so that, if the life has been good, so too will the death; and if the life has been bad, so too will the death. Therefore, whoever wishes to find out how his death shall be, he need only look at his life and thus shall he know that his death will be as his life.)

* * *

When taken in the context of other sermons on the themes of penance, repentance, preparation for and reception of the eucharist, the sermons that Gahan, Gallagher and Goonan preached on death may be seen as part of a wider religious and pastoral project. The church was anxious not only to promote its teaching and doctrine on the afterlife but also to encourage the faithful to engage with the concept on a daily basis, as opposed to putting preparation for death off until the final hours. Recourse to the other sacraments, principally confession and eucharist, was the way to achieve this end. This also provided the clergy with a means of exerting a degree of control over their flock except, of course, when they deviated from the path of righteousness. However, the sinner might always be encouraged back to the straight and narrow path through the reconciliation available in confession. Leading good Christian lives was also conducive to the maintenance of good order in normal civic society and, as the Catholic clergy began to emerge from the penal law era and to re-establish their position in public life towards the end of the eighteenth century, their influence in this regard could not be ignored. Death, as portrayed in the sermons of these preachers, was therefore not only a matter for the individual and the church but, by extension, for the entire community. In reminding the faithful of the daily tension between life and death, these preachers may have prioritized and emphasized the individual's personal responsibility for the salvation of their own soul but both church and society benefitted as a result.

Momento mori: photography and loss in Dublin

ORLA FITZPATRICK

According to Jay Ruby, whose work *Secure the shadow* was one of the first to seriously consider the phenomenon of post-mortem photography, portraits of the dead 'afford those in the business of adjusting to the loss of someone they cared for a chance to both remember and accept that which is final'.[1] Within the Irish context little has been written about the practice and this is partially due to the scarcity of extant examples.[2] In addition, folklorists and anthropologists have concentrated upon the traditional and the rural aspects of mourning with a particular emphasis upon the wake. The material culture of urban death has received little attention; however, examples of Dublin post-mortem photography do exist and this essay will consider two such images: first a portrait taken by the Dublin photographic studio of William McCrae at the beginning of the twentieth century and another by an anonymous photographer showing Patrick Lawrence Doubleday who died in the city in March 1894, before his second birthday.

* * *

From the medium's inception in 1839, photography was utilized to create post-mortem portraits. In the United States, both the early daguerreotype process and its less expensive counterpart, the tintype, were employed to commemorate and record images of deceased family members. Ruby does not note any circumscription upon post-mortem photographs among Catholic communities and his study includes several examples from both Italian and Irish Catholics. As mentioned above, the high importance placed upon funerals and the waking process in Ireland is widely acknowledged by historians and folklorists alike.[3] The emphasis upon the rituals of the wake,

1 J. Ruby, *Secure the shadow: death and photography in America* (Cambridge, MA, 1995), p. 7. See also: S. Burns, *Sleeping beauties: memorial photography in America* (New York, 1990); G. Batchen, *Forget me not: photography and remembrance* (New York, 2004) and *Suspending time: life – photography – death* (Tokyo, 2010). 2 The phenomenon does not appear in the standard Irish photo-histories: E. Chandler, *Photography in Dublin during the Victorian era* (Dublin, 1980); E. Chandler & P. Walsh, *Through the brass lidded eye: photography in Ireland, 1839–1900* (Dublin, 1989); E. Chandler, *Photography in Ireland: the nineteenth century* (Dublin, 2001) or J. Carville, *Photography and Ireland* (London, 2011). 3 See N.

month's mind masses (a requiem mass celebrated about one month after the person's death) and anniversaries has led to Ireland being described as a funereal society. In addition to traditional Irish customs, a cult of mourning permeated both Victorian and Edwardian societies with strict codes modifying the behaviour of the bereaved with regards to their dress and social activities. It is within this context that the McCrae post-mortem photograph, and another showing Patrick Lawrence Doubleday, will be evaluated. As both photographs depict young children, the high child mortality rates in the city of Dublin will also be referred to.

Unlike cultures such as that of Mexico, Irish mourning practice in recent centuries did not, until the mid-twentieth century, include the use of icons or visual representations of the dead. Photographic portraits were incorporated into the memorial and commemorative cards that marked the martyrdom of the leaders of the 1916 Easter Rising; however, these objects were publically circulated for mass consumption and differed from the memorial cards commissioned for private circulation among family and friends. In his discussion of the cultural construction of death in Ireland, Taylor, in reference to the death of a bachelor farmer in rural Donegal in the late 1980s, notes that 'once the wake is over, however, Conny will not be represented on the walls of his cottage by any image, for traditionally no such iconography mediates social memory in the rural Irish world'.[4] The dead are generally remembered through an oral rather than a visual tradition with mourners retelling stories in which the departed features as the main protagonist. However, Taylor also noted that recent memorial cards combined photographic portraits of the deceased with prayers and religious iconography. Mary Ann Bolger in her study of Irish memorial cards states that photographic images were incorporated, by the general population, from the 1940s.[5] These images were taken before death and the memorial card photograph is 'accepted as part of a system that establishes an official, sanitized identity for the deceased'.[6] In contrast, post-mortem portraits fulfil a different function and 'are truly liminal pictures of the past, of those who lived before us, uniquely preserving the last possible sight of the deceased, and offering a final possibility of having the dead within the circle of living'.[7]

Witoszek & P. Sheeran, *Talking to the dead: a study of Irish funerary traditions* (Atlanta, GA, 1998). **4** Taylor, 'Bás In Éirinn: cultural constructions of death in Ireland', *Anthropological Quarterly*, 64:4 (1989), p. 184. **5** M. Bolger, 'The ephemera of eternity: the Irish Catholic memorial card as material culture' in L. King & E. Sisson (eds), *Ireland, design and visual culture: negotiating modernity, 1922–1992* (Cork, 2011), p. 242. **6** Ibid., p. 243. **7** L. Kurti, 'For the last time: the Hiltman-Kinsey post-mortem photographs,

An examination of photographers' advertisements in the national press does not reveal any announcements offering the service of photographing the dead. The absence of advertisements perhaps points to sensibilities and social prohibitions surrounding the photographing of the dead, although historians have noted that the Victorians and Edwardians did not shy away from the subject. In the United States, Ruby and others have also highlighted the fact that notices and advertisements for post-mortem portraits declined or became less direct in the late nineteenth and early twentieth century. This was partially due to changing cultural attitudes towards death and also a decline in the number of people who did not have their likeness captured while alive.

* * *

In the absence of a large number of examples, this piece will involve detailed case studies of two post-mortem images of children taken *c.*1890 and 1910. The first study examines two variant images taken by the Scottish-born photographer, William McCrae (1866–1927), who lived and worked at Berkeley Road, Dublin.[8] McCrae was a member of the United Free Church of Scotland, a Presbyterian evangelical group who were in existence from 1900. Census returns show that he lived with his Irish wife, Rebecca (née White), who since their marriage in 1887 had given birth to at least eleven children. Examples of McCrae's photographic output reveal the usual family portraits and the commemoration of special events such as weddings. He does not appear to have advertised in any of the national or local newspapers. By 1916, McCrae had opened a second studio at the fashionable location of Grafton Street, an indication that his photographic practice was a successful one. The business was continued by his sons, one of whom recorded the aftermath of the North Strand bombings in 1941.

The post-mortem portrait shows an unnamed young girl and was taken *c.*1890–1910. Children were the most common subjects for post-mortem photography as they were less likely to have been portrayed while alive. Such images acted as material representations of the young life and became treasured mementos fulfilling what Edwards has called the memorial role of photography.[9] These images were for private consumption and seldom circulated outside the family circle. The McCrae images under discussion show

1918–1920', *Visual Studies*, 27:1 (2012), p. 92.   **8** These photographs are part of the collection of the National Museum of Ireland – Country Life, Castlebar, Co. Mayo.   **9** G. Batchen, 'Ere the substance fade: photography and hair jewellery' in E. Edwards (ed.), *Photographs, objects, histories: on the materiality of images*

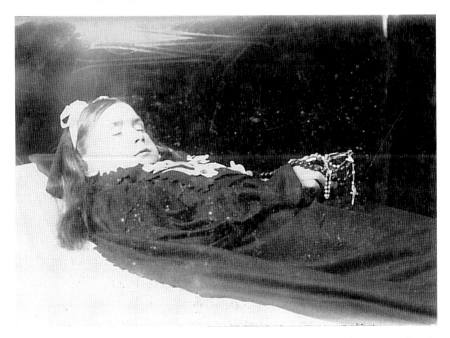

22 Post-mortem young girl *carte de visite*. Post-mortem photograph of a young girl with rosary beads and prayer book, taken by Dublin photographer William McCrae, *c.*1890–1910 (reproduced courtesy of the National Museum of Ireland).

variant views of a young girl laid-out in a traditional shift similar to that described by Brendan Behan in his short story *The confirmation suit*:

> They were like a brown shirt, and a hood attached, that was closed over the person's face before the coffin lid was screwed down. A sort of little banner hung out of one arm, made of the same material, and four silk rosettes in each corner, and in the middle, the letters I.H.S., which mean, Miss McCann said: 'I have suffered'.[10]

She appears to be aged between 8 and 12 and her hands are intertwined around multiple sets of rosary beads. This practice was noted by O Súilleabháin[11] and also by Ridge who recorded that rosary beads and devotional items such as scapulars, medals and prayer books were sometimes placed in the coffin with

(London, 2004), pp 32–47. **10** B. Behan, 'The confirmation suit' in M. O'Rourke Murphy & J. MacKillop (eds), *Irish literature: a reader* (New York, 1987), p. 348. **11** S. O Súilleabháin, *Irish wake amusements* (Cork, 1967), p. 14.

the corpse.[12] Her hair is lovingly adorned with a ribbon, as was fashionable during this period. The child was photographed before being coffined and lies on a plinth or a table, which is covered with a sheet. Only one of the photographs provides a clear picture of the girl's features (fig. 22) and the other suffers from over-exposure and does not provide a good likeness. Together they present an overall impression of the decorum and propriety adhered to in the laying-out of her body.

The solemn scene, with its carefully arranged religious objects, conveys the notion of a 'good death' within the rites of the Catholic Church. The image transmits codified religious and cultural symbols and, to the initiated, immediately demonstrates that this child was a Catholic. The photograph does not reveal any clues as to the setting and there are no background details that would reveal whether it was taken in a domestic or institutional location. Traditionally, an Irish wake would last two nights during which time the corpse was not left alone and family, neighbours and friends maintained a vigil until the body was removed to the church. As stated it is not clear whether or not this photograph was taken at the child's home or at a hospital which would have precluded the usual wake from taking place.

Ridge has remarked that the traditional two-night/three-day wake began to decline, in rural locations, from the 1920s onwards and that this was mainly due to opposition from the clergy who wished to control the excesses of alcohol consumption associated with them.[13] However, as late as 1977 the photographer, John Minihan, recorded a traditional home wake in his native town of Athy, Co. Kildare, and this series of photographs included many of the features described by folklorists and anthropologists: covering of mirrors, putting out of fires, stopping of clocks.[14] In contrast to the McCrae images, Minihan's series was produced as part of his photographic practice and were not commissioned by the bereaved family.

A sub-genre within post-mortem photography includes portraits that attempt to depict the deceased as living. For this type of image the photographer often propped-up the corpse as if sitting in a natural pose. Sometimes closed eyes were over-painted as if open; these efforts tended to be unsuccessful and the resulting portraits appear unnatural and inept. Neither the McCrae portrait, nor the post-mortem image of Patrick Lawrence

---

12 A. Ridge, *Death customs in rural Ireland: traditional funerary rites in the Irish midlands* (Galway, 2009), p. 96. **13** Ibid., p. 91. **14** 'The wake of Katy Tyrrell, Athy, County Kildare, 1977' in John Minihan, *Shadows from the Pale: portrait of an Irish town* (London, 1996), pp 54–63.

Doubleday, which will be discussed later, attempt to portray the deceased as living. Instead, the children are shown as if sleeping, albeit surrounded by the paraphernalia of death (the Doubleday child is depicted in a coffin and the image by McCrae shows a young girl in a shroud).

Fernandez has remarked upon the inherent contradiction that such images contain. Although the children appear to be 'sleeping', a widely used euphemism for death in the nineteenth century, there is no escaping the fact that they are deceased:

> At first glance, all seems natural. We find another sleeping child dressed in Sunday clothes, ready for display. But something breaks with the intended sentimentalized rendering of social identity. In this particular example, the labour behind the arrangement does not disguise the moment of death. Rather than beautification and aliveness, we confront the overwhelming materiality of the corpse. The corpse is not camouflaged but contemplated as a key moment in the process of mourning.[15]

Fernandez considers such images to be part of the first phase in the development of mourning photography which concentrated upon the body of the departed. Later photographic practices emphasized the funeral process (flowers, caskets and mourners) and coincided with the rise of professional undertakers.

* * *

According to a history of the Dublin undertakers, Nichols, the city's street directories did not list 'undertakers' as a separate profession until 1865.[16] Up until then families organized funerals without the assistance of a professional undertaker. They would engage the services of a coffin maker. Until well into the twentieth century, most people in Dublin died at home and the family would either carry the coffin to the church or hire a hearse from a coach owner.[17] Nichols and Howard note that

> A funeral trade offering a more complete service did not begin to gain acceptance with the population as a whole until the nineteenth century

---

15 I. Fernandez, 'The lives of corpses: narratives of the image in American memorial photography', *Mortality: Promoting the Interdisciplinary Study of Death and Dying*, 16:4 (2011), p. 350.   **16** G. Nichols & P. Howard, *Past Nichols the undertakers: six generations of a Dublin family business, 1814–2014* (Dublin, 2014), p. 77.   **17** Ibid., p. 95.

... Funeral directors as we know them today (Nichols, Fanagans, Masseys, Corrigans being the oldest firms) began life as providers of funeral transport, but changed as they expanded their operations to include the supplying of coffins, offering a chapel of repose on their premises, arranging the opening of the grave and contacting the newspapers.[18]

This development is in keeping with Ariès' work *The hour of our death*, which acknowledges that by the twentieth century the emphasis had switched from the corpse to the funeral process and paraphernalia, and that this is partially the reason why nineteenth-century post-mortem portraits can appear abhorrent to contemporary viewers.

McCrae noted on the verso of his photographs that his studio was situated opposite the Mater Misericordiae Hospital. This location, and his proximity to the nearby Temple Street Children's Hospital, may have facilitated the taking of post-mortem portraits. McCrae's studio was one of twenty-two operating in Dublin in 1901.[19] From the 1860s onwards Dublin had a vibrant photographic trade which offered portraits at prices affordable to most sectors of society. Advertisements show that Dublin photographic studios produced mourning jewellery which incorporated photographic portraits with locks of hair and other items. These types of photographic objects offered the mourner a tactile as well as a visual engagement with their loved one which allowed 'touch to become real and continuous, with the hair of the photographed subject resting on the skin ... as a physical, permanent, and public reminder of the otherwise missing subject'.[20]

Neither McCrae nor any of the Dublin photographers provided written accounts of how they undertook post-mortem photography. However, Josiah Southworth, a photographer practising in Illinois in the 1870s, revealed the manner in which he conducted such assignments:

> This is a matter which is not easy to manage; but if you work carefully over the various difficulties you will learn very soon how to take pictures of dead bodies, arranging them just as you please. When you have done that the way is clear, and your task easy. The way I did it was just to have them dressed and laid on the sofa. Just lay them down as if they were in a sleep.[21]

---

18 Ibid., pp 162–3.   **19** Figure derived from photographic studios listed in Dublin street directories. **20** G. Batchen, *Suspending time*, p. 120.   **21** J. Southworth, 'A panel discussion on technique', *Philadelphia*

23 Post-mortem *carte de visite*, verso – with details of the Dublin studio who took post-mortem photo (reproduced courtesy of the National Museum of Ireland).

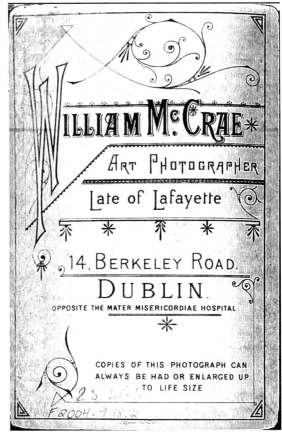

McCrae's post-mortem portrait of the young girl is in the cabinet card format which consisted of a thin photograph mounted on a card measuring 108 by 165 mm (4¼ by 6½ inches). It replaced the smaller and earlier *carte de visite* format and peaked in popularity between 1890 and the 1900s, although its use continued into the early 1920s. McCrae's name and the studio address appear in gold foil lettering on a black or dark green background. The verso, or back, of the card provides further information such as the fact that the photographer had previously worked at another Dublin studio – Lafayette (fig. 23). This is printed in several styles of lettering including one typeface with a marked art nouveau influence.[22] The existence of the photographer's promotional and business information alongside the hallowed image of the dead child is

Photographer, V10 (1873), reproduced in J. Ruby, *Secure the shadow: death and photography in America* (Cambridge, MA, 1995), p. 54. **22** The art nouveau influence can be seen in the text which reads: 'Art photographer, late of Lafayette.'

somewhat incongruous and, when evaluated as a whole, the object represents a mixture of the sacred and the profane.

The McCrae family, although middle class, experienced the reality behind the high childhood mortality statistics in the city. Death notices and church records reveal that three of the photographer's children were to die before the age of 10. A daughter, Rebecca McCrae, died at the age of 2½ on 20 October 1899. The only trace she leaves is a church record showing that it cost her father £1 10s. to have a headstone erected in the graveyard of St George's Church, Dublin. A death notice in the *Irish Times* on 20 April 1907 reads as follows: 'McCrae at Berkeley Road, suddenly of bronchitis, Gilbert Proctor McCrae, seventh son of W. and Rebecca McCrae, born Christmas Day, 1906'. The McCrae's youngest child, Victor Roberts, died in hospital of infantile paralysis on 8 November 1910 aged 9 years and 9 months. He was predeceased by his mother who died of pneumonia in January 1908 at the age of 41. According to Ó Gráda, as self-employed Presbyterians living in an adequate standard of accommodation, the McCraes were in a cohort that experienced fewer infant and child deaths than most. Dublin during this period did have a higher rate of child mortality than comparable English cities and it doubtless impacted upon all sectors of society. Both Daly[23] and Ó Gráda have noted that sanitary conditions and life expectancy did begin to rise in the early twentieth century although 'In 1909, for example, the overall death rate in Dublin's relatively affluent southern suburbs was 16 per thousand while in North City No. 2 District, comprising part of the inner city to the north of the Liffey, it was 24.7 per thousand'.[24] Perhaps the McCrae and the Doubleday families' proximity to this district lessened the impact of other factors (religion, class and income) that would have protected them from succumbing to disease.

Another extant example of Dublin post-mortem photography is in the collection of Aida Yared and it is reproduced on her website, which illustrates James Joyce's novel *Ulysses* with images contemporary to 1904.[25] A post-mortem portrait of Lawrence Patrick Doubleday, 71 Aughrim Street, Dublin, in his coffin is used to illustrate a passage relating to the death of Rudy, the young son of Bloom, the main character in the novel. The photograph shows

---

23 M. Daly, *Dublin, the deposed capital: a social and economic history, 1860–1914* (Cork, 1984). **24** Cormac Ó Gráda, 'Infant and child mortality in Dublin a century ago', *Centre for Economic Research Working Paper Series*, University College Dublin (Dublin, 2002), p. 2. **25** http://www.joyceimages.com/chapter/6/?page=5, accessed 5 May 2015.

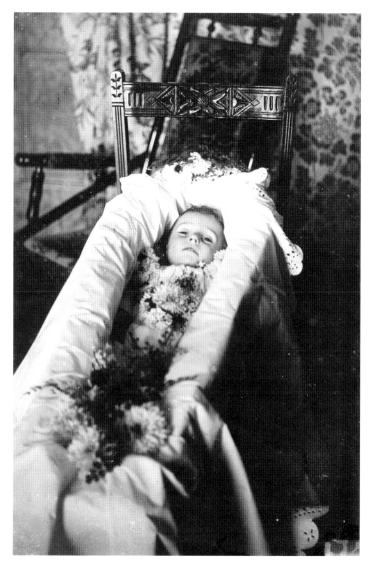

24 Post-mortem infant surrounded by flowers, taken by a Dublin photographer. On the back of the photo is written 'Lawrence Patrick, died – March 28th 1893' (reproduced courtesy of joyceimages.com).

a boy, dressed in white, in what appears to be a domestic setting although the furniture may be that of a photographic studio. The child is less than 2 years of age. He was born in October 1892 and died in March 1894. In contrast to the young girl photographed by McCrae this boy is from a Church of Ireland family and his English-born parents attended the nearby church of St Paul's, North King Street. There is no sign of any religious or devotional items and the white-lined coffin is adorned with flowers. The image does not include a photographer's credit although, like the McCrae image, it is in the cabinet card format. A hand-written inscription on the verso of the card records the child's date of death, name and address. This has a poignancy lacking in the McCrae cabinet card, which contains only the photographer's promotional notice. As Batchen records 'even in their most prosaic form, hand-written inscriptions conjure the voice of the writer, adding an imagined sound to the senses of touch and sight'.[26] Lawrence's father's occupation is listed on the child's baptism certificate as that of commercial traveller although he was described, at the time of his death in 1908, as the director of a catering firm called Dickeson and Co. Ltd.[27] Census returns also reveal that the family lived in a class 2 type dwelling and that they were the sole occupants of the house. Again, this places them outside those living in over-crowded tenements where figures for child mortality were even higher.

Another example of domestic Irish post-mortem photography, although not undertaken by a studio or a professional photographer, exists within the Clonbrock photographic collection at the National Library of Ireland's photographic archive.[28] The collection consists of over 2,000 photographs charting life on the landed estate of the Dillon family at Clonbrock, Ahascragh, Co. Galway, between 1860 and the 1930s. In 1912, Edward (Ned) Crofton died at the family's home. His sister Augusta Crofton Dillon was, like Edward, a keen amateur photographer. From the 1860s, the family appear to have photographically recorded nearly all aspects of their life and it does not seem that unusual that they would photograph their departed uncle. The images show an elderly man laid out in his bed. A calendar in the background gives the date of death and the bedspread has been strewn with flowers. It is to be imagined that this image was for private consumption only and its creation was facilitated by the fact that the family had both the cameras and the expertise to record his death.

* * *

In Ireland, as elsewhere, the taboo on photographing the dead is sometimes lifted when an individual has died while engaged in revolutionary activities or

26 Batchen, *Suspending time*, p. 21.   **27** *Irish Times*, 11 Aug. 1908.   **28** Clonbrock Collection, NLI, NPA: Clon1403 to Clon1405.

for political causes. Within this context, photographic portraits of the deceased are utilized for their propaganda purposes with images made available publicly and used to further the victim's cause. Paige Reynolds refers to the funeral of the Fenian leader Jeremiah O'Donovan Rossa, whose body was returned from the United States of America for interment in Glasnevin Cemetery in August 1915. The funeral was attended by many thousands of Dubliners and the graveside oration by Patrick Pearse, a future leader of the Easter Rising in 1916, was used to rouse republican feeling. Reynolds states that 'like other Irish nationalists, Pearse understood that the emotions generated by a hero's funeral might be harnessed into political action'.[29] She also outlines the use of mass media and how notions of martyrdom were intertwined with concepts of spectacle in the funeral of Cork's Lord Mayor, Terence MacSwiney, who died on hunger strike in 1918:

> His heroic corpse was traditional in its capacity to bring people together in shared time and space, and modern in its capacity to shape an international community … by offering audiences myriad points of identification, the display of his corpse allowed ostensibly antagonistic citizens in England and Ireland access to shared feeling of Irishness.[30]

Both funerals were photographed in detail. The firm of Keogh Brothers Ltd captured images of O'Donovan Rossa's closed coffin lying-in-state in the City Hall and recorded the funeral procession through the city en route to Glasnevin. MacSwiney's body lay in state in St George's Cathedral, Southwark, London, before travelling to Cork. Photographs of his open coffin in his native city, and of the procession that followed, were internationally distributed. Other notable examples include the photographs taken of the public lying-in-state of Michael Collins at Dublin City Hall in August 1922. The series of photographs of Collins, who was killed during the Civil War, includes images showing his brother, Seán, during a private moment of grief. Such funerals represent the merger of private and public or national concerns. In incidents such as this the body no longer remains the preserve of the family and privacy is superseded by the nation or group's right to commemorate and immortalize the figure who has died for a particular cause.

More recently, the republican hunger strikers who died in Northern Ireland in 1981, were often laid out in their family homes in open coffins and their

29 P. Reynolds, *Modernism, drama, and the audience for Irish spectacle* (Cambridge, 2007), p. 130.   **30** Ibid.,

photographs were widely distributed – for example, the front page of *An Phoblacht: Republican News* on Saturday, 15 August 1981, featured a close-up photograph of the face of the dead hunger striker Thomas McElwee. Often surrounded by members of their organizations in paramilitary uniforms, this type of image was taken by those on both sides of the conflict; for example, the leader of the Loyalist Volunteer Force, Billy Wright, who was killed in the Maze prison on 1997, was photographed lying in an open coffin flanked by masked and armed LVF members. In these examples, the grieving process has moved from one undertaken within the confines of a closed familial group to being a public event. Aytemiz has also noted that the restrictions on photographic portraiture that exist in Islamic countries, such as Turkey, are sometimes lifted when a person has died as a result of a natural disaster or in times of war.[31] In these cases the deaths were exceptional and their depiction photographically was judged to be for the common good. A similar event was the sinking of the *Lusitania*, which took place off the coast of Cork in 1915. Photographs of the victims, who included many children, appeared in newspapers throughout the world. The propaganda value of these images, which showed the victims of German aggression at a time when America's entry into the First World War was uncertain, would have been welcomed.

In conclusion, post-mortem photography does not appear to have been a common occurrence in Ireland, and the scarcity of surviving images would indicate that they remained within private domestic circulation or were destroyed as such images became distasteful to modern sensibilities. Even though the 'cult of death' is said to permeate Irish culture and traditions, the visual representation of the deceased does not appear to have been central to the grieving process in the period under consideration. The Dublin examples discussed here are very much in keeping with the type of post-mortem images created in both Victorian Britain and in the United States. Increasingly, in Ireland, as in other countries, exceptional circumstances such as political or revolutionary martyrdom or large-scale disasters, removed the prohibition on photographing the corpse and images were produced for public consumption. It is perhaps these images, which intertwine notions of republicanism and martyrdom, that are the best known post-mortem photographs within the Irish context.

pp 140–1.   **31** P. Aytemiz, 'Death photography in Turkey in the late 1800s and early 1900s: defining an area of study', *Early Popular Visual Culture*, 11:4 (2013), pp 322–41.

'Well may we be proud of him': living with the deaths of the Easter Rising leaders, 1916–17

BRIAN HUGHES

The death, by firing squad, of fourteen men in Kilmainham Gaol between 3 and 12 May 1916 shaped the course of twentieth-century Irish history. Almost immediately, they were celebrated in print, speech and song and their place in the narrative of the struggle for Irish independence is well-documented. Behind all death, however, is a family left behind to grieve and mourn. For some of the relatives of the Rising leaders, their martyred husband, son or brother became integral to their own public persona. Notably among the surviving members of the Pearse family, the ghosts of Patrick and Willie loomed large and dominated their lives in a way that is, perhaps, quite poignant. Patrick's legacy even led to a series of legal squabbles between his sisters Margaret and Mary Bridget Pearse.[1] Several relatives went on to have significant careers in public life and republican activism and, indeed, some had been active before the Rising in various capacities. This essay, however, will focus on the public and private words of the adult relatives – wives, parents and siblings – of the men shot in Dublin (thus excluding Sir Roger Casement and Thomas Kent)[2] over the twelve months that followed the Rising. It is not possible to trace the thoughts and feelings of all, and private expressions of grief remain, for the most part, private, but a study of the surviving documents offers some revealing themes and it is these themes that will be explored in this essay. While all were affected by the unique circumstances surrounding the 1916 executions, it will be seen that responses fall largely into two categories: those who embraced and received comfort from their Catholicism and the cult of martyrdom and those for whom such solace was more difficult to find. In addition, it will be seen that the executions presented unique opportunities to relatives but they also created challenges for those wishing to partake in traditional mourning rituals.

* * *

---

1 Ruth Dudley Edwards, *Patrick Pearse: the triumph of failure* (London, 1977), p. 333. **2** Sir Roger Casement was hanged in Pentonville Prison in London and Thomas Kent was executed by firing squad in Cork Detention Barracks.

A desire to keep the political movement going, and to capitalize on growing popular support for what had previously been a minority position, was a notable driving force for the activity of many of the bereaved of Easter Week. Jack Plunkett (brother of Joseph Mary) and Henry O'Hanrahan (brother of Michael) served terms of imprisonment for their own part in the Rising. Count Plunkett (father of Joseph) was also held in Richmond Barracks before being deported to Oxford with his wife. He then ran successfully in the Roscommon by-election in May 1917 and was joined on the campaign trail by his wife and by Mrs Margaret Pearse (mother of Patrick and Willie), Áine Ceannt (widow of Eamonn Ceannt), Kathleen Clarke (widow of Tom Clarke) and Eily O'Hanrahan (sister of Michael O'Hanrahan).[3] Clarke's public role was, perhaps, most remarkable of all. She suffered a miscarriage shortly after the loss of her brother (Ned Daly) and husband, from whom she had kept the pregnancy a secret so as not to burden him.[4] Having been left Irish Republican Brotherhood money for the purpose of looking after dependents, she became a founder member and president of the Irish Volunteer's Dependents Fund (IVDF), even continuing to work from her hospital bed.[5] The fund's committee was weighted heavily towards those bereaved by the Rising and also included Madge Daly (sister of Ned Daly and Kathleen Clarke), Áine Ceannt, Mrs Pearse, Muriel MacDonagh (widow of Thomas MacDonagh), Eily O'Hanrahan, Lila Colbert (sister of Con Colbert) and John Daly (uncle of Ned Daly).[6] Joseph MacDonagh (brother of Thomas) offered his services to another dependents' organization, the Irish National Aid Association, although his civil service position precluded him from openly canvassing for subscriptions.[7] These connections were mutually beneficial, affording legitimacy to the IVDF but equally offering relatives the opportunity, as the committee put it, to act 'as their dead husbands, sons and brothers would desire'.[8] As early as 30 May, Madge Daly wrote of doing 'what lies in our power to forward the final act'.[9] 'If our hopes for Ireland's future are fulfilled, the sacrifices will have been well worth the making', wrote Kathleen Clarke to Capuchin priest Fr Albert Bibby in October 1916.[10] Relatives do not seem to have questioned the priorities of the leaders of the Rising or the wisdom of placing their lives in

3 *Irish Independent*, 5 May, 7 May 1917. **4** Margaret Ward, *Unmanageable revolutionaries: women and Irish nationalism* (2nd ed., London, 1995), p. 117. **5** Ibid. **6** *Irish Independent*, 19 June 1916. **7** Joseph MacDonagh to Louise Gavan Duffy, 2 June 1916 (NLI, Thomas MacDonagh Family Papers, MS 24,376/1). **8** Caoimhe Nic Dháibhéid, 'The Irish National Aid Association and the radicalization of public opinion in Ireland, 1916–1918', *Historical Journal*, 55:3 (2012), p. 710. **9** Madge Daly to the chairman of the Limerick Board of Guardians, 30 May 1916 (The Daly Papers at the Glucksman Library, University of Limerick, Madge Daly Papers, folder 43). **10** Kathleen Clarke to Fr Albert Bibby, 7 Oct.

danger by taking part in armed revolt. While such thoughts may have been quietly expressed in private, there is no surviving record of any bitterness or anger towards the leaders by relatives, even among those who had lost a breadwinner. There is also little to suggest that relatives used their new status for personal gain, with the exception being Con Colbert's brother Michael's fraudulent claim that he had lost his job as a horse rider and trainer owing to connections with the Easter Rising (he had, in fact, lost his license before the Rising).[11]

Recognizing that their loved one had died in a worthy cause was a crucial part of rationalizing and accepting their loss. In a letter to Madge Daly in June 1916, Ernest Blythe declared that, 'the people whose relatives have died for Ireland have a consolation that nobody in Ireland has had for a long time'.[12] Maria Heuston, mother of Seán Heuston, and Madge Daly were two who very quickly articulated the idea that the executions had significantly advanced the cause of Irish freedom and were worth their own individual suffering. Mrs Heuston told the *Gaelic American* newspaper that the dead had 'done more to further freedom for Ireland than all the parliamentary work of half a century'.[13] She was unequivocal that physical force was the right course of action, even if she did admit that he was 'too young to die such a cruel death ... he had my blessing ... He was our breadwinner, too. But all considerations were forgotten when Ireland called him.'[14] In May 1916, in reply to the Limerick Board of Guardians who had passed a vote of sympathy to the Daly family, Madge Daly thanked them but added:

> I regret that your vote was not one of congratulation that God gave our men the opportunity & the strength to play their great parts. Knowing that the shooting of such heroes by the British government has saved the soul of Ireland. We are willing and proud to pay our share of the sacrifice, and believe ... our martyrs died happy believing that their fight is the first great step toward complete freedom.[15]

Such comments could be put down to a public attempt to justify the Rising and use of physical force, but similar sentiments can be found within private correspondence.

1916 (Irish Capuchin Provincial Archive (ICPA), Fr Albert Bibby Papers, CA/IR/1/1/2/2/2). **11** Nic Dháibhéid, 'The Irish National Aid Association', pp 720–1. **12** Ernest Blyth to Madge Daly, 19 June 1916 (Daly Papers, folder 4). **13** John Gibney, *16 lives: Seán Heuston* (Dublin, 2013), pp 171–2. **14** Ibid., p. 172. **15** Madge Daly to the chairman of the Limerick Board of Guardians, 30 May 1916 (Daly Papers,

The reported bravery with which Thomas MacDonagh faced the firing squad (he had, in the words of an attending officer, 'died like a prince')[16] seems to have comforted his siblings. Four days after the execution of his brother, Joseph MacDonagh, later a member of the first Dáil, urged his sister Mary to 'Be strong of heart. Tom died heroically.'[17] Mary wrote to another brother, Jim, in September and proclaimed that she could not yet 'realise the awful tragedy that has taken him from us forever' but passed on an equally defiant message:

> His last book is nearly ready. & in the preface, it is said, 'They all died bravely, but MacD died like a prince'. Well may we be proud of him, & his name will ring down the centuries as a hero. His name is revered & hallowed in Ireland as Emmet's.[18]

For Maud Gonne, the heroic death of her estranged husband John MacBride did not so much offer consolation as redemption. Although in the years prior to the Rising she had lost few opportunities to denigrate MacBride, she took to using his surname after his death.[19] On 11 May she wrote to American lawyer John Quinn that 'my husband is among those executed … he has died for Ireland … I remember nothing else … his son will bear an honoured name.'[20] Similarly, she wrote to W.B. Yeats that by his death MacBride had 'left a name for [Seán] to be proud of. Those who die for Ireland are sacred. Those who enter Eternity by the door of Sacrifice atone for all – in one moment they do more than all our effort'.[21] She even took to writing to the Paris press about an article that appeared in the *Daily Mail* that she felt was intended to 'dishonour the memory of one of those who gave his life for the Irish cause', noting, 'I separated from my husband for personal reasons, but I don't want the memory of him to be dishonoured.'[22] What was most important for Maud Gonne was that the nature of his father's death had created a legacy for her son Seán. In that way, John MacBride was more useful in death than he had been in life.

* * *

folder 43).   **16** James Stephens, preface to *The poetical works of Thomas MacDonagh* (London, 1916), p. xii.   **17** Joseph MacDonagh to Mary MacDonagh, 7 May 1916 (NLI, Thomas MacDonagh Family Papers, MS 20,476/2).   **18** Mary MacDonagh (Sister Francesca) to Jim MacDonagh, 5 Sep. 1916 (ibid., MS 44,322 (5)). She was referring to *The poetical works* and Stephens' preface.   **19** Dudley Edwards, *Patrick Pearse: the triumph of failure*, p. 328.   **20** Quoted in Elizabeth Keane, *Seán MacBride: a life* (Dublin, 2007), p. 27.   **21** Maud Gonne to W.B. Yeats, 11 May 1916, in Anna MacBride White & A. Norman Jeffares (eds), *Always your friend: the Gonne–Yeats letters, 1893–1938* (London, 1993), p. 375.   **22** Copy of letter from Maud Gonne to the French press in ibid.

The leaders of the Rising were, as Fearghal McGarry has pointed out, quickly venerated in much the same way as traditional Catholic martyrs, and the Catholic Church was one of the first means through which sympathy for the rebels was publicly demonstrated.[23] Relatives played a part in this process – the *Catholic Bulletin*, for example, published photographs of the widows and children of some of the executed men – but they were also influenced by it.[24] Lillie Connolly and Muriel MacDonagh (widows of James Connolly and Thomas MacDonagh respectively) were both received into the Catholic faith in late 1916.[25] Sister Mary Heuston, a Dominican nun and sister of Seán Heuston, referred to the conversion to Catholicism of rebels like Constance Markievicz, remarking that the 'number of conversions certainly proves the excellent religious foundation of their patriotism'.[26] Crowds turned out for requiem masses in large numbers, particularly month's minds and around the first anniversary. These services were an important public demonstration of support for the Rising and their popularity provided spiritual comfort for relatives. Mary Heuston noticed 'a great many anniversary masses' in May 1917, 'Indeed they have been kept up during the year & I am sure are [*sic*] dead ones will obtain many graces for the land they gave their lives for … certainly they have got more prayer than most people can dare to expect. The spirit still lives on.'[27] Lillie Connolly told Fr Albert Bibby, 'you were very good to let me know that you were able to arrange for so many masses. Thank God you were able to do so', while in a letter to Fr Aloysius Travers, Lila Colbert wrote, 'I am glad to see the poor martyrs are not forgotten. I wish I could be present in Church Street tomorrow for Mass.'[28] Áine Ceannt praised Fr Albert for saying a mass in Irish as 'I felt how pleased poor Eamonn would be. He never I believe made any announcement without first speaking his own language.'[29]

Much of the comfort derived from this process was informed by the personal faith of individual relatives. Seán Heuston's siblings Mary and Michael, and Thomas MacDonagh's sister Mary, were members of religious

23 Fearghal McGarry, *The Rising, Ireland: Easter 1916* (Oxford, 2010), p. 282.   **24** *Catholic Bulletin*, 7:12 (1916).   **25** Declaration of Lillie Connolly into the Catholic faith, August 1916 (ICPA, Fr Aloysius Travers Papers, CA/IR/1/3/3/1); Declaration of Muriel MacDonagh into the Catholic faith, October 1916 (ibid., CA/IR/1/3/3/3). Lillie Connolly told Fr Aloysius that 'I started the Catholic Belief this morning. Taking it from the beginning I will study it right through': Lillie Connolly to Father Aloysius Travers, 25 Aug. 1916 (ibid., CA/IR/1/3/3/2).   **26** Mary Heuston to Fr Albert Bibby, 6 May 1917 (ibid., Fr Albert Bibby Papers, CA/IR/1/1/2/2/6).   **27** Ibid.   **28** Lillie Connolly to Fr Albert Bibby, 30 Apr. 1917 (ibid., CA/IR/1/1/2/2/5); Lila Colbert to Fr Aloysius Travers, 5 May 1917 (ibid., Fr Aloysius Travers Papers, CA/IR/1/3/4/2).   **29** Áine b. É. Ceannt to Fr Albert Bibby, 9 May 1917 (ibid., Fr Albert Bibby Papers, CA/IR/1/1/2/2/7).

orders (although Mary seems to have endured some hostility from her colleagues in the aftermath of the Rising).[30] Henry O'Hanrahan had fought alongside his brother Michael and reassured his mother from Portland Prison that 'I am and will be alright please God & as for poor Míceal is he not better off. When we started we were all prepared to go under & had confession in Jacob's on the Tuesday & Wednesday ev[enin]gs that we were there. We had the priests very often.'[31] Madge Daly was comforted 'picturing all the fine times Tom & Sean & Ned and he [her Uncle John Daly] and thinking that some day we shall all be reunited.'[32] But among some of the relatives it is clear that the status of the leaders of the Rising as Catholic martyrs was not only personally comforting, but politically significant. Maud Gonne's overriding concern in the aftermath of her husband's death was his public image and, in a letter to W.B. Yeats, she insisted that an Abbey actor was 'misinformed about my husband's last words & refusal to see a priest, it would be so unlike all I know of him … for all his life he had been, with occasional lapses perhaps, [a] practical Catholic & a very convinced one, even when he failed to act upon the teaching of the Church.'[33] In May 1917, Mary Heuston was pleased to note that there 'seems to have been a revival of the religious as well as the National spirit during the past twelve months'.[34]

* * *

Not all of the relatives openly embraced the exalted position that came from such close association with the Easter Rising. The reluctance of some widows to have their pictures published in the December 1916 issue of the *Catholic Bulletin* was attributed in an editorial to 'their natural desire for retirement and their strong aversion to the notoriety of the press'.[35] Neither were all at ease with their loss. It was those relatives who were politically or publically active who seem to have shared a more positive outlook, reflected in their demeanour in the year after the executions. In a letter to Terence MacSwiney, Madge Daly wrote: 'I was in Dublin yesterday and met Mrs Pearse. She is splendid and reminds me very much in her kindly ways of my grandmother. I think [she] also could not think or say or do an inkind [*sic*] thing to anyone and she bears

30 Joseph MacDonagh to Mary MacDonagh, May 1916 (NLI, Thomas MacDonagh Family Papers, MS 20,674/2).   **31** Henry O'Hanrahan to his mother and sisters, 15 May 1916 (ICPA, Fr Albert Bibby Papers, CA/IR/1/1/1/5).   **32** Madge Daly to Fr Thomas Wall, 17 July 1916 (MAI, Bureau of Military History Contemporary Documents, Fr Thomas Wall Collection, CD 323/1/1).   **33** Maud Gonne to W.B. Yeats, June 1916, in MacBride White & Jeffares, *Always your friend*, p. 382.   **34** Mary Heuston to Madge Daly, 12 May 1917 (Daly Papers, folder 39).   **35** *Catholic Bulletin*, 6:12 (1916), pp 694–5.

all so well.' In comparison, the rather less political 'Mrs M[acDonagh][36] seems not yet recovered from the shock. She is so quiet'.[37] This is suggestive not only of the character of the relatives who put themselves forward in public but also of the power of a firm belief in the cause to ease personal grief.

Jim MacDonagh's letter to his sister-in-law Muriel MacDonagh in May 1916 is, perhaps, akin to a more common reaction to death: 'I don't really know how to write & express our deep sympathy in your great sorrow, indeed yours is a heavy cross to bear. Poor Tom! Always the most kind & gentle of men … Eva feels she is unable to write as she would like she was so fond of Tom.'[38] For Mary Brigid Pearse, her brothers' martyrdom offered no comfort. Unlike her mother and sister, Mary Brigid had been opposed to Patrick and Willie's militarism. She, as Ruth Dudley Edwards has put it, 'did not yet have the consolation of believing that her brothers had been martyred to glorious purpose'.[39] Her failure to fully embrace their stand only served to exacerbate her nervous condition.[40] Agnes Mallin (wife of Michael) wrote to Irish Citizen Army member Lily McAlerney congratulating her on her recent wedding but confided that 'I am not feeling very fit myself this is the anniversary of my wedding the <u>26 of April</u> I do often wish our dear God would take me to [my] husband but that is sinful'.[41] In October 1916, Kathleen Clarke described how her mother had been affected by the loss of her son Ned: 'she has become an old woman suddenly. Up to now she looked as young as any of us and was full of energy. Now she is tired all the time and life seems a trouble to her.'[42] Clarke's own miscarriage was one of a number of serious health issues suffered by relatives and children in the months and years following the Rising and is reflective of a period of intense stress and personal trauma. A biographer of Seán MacBride has suggested that the enteritis he contracted shortly after Easter Week was 'probably as a result of the emotional trauma of recent events'.[43] Donagh MacDonagh also spent a prolonged period in hospital in 1916 and 1917, having contracted tuberculosis earlier in the year.[44] Agnes

36 The reference appears to be to Muriel MacDonagh, but may alternatively have been to the equally reserved Agnes Mallin.   **37** Madge Daly to Terence MacSwiney, 27 July 1916 (University College Dublin Archives (UCDA), Terence MacSwiney Biographers, P48c/18).   **38** James MacDonagh to Muriel MacDonagh, May 1916 (NLI, MacDonagh Family Papers, MS 10,854(7)).   **39** Dudley Edwards, *Patrick Pearse: the triumph of failure*, p. 328.   **40** Ibid.   **41** Una [Agnes] Mallin to Lily McAlerney, 25 Apr. 1917 (MAI, Military Service Pensions Records, 34/28861). Underlining appears as in the original. The phrase echoes one of her husband's in his final letter to her: 'oh if you were only dieing with me but that is sinful': Brian Hughes, *16 lives: Michael Mallin* (Dublin, 2012), p. 232.   **42** Kathleen Clarke to Fr Albert Bibby, 7 Oct. 1916 (ICPA, Fr Albert Bibby Papers, CA/IR/1/1/2/2/2).   **43** Keane, *Seán MacBride*, p. 28.   **44** Nic Dháibhéid, 'The Irish National Aid Association', p. 717.

25 The Mallin family in mourning (reproduced courtesy of Kilmainham Gaol Museum).

Mallin described the breakdown of her health in the 1920s as 'a direct result of 1916' and Muriel MacDonagh drowned after suffering a heart attack while swimming in 1917.[45] The uniquely traumatic events surrounding the executions, which themselves followed a week of worry and anxiety, played a part here. Death sentences came as a shock to some – Agnes Mallin had believed that her husband would be deported rather than shot; Maria Heuston had believed 'they would not execute boys' and the O'Hanrahan sisters arrived at Kilmainham Gaol having been told their brother would be deported, only for the Dalys to warn them to prepare for the worst[46] – and final meetings, when they took place at all, were short, happened late at night and conversations were timed and monitored.[47]

The exceptional circumstances of the Rising further served to deny the relatives access to some of the most common, traditional means of grieving a

45 Una [Agnes] Mallin to 'Secretary, Ministry of Pensions', 22 Oct. 1928 (MAI, Military Service Pensions Records, W1/D/322); Nic Dháibhéid, 'The Irish National Aid Association', pp 717–18.   **46** Hughes, *Michael Mallin*, p. 174; Gibney, *Seán Heuston*, p. 172; Michael Foy & Brian Barton, *The Easter Rising* (1st ed., Stroud, 1999), p. 363.   **47** McGarry, *The Rising*, p. 274.

26 Kathleen Clarke (née Daly), widow of executed 1916 leader Tom Clarke, in mourning dress with her sons. An active Republican, she became a TD and was the first female Lord Mayor of Dublin (reproduced courtesy of the National Library of Ireland).

death. Four of Seán McDermott's five sisters had emigrated to America and, like so many other Irish families, could not visit their brother's physical remains, but it was impossible even for relatives in Dublin to carry out the most basic mourning rituals. Kathleen Clarke unsuccessfully requested the return of her husband's body to 'enable me to pay him the last sad rights'.[48] General Sir John Maxwell refused a similar request for the return of the remains of Patrick and Willie Pearse on the grounds that it would create a shrine and cause disturbance.[49] Securing the return of personal items was troublesome. Madge Daly had to write to the military barracks in Omagh, Co. Tyrone, to trace money left by her brother before his execution.[50] Áine Ceannt made repeated enquiries about a bicycle, thermos flask, topcoat and knapsack left by her husband in the South Dublin Union.[51] Over the course of a year she also made a concerted effort to retrieve possessions allegedly stolen in two raids on her home during the Rising, with seemingly little success.[52] The reason for all this effort is made clear in a letter to a prison official:

> In reply to yours of the 31st ult. offering me compensation for the loss of goods the property of my husband the late E. Ceannt kindly note I applied for the return of his kit etc that I might keep them in memory of him. The goods in question were dear to me as his property but failing their return no money would compensate me. I send you back herewith your form unsigned.[53]

 When a claim was made on Eamonn's life assurance the following reply came from the assistant secretary of the Scottish Life Assurance Society: 'the society is advised that in view of the circumstances of the death of the assured they are under no liability in respect of these policies', and it is revealing that this piece of correspondence has survived among Áine's papers.[54] Similarly, Joseph Plunkett's will was declared void and this, allied to her estrangement from her parents and difficult relationship with her mother-in-law, meant that his wife

---

48 Kathleen Clarke to the commandant, Kilmainham Detention Barracks, 3 May 1916 (Daly Papers, folder 65b); Kathleen Clarke to the US Consul, Dublin, 3 May 1916 (ibid.).   **49** Dudley Edwards, *Patrick Pearse: the triumph of failure*, p. 329.   **50** Madge Daly to Lieutenant-Colonel G.P. Stewart, 23 May 1916 (Daly Papers, folder 39).   **51** Handwritten reply by Áine Ceannt on W.J. Lennon to Áine Ceannt, 11 May 1916 (NLI: Papers of Éamonn and Áine Ceannt and of Kathleen and Lily O'Brennan, MS 41,480/1).   **52** See correspondence contained in Papers of Éamonn and Áine Ceannt and of Kathleen and Lily O'Brennan (NLI, 41/480/1).   **53** Áine Ceannt to Major C. Harold Heathcote, 12 Feb. 1917 (ibid.).   **54** Assistant secretary, Scottish Life Assurance Society, to Áine Ceannt, 13 May 1916, 3 Aug. 1916 (ibid.).

Grace struggled financially, relying heavily on income from the dependent's funds.[55]

* * *

Much has been written about the executions of the leaders of the Easter Rising. It is, however, the cultural and political significance of the executions that continues to draw attention, while the consequences for those closest to the dead are rarely, if ever, explored. Mourning the loss of a loved one is usually a private, internal affair. It is the historical significance that was attached to the executions in Dublin in May 1916 that has prompted this study. Letters and documents that may not have made it into the public domain in the case of ordinary deaths were preserved, while the families of the dead were automatically afforded an important place on the post-Rising public stage. Relatives of the 1916 leaders were offered a rare form of consolation and an opportunity to further the aims for which their loved one had died. Political activism and a strong belief in the same ideals seem to have been an important determinant in the reactions of the bereaved and gave them a greater acceptance of the loss they had suffered. This was not, however, a comfort felt by all. There were some relatives who struggled to find relief in the cause. Where all did share a common experience was in the practical process of dealing with a death. The absence of a funeral or a grave to visit, and the difficulties in securing the return of personal possessions, made mourning and grieving in the traditional way largely impossible. Each relative dealt with death in his or her own way, but in other respects, all shared a unique and remarkable experience.

---

55 Nic Dháibhéid, 'The Irish National Aid Association', pp 715–16.

Appendix 1: The Representative Church Body Library, Dublin: a Church of Ireland perspective on death

RAYMOND REFAUSSÉ

Following the Elizabethan Reformation the Church of Ireland, rather than the Church of Rome, was confirmed as the official church of the state. In consequence it was the Church of Ireland that was left in possession of church buildings and graveyards, it was in the Church of Ireland alone that acts of worship could take place, and it was only Church of Ireland clergy who could conduct those acts of worship and who could perform related pastoral functions. In theory this situation obtained in full until the introduction of Roman Catholic relief acts in the late eighteenth and early nineteenth centuries, although the extent to which it was enforced remains a matter of historical debate. However, while it may be a matter of debate as to where and when Catholics and Dissenters were allowed to conduct their own religious services in their own church buildings what is certain is that no churches or graveyards were transferred to them from the Church of Ireland and, with the exception of the Huguenot communities who had graveyards in Merrion Row and Peter Street, and the Quakers, who had a burial ground in Blackrock, all the graveyards in the city and suburbs of Dublin were administered by the Church of Ireland. The Church of Ireland may have been a minority religion but it held a majority stake in the business of death and dying.

This was initially obvious in the liturgy of death. *The Book of Common Prayer* was the prescribed liturgy of the established church and therefore its use was mandatory in Church of Ireland churches and graveyards. Within it the orders for the visitation and communion of the sick and, especially, the order for the burial of the dead set out in a stark and measured way what was to be said and what was to be done. Gone were the elaborate requiems of the Roman Church and in their place was a liturgy of death that concentrated on prayers and the recitation of passages of scripture. The dead being with God had no need for prayer and so the focus of the liturgy was on providing comfort for the bereaved. The evolution of this liturgy can be traced through the many editions of the *Book of Common Prayer* and while the essence of the burial service changed little there were subtle changes from time to time with, for example, the addition of passages of scripture, and the appearance in the eighteenth century of the rubric advising that the office was not to be used for those who had died unbaptized, were excommunicated or had committed suicide. However, these strictures apart, the 1634 canons (often printed in the *Book of Common Prayer*) made clear that Church of Ireland clergy could not refuse to bury any corpse that was brought to a church or churchyard, providing appropriate notice had been given and that the burial rite was in accordance with the *Book of Common Prayer*.[1] The Watson Collection of prayer books in the RCB Library provides a convenient overview of the evolution of the liturgy of burial.[2]

As well as ordering the liturgy of death, the Church of Ireland also regulated the keeping of the records of death. A system of public registration was introduced in 1617 and seems to have operated for a short time but no records of it of have survived[3] and it was not until 1864 that the civil registration of deaths began – before then Church of Ireland registers of burials were, in effect, the official records of deaths. The 1634 canons required that every church should have a 'parchment book' for recording christenings, weddings and burials. The book was to be kept in a 'sure coffer, with three locks and keys' – one key for the minister and one for each of the churchwardens, 'so that neither the Minister without the Church-wardens, nor the Church-wardens without the Minister shall at any time take that Book out of the said coffer'. Every Sunday, after morning and evening prayer, the minister, in the presence of the churchwardens, was to enter the details of those who had been baptized, married or buried during the previous week, and each year, within one month after 25 March, the churchwardens were to transmit to the bishop an annual return of baptisms, marriages and burials for preservation in the diocesan registry.[4] Prior to this there does not seem to have been any requirement to keep parish registers even though similar regulations had been in place in England since 1538.[5]

Registers had been kept in some Dublin parishes before the promulgation of the 1634 canons. The burial records of the parish of St John the Evangelist,

1 *Constitutions and canons ecclesiastical treated upon by the archbishops and bishops, and the rest of the clergy of Ireland; and agreed upon by the King's Majesty's licence in their synod begun and holden at Dublin, Anno Domini, 1634*: canon xiv. **2** *The Watson collection of prayer books and related liturgical works given by Edward John Macartney Watson, M.D.* (Dublin, 1948). **3** James Mills (ed.), *Registers of the parish of St John the Evangelist, Dublin, 1619–1699* (Dublin, 1906 & 2000), pp iii–iv. **4** *Constitutions and canons ecclesiastical*, canon xlvi. **5** Richard Burn, *The ecclesiastical law* (9th ed., London, 1842), vol. iii, pp 459–60.

centred on the parish church in Fishamble Street, begin in 1619 and are the oldest surviving registers in the Church of Ireland. Those of St Bride, destroyed in the fire in the Public Record Office of Ireland in 1922 but surviving in a printed edition, began in 1633 while there was a register for the parish of St Nicholas Without beginning in 1631, which was also lost in 1922. However, the new regulations had little immediate effect – only the parish registers of St Michan, beginning in 1636, might reasonably be supposed to be a product of the 1634 canons and so the burial records of the Dublin city parishes date largely from the late seventeenth and early eighteenth century. Most of these have survived – only six out of nineteen sets of records were destroyed in 1922 and of those which were lost most have survived, at least in part, in copy form. All of them, plus the registers of the two cathedrals, Christ Church and St Patrick's, have been transferred to the RCB Library.[6] In 2009 these registers were digitized as part of a genealogical project sponsored by the Department of Arts, Heritage and the Gaeltacht and they are available on the free government website, www.irishgenealogy.ie

All of the city parishes had burial records since they all provided facilities for burial either in the church or in a surrounding churchyard – the one exception is St George's parish whose graveyard is not adjacent to the church in Hardwicke Place but in Whitworth Road in Drumcondra. However, the situation is somewhat different in the suburbs – some of the churches have graveyards, some do not. Those parishes with graveyards largely pre-date the opening of the cemeteries in Mount Jerome and Glasnevin and so, for example, the burial records of Donnybrook are extant from 1712, those of Glasnevin begin 1793 and those Irishtown in 1812. Some of the later churches did not need graveyards because of the availability of the commercial cemeteries and so there were no burial facilities in, for example, Sandford (Ranelagh), Zion (Rathgar), or especially in Harold's Cross church, which was built beside the gates of Mount Jerome. In other cases graveyards were not needed because new parishes had been carved out of existing parishes that already had graveyards in which families had historic rights of burial. So, for example, there are no graveyards surrounding the churches in Dun Laoghaire, Glenageary or Kill o' the Grange as they were served by Monkstown, the

---

6 An outline list of these registers is available on the RCB Library pages of the Church of Ireland website – www.ireland.anglican.org. For a fuller treatment of the records of Dublin city graveyards see Raymond Refaussé, 'Gone but not forgotten – the Church of Ireland graveyards in the city of Dublin', *Dublin Historical Record*, 68:1 (Spring/Summer 2015), pp 84–96.

burial registers of which are extant from 1679. The burial records of the suburban parishes have largely been transferred to the RCB Library.[7]

Both the city and suburban graveyards did have one common feature – during the second half of the nineteenth century they began to fill up. This was more marked in the city parishes. There were no burials in St John's after 1850, St Mary's was closed in 1858, as was St Nicholas' Within in 1875, and St Peter's in 1883 with only St George's and St James' accepting burials in the twentieth century. Similarly, in the suburbs, Irishtown graveyard was closed in 1872, Clontarf in 1875 and Donnybrook in 1916. Thereafter, Church of Ireland burials took place largely in the public cemeteries and it was their records rather than the records of churches and cathedrals which became the principal sources for information on burials.

Burial records were, initially, terse. The 1634 canons required only the name of the person being buried to be recorded although since the registers were kept chronologically the date of burial was also recorded. It was not until the nineteenth century with the introduction of pro-forma registers that there was an agreed recording formula – name, abode, date of burial, age, name of clergyman. However, because the early burial registers were simple 'parchment books' there was the potential for variations in recording practice. So, for example, in St Peter's they were recording addresses by the 1770s[8] and in St Werburgh's, by the 1780s, they were recording ages.[9] Rarely were causes of death recorded and usually only in the context of a particular disaster – for example, in the register of St Paul's Church in North King Street there is an entry for the burial of Lt Col. Browne, 'barbously murdered by an armed banditti' during the Emmet Rebellion,[10] while the register of St Patrick's Cathedral records the burial of Captain John MacNeill Boyd, Commander of HMS *Ajax*, who was drowned at Kingstown Harbour in 1861.[11]

Although the graveyards of the Church of Ireland were to serve all the parishioners, irrespective of religion, this is not always apparent from the burial registers due to differences in recording practice. In some parishes, and St James' is good example of this, there were many Roman Catholic burials that were recorded in the registers and sometimes specifically noted as being 'RC'. In other parishes it appears that only Church of Ireland burials were recorded. Furthermore, while all the parishes with graveyards had burial registers none

7 An outline list of these registers is available on the RCB Library pages of the Church of Ireland website – www.ireland.anglican.org.   8 RCBL P45/1/3 et seq.   9 RCBL P326/1/2 et seq.   10 RCBL P273/1/4.
11 J.H. Bernard & Raymond Refaussé (eds), *Register of the cathedral of St Patrick, Dublin, 1677–1869*

have graveyard registers (registers which record who is buried in each plot) or accompanying graveyard maps which record the position of each plot. So while from the burial registers it is possible to discover who was buried in a particular graveyard it is not possible to be sure where the burial took place within the graveyard unless there is a gravestone.

If a church did not have a functioning graveyard it was not required to have burial registers – the requirement was to record burials in the church or churchyard not funerals in the church where the burials took place elsewhere. However, some churches used pro-forma burial registers to record funerals. More usually, however, funerals were recorded in preachers' books, the record volumes that detailed all the services in each church, and in parish magazines. Both preachers' books and parish magazines date largely from the late nineteenth century, although they tend to be more productive sources from the mid-twentieth century.

Just as the established Church of Ireland controlled the liturgy and the recording of death so too, by virtue of having custody of the churches and churchyards, it controlled the memorialization of death on gravestones and memorial plaques, and on church furnishings and stained glass windows.[12] In stark contrast to the terse entries in the burial registers, the memorials often had much to say about the family, personality, achievements and place in society of the deceased. However, these sources have not fared well with the passage of time. Only 5 out of the 20 city churches that had burial records are still Church of Ireland churches,[13] 5 have totally disappeared,[14] another 4 survive only as fragments,[15] and the remainder have been converted to other uses.[16] In most instances their graveyards have disappeared – built over, turned into car parks or converted into public parks, sometimes with the gravestones remaining, sometime not. The fate of interior memorials is not dissimilar – many destroyed, some moved to other locations, some left in situ in newly secular circumstances that are scarcely appropriate, as is the case with

(Dublin, 2007), p. 204.   **12** Church of Ireland stained glass windows have been photographed and catalogued at www.gloine.ie.   **13** St Ann's (Dawson Street), St Audoen's (Cornmarket), St Catherine's (Thomas Street), St Michan (Church Street), St Werburgh (Werburg Street).   **14** St Bride (Bride Street), St John (Fishamble Street), St Nicholas Without (north transept of St Patrick's Cathedral), St Peter's (Aungier Street), St Thomas (Marlborough Street).   **15** The framework of St Nicholas Within still stands at the top of Nicholas Street, the tower of St Michael's was incorporated into the Synod Hall, the tower of St George's chapel of ease still stands in Hill Street and St Luke's, after repeated acts of vandalism, remains in a semi-ruinous condition in the Coombe.   **16** St Andrew's (St Andrew Street), until recently a tourist office; St George's (Hardwicke Place), an office building; St James (James' Street), soon to be a distillery; St Mark's (Pearse Street), an evangelical church; St Mary's (Mary Street), a pub and restaurant; St Paul's (North

St Mary's, now a bar and restaurant. Changes in the suburbs have been less dramatic with fewer church closures, which, when they did occur, involved sympathetic internal alteration – for example, when Harold's Cross church became the Russian Orthodox church of the Holy Apostles Peter and Paul although the seating was largely removed the memorials and windows were left intact.

Many of the losses in the city took place before the heritage lobby was as developed as it now is and so there is no photographic record of Dublin gravestones and memorials[17] and there has been no systematic programme to transcribe them. In some instances vestry minute books can be helpful, especially in relation to memorials that have been moved to other locations, but often not. There was no requirement on the part of the parishes to record such information and the re-location of memorials was often arranged in an informal fashion and not recorded. Yet, in an informational sense, much has survived, especially in the *Journal of the Association for the Preservation of the Memorials of the Dead*, while in the RCB Library there are many partial records, both photographic and textual, of gravestones and memorials, often the work of unusually diligent parish officers or concerned well-wishers.

So, from the perspective of the Representative Church Body Library, death and dying in Dublin may be interpreted through the liturgy of death as evidenced in the successive editions of the *Book of Common Prayer*, through the recording of death in the burial registers of the cathedrals and parish churches and through the memorializing of death on gravestones and memorials in churches and churchyards. While accidents of history and the ravages of time have combined to ensure that these records are incomplete, nonetheless they represent, at least by Irish standards, a substantial body of evidence that would repay careful investigation.

King Street), an enterprise centre).   **17** A photographic record, in the RCB Library, of the memorials in St Mary's Church, Mary Street, commissioned from the Irish Architectural Archive, is a good example of what could have been achieved.

Appendix 2: An overview of the Glasnevin Board minutes

PATRICIA BEDLOW

Glasnevin Trust's minute books date from 1827 and were compiled at committee offices in Ormond Quay, Parnell Square and, later, Glasnevin (Prospect) Cemetery. Not only do they present the historical record of the governance and administration of Goldenbridge and Glasnevin cemeteries, they also provide glimpses into issues affecting the political, social, military and economic history of Dublin. For example, the minutes convey the reaction of staff to the 1916 Rising and its impact.

The cemeteries, which are non-denominational, were established by Daniel O'Connell as part of his campaign to gain greater freedoms for Catholics in Ireland. A committee was established to oversee the administration of the cemeteries, its membership included individuals from the legal, political and medical professions, as well as the clergy. Prior to June 1839, decisions were made relating to the administration of the cemeteries at the Catholic Burial Committee's weekly meetings. The system changed in June 1839 with the establishment of a Rotation Committee. The Rotation Committee comprised members of the Catholic Burial Committee, and later the Dublin Cemeteries Committee, who attended meetings on a rotational basis. After the introduction of the Rotation Committee, the larger committee met in full at monthly meetings, referred to as General Committee Meetings.

As a result of this system of administration, and the establishment of a number of subcommittees, Glasnevin Trust Archive holds several series of minute books, including the minute books of the General Committee, Rotation Committee, Visiting Committee and Special Subcommittees. All committees reported to the General Committee. The duty of the General Committee was to address motions of importance presented to it. The committee's minutes record monthly burial statistics and accounts, they raise issues relating to the administration of the cemeteries and include transcriptions of letters received from external correspondents, including letters from businesses, plot owners and relatives of those interred in the cemeteries. Also recorded in the minute books of the General Committee are

Glasnevin Trust Archives	
Grant Ticket Books	Includes applications for the purchase of plots in Goldenbridge and Prospect cemeteries and grants issued by the Dublin Cemeteries Committee for the right of burial in the cemeteries.
Interment Orders	Includes the informant's name and relationship to the deceased and grave owner, the funeral time, fee charged, the name of the person to be interred, their age, address, rank or occupation, marital status, cause of death and coffin size.
Interment Registers	Includes the date of interment, plot number, sex, religion, rank or occupation, marital status, cause of death, and the name and residence of the informant.
Letter Books	Record outgoing letters of the Dublin Cemeteries Committee.
Minute Books	Record the business transactions of the Dublin Cemeteries Committee.
Monument Plans	Includes applications made to the committee for permission to erect monuments, and sketches of the proposed monuments.

the minutes of Special Monthly Meetings, held when additional time was warranted to deal with specific issues, for instance, the election of a new committee member.

The Rotation Committee was concerned with the daily administration of the cemeteries, including issues relating to finance, human resources and record keeping. These minutes relate to monuments and inscriptions, the concerns and applications of the public, the recommendations of the Visiting Committee and the maintenance of the cemeteries and their labourers' cottages. The Visiting Committee was responsible for inspecting the cemeteries. This committee's minutes inform us of inspections held, issues of concern noted during inspections and the committee's recommendations. Special Subcommittee Minute Books include the minutes of special subcommittees formed by the Dublin Cemeteries Committee. Examples include the minutes of the Law and Land Committee, the Buildings Committee and the Walkways and Trees Committee. An informative account of the work of the Dublin Cemeteries Committee, including sources for research, is Carmel Connell's *Glasnevin Cemetery, Dublin, 1832–1900*, in the Maynooth Studies in Local History series (2004).

Enquiries concerning access to the archives of Glasnevin Trust, including the minute books, may be addressed in writing to Glasnevin Trust's Resident Historian at Glasnevin Cemetery Museum. **Email:** info@glasnevintrust.ie

For researchers interested in accessing the Trust's Interment Registers, these have been digitized and may be accessed online at http://www.glasnevin trust.ie/genealogy. Genealogical enquiries may be addressed to the museum's Resident Genealogist. **Email:** genealogy@glasnevintrust.ie

Appendix 3: The cost of dying: a case study from an undertaker's archive

LISA MARIE GRIFFITH & CIARÁN WALLACE

Nichols Funeral Home operates today at 29/31 Lombard Street, Dublin 2. The firm has been in operation for over two centuries and has passed through the hands of six generations of the Nichols family. It originated as a stable livery and its records allow us to see how the profession of undertaker emerged in the mid-nineteenth century into the role that we are familiar with today. Records of invoices and burials survive from the late nineteenth century allowing us to gauge how traditions surrounding death and burial have changed from the nineteenth century into the twenty-first century. It is possible to detect medical crises within the city, such as the outbreak of Spanish Influenza in 1918. The archive can also tell us much about broader changes in society and how the rise of hospital care, the arrival of city-wide cemeteries and the dominance of the motor car could impact on the burial and funeral arrangements of Dubliners. While these records can highlight the history of the Nichols family firm, they also hint at an untapped social and medical history resource for the city. Dublin has a number of long-running and historic undertaker businesses such as Fanagan's, established in 1819, and Corrigan's, founded in the late 1800s. It is likely that many of these firms preserve their records and that they can shed light on death, dying and burial in Dublin.

* * *

The founder of the Nichols family undertaker business was Joseph Nichols, a Quaker, who was born in Warwickshire in 1777, and moved to Dublin in 1814.[1] Joseph rented premises at 4 Lower Merrion Street (now Lincoln Place). His initial enterprise was providing horses and renting space in his livery stable.[2] Dublin was a busy city and a ready availability of transportation kept the city running. Livery stables like Nichols' would have been much in demand. Horses were used for industry as well as transportation and 'the city

---

1 Gus Nichols and Paula Howard, *Past Nichols the undertakers: six generations of a Dublin family business 1814–2014* (Dublin, 2014), pp 26, 33. 2 Nichols and Howard, *Past Nichols the undertakers*, p. 47.

streets were filled each day with horses drawing a wide variety of vehicles'.[3] The business expanded throughout the century. Joseph rented carriages as well as horses, and progressed to providing taxi coaches by 1828. On his death in 1845, Joseph left this thriving business to his nephew, James.

The business began to diversify in the second half of the nineteenth century and by 1857 the family were advertising as undertakers, as well as providing their livery stable service. The business provided carriages as mourning coaches for funerals before this, and we know that the horses had been hired to coffin makers as well as being used to draw hearses.[4] Nevertheless, this represented a significant diversification for the business and undertaking would become their primary focus. The advertisement of 'undertaking' for the Nichols' livery was part of a wider movement to recognize the services of 'undertakers' in its own right. In the Nichols' family history they point to the gradual evolution of the trade:

> It took longer for undertaking to be considered a separate trade in Ireland. Undertakers, including James Nichols, were listed for the first time in the trade section of Dublin directories in 1865. Prior to this, they were listed under 'Coffin Makers and Undertakers' or 'Coach, Gig, and Car Proprietors and Undertakers'.[5]

This gives us some idea of where the overlap in livery stables and undertaking started – provision of coaches and transportation for funerals – and how the Nichols family business evolved to become wholly concerned with undertaking. It also represents a change in the habits and fortunes of Dublin's population. They could now afford to hire a company for funeral services. Families were less likely to take care of their own dead but began to involve professionals. Previously, the bereaved had arranged the removal of the deceased (primarily from the family home where they had died) to the church and the opening of a burial plot.[6]

The rise of the funeral director may also have come about because of a wider change in burial practice. From the early nineteenth century it became more usual for people to be buried in the large cemeteries outside the city, rather than in local church graveyards (see introduction). This created a greater demand for transportation from the local church, where the funeral service took place, to cemeteries like Glasnevin or Mount Jerome. This need for

---

3 Ibid., p. 60.   **4** Ibid., pp 66–7.   **5** Ibid, p. 77.   **6** Ibid.

transportation made undertakers a crucial expense in any funeral. From the late nineteenth and into the twentieth century, there was also an increase in the number of people dying in hospitals and state institutions, rather than in their own home. Such funerals required transport for the remains of the deceased, and for the family and friends, to the cemetery. Following interment, the undertaker's coaches were required to bring the bereaved home or, perhaps more typically, to some place of refreshment. There was also a financial element to the increased take up of the funeral director's services. They tailored their service to the financial needs of each family and were prepared to work on credit, enabling families pay off their bill gradually, sometimes over many small instalments. This was very important. Dublin's two Poor Law Unions provided for the burial of those who were too poor to cover the cost of their own funeral, but a pauper funeral was looked down upon and was felt to bring great shame to a family. Most would rather undergo the expense of a funeral than have their loved one buried in an unmarked pauper's grave.

By the end of the nineteenth century, the service offered by undertaker firms, or by the funeral director, included preparation of the body (if required), transport from place of death to the firm's own mortuary chapel, or to a chapel linked with the deceased person, the provision of a coffin, arranging the opening of the grave and placing advertisements in newspapers to announce the death. The Nichols' family history notes that 'embalming did not gain ground' until the second half of the twentieth century.[7] Before then, the deceased were generally interred within a day of their passing. By the mid-1880s Nichols' business was spread over six properties; including premises on Mark Street near St Mark's Church, on Lombard Street, on Great Brunswick Street and another on Denzille Street. They had yards at Lincoln Place and off Merrion Street Lower.[8] As well as being close to upper-class residential areas like Merrion Square, with their prosperous clientele, these premises were close to the new railway terminus at Westland Row. Travellers into the city may have stopped at the livery stables to hire horses for their business in the city or its outer suburbs. The family added a coffin-making factory in 1890 at the Lombard Street premises. This was a trend that was followed by other city undertakers such as Fanagan's and Corrigan's. Coffin makers were traditionally located around Cook Street. In fact, in 1836, 16 of the 19 city coffin makers were located on the street.[9] This may reflect the concentration of churches in the old city, while the location also enabled timber to be carried upriver to the workshops.

7 Ibid., p. 163. 8 Ibid., p. 47. 9 Ibid., p. 160.

With the expansion of the rail and tram systems, both cheap and reliable services, there was a decreasing demand for carriages and horses in the city and Nichols' business began to focus on its role as an undertaker. The decline of the horse can be seen in 1948 when the business ceased using horses for drawing their hearses. The last coach and pair was used by the firm on 18 January 1948: 'After 134 years of faithful service on the city streets, the connection between the Nichols family and its horses was finally broken'.[10] By 1952, every undertaker in the city had ceased to use horses. In the 1970s, however, there was a revival of interest in the tradition of the horse-drawn hearse and Massey's undertakers re-introduced them. Other city undertakers followed suit.[11] With the move to motorized hearses, the extensive stables that had been managed by Nichols were no longer required and the business contracted.

At his death in 1873 James Nichols left the family business to his wife, Anne. With three grown-up sons this may seem unusual but as a Quaker James was recognizing his wife's equal standing to himself, as well as her capability to run the business. When Anne died in 1893, the business was left equally to her sons Charles and James. They renamed the business J & C Nichols in 1900, and it trades to this day under that name.[12] James, however, branched out on his own and in 1901 set up as a merchant, leaving Charles to run the undertaking business.[13] In 1933 Charles died, and was succeeded by his son Richard (known as Dick) who inherited a 'robust and financially sound' business.[14] One of the biggest projects that the family undertook during this period, and a further indication of the ever-expanding role of the undertaker, was the renovation of the vaults of St Michan's on Church Street in 1940. A principal part of this was re-coffining the Sheares brothers (prominent United Irishmen, executed following the 1798 Rebellion, see plate 17).[15] In 1953 Edward took over from his father, Richard. Edward would train his son Charles Edward up to the family profession as well.

In the 1970s the firm was responsible for re-interring 500 bodies from the Huguenot Cemetery on Bishop Street to Mount Jerome Cemetery (see plate 16).[16] In the 1990s they were involved in another important city re-interment. The Anglican church of St Mary, on Mary Street, had been purchased in the 1980s by a developer. The development of the church for secular purposes necessitated the removal and re-interment of bodies buried in the church vaults and surrounding graveyard. This was carried out by Gus Nichols, who

10 Ibid., p. 146. 11 Ibid., p. 147. 12 Ibid., p. 104. 13 Ibid., p. 106. 14 Ibid., p. 153. 15 Ibid., p. 165. 16 Ibid., p. 183.

took over the business from his father in 1996. The firm has also carried out work on the Christ Church Cathedral and Pro-Cathedral vaults. Today, Nichols operates from the Lombard Street premises and the firm celebrated its 200th anniversary in 2014.

* * *

Nichols' company records stretch back to 1889, the older records are held in the National Archives of Ireland,[17] and those from 1920 are held in Nichols' current premises on Lombard Street East. A brief survey of the firm's modern records gives an interesting insight into the changing nature of the undertaker's role in life and death in twentieth-century Dublin. The central location of the Nichols' premises meant that they built up a sizeable Catholic clientele in the densely populated inner city. Perhaps the family's Quaker roots attracted Protestant clients, among both working-class families living near the docks and those wealthier families living in the more prosperous outer suburbs. As a result, the records show everything from basic funerals – involving just the transport of a plain coffin – to the more elaborate obsequies with a silk-lined casket and numerous carriages.

We have taken the Nichols' archive as a sample in which to explore the type of information, both quantitative and qualitative, that may be found in undertaker records, and to draw some tentative conclusions about social and economic conditions in the city during the twentieth century. A representative sample of the accounts books from 1920 to 1985 was selected, with the records for January of each fifth year being examined. These accounts give the name and address of the client, the name of the deceased and the cost of the services provided. Funerals are recorded in varying levels of detail, apparently at the discretion of the individual clerk; however, more elaborate burials are typically itemized more fully. A regular interment might be listed as, 'Paid for by C.R. Esq., Grosvenor Square, Rathmines, for funeral of late Mrs M.C. at Mount Jerome, cost £15 7s.',[18] or an entry may show greater detail, 'Paid for by Coall, Talbot & Son, Kingstown for Charles E.W.B. from The Rest, Camden Row, to Dean's Grange, included a hearse, 2 carriages and attendant. Cost £11 10s.'[19] As the years progressed, however, the tendency was to record all funerals, regardless of cost, in greater detail.

17 NAI Catalogue Number: BR Dublin 19.   **18** Nichols' Account Book, 19 Jan. 1920. All names have been anonymized for the purposes of this research.   **19** Nichols' Accounts, 10 Jan. 1920.

The changing face of the city can be seen in some entries; an early example of a motorized hearse appears in 1925 for the funeral of A. S. Esquire of Eaton Square, Terenure, for his funeral 'from above to Torgeny, near Ballymahon, Co. Longford, for Motor hearse. Cost £34'.[20] Presumably, the great distance to the burial site meant that a motor hearse was the simplest option. This entry also raises the issue of deaths in Dublin requiring burial beyond the city, and the burials in Dublin of those dying elsewhere. For these more complicated logistical arrangements an undertaker was essential, with shipping charges, official paperwork, storage and delivery involved all along the route. A funeral to the City Cemetery, Belfast, in 1955 cost £77 3s. while handling remains arriving from Britain in the same year amounted to only £6 15s. 6d. In this case the bulk of the arrangements (and presumably the cost) had been handled by the dispatching undertaker, so Nichols' accounts show 'Deceased A. T., from the W[estland] Row Station to our yard and then Deans Grange, phone call and telegrams to Undertakers, Budleigh Salterton, Devon. Paid for by G. C. T., Marlborough Road, Donnybrook and Mount Street Club. 1 hearse, 1 attendant, 1 van, 2 attendants at the rear.'[21] The inclusion of telegrams, and later telephone calls, as items on the bill becomes more common for such long-distance funerals in the mid-twentieth century. More frequently, however, such communications costs relate to placing death notices in London or Belfast newspapers. Placing of death notices appears as an itemized part of the undertaker's bill from the early 1950s but, given how popular and long-standing the death notice is, it seems likely that they provided this service from before this date. The *Irish Times*, and its sister title the *Evening Mail*, appear frequently and suggest a middle- or upper-class clientele. The *Evening Herald*, the local city newspaper, is also mentioned regularly with the *Irish Press* appearing less often. Notices in London newspapers, *The Times* and the *Daily Telegraph*, accompany some more expensive funerals. The absence of any notices in Irish provincial newspapers indicates the strongly urban nature of Nichols' business.

Occasionally, family tragedies are encompassed in a few words. 'Cost of funeral £1 8s., for child-coffin 2.4, J. T. deceased, Paid for by Mr T. Ringsend Park, 2 vans and coffin from Sir P. Dunns Hospital to Glasnevin',[22] and 'Paid for by Mr E. B., Pearse House. 2.4 plain silk sheet, coffin, for C. B. at Children's Hospital, Harcourt St. £9',[23] being just two examples. A similar tragedy, which

20 Nichols' Accounts, 2 Jan. 1925.   **21** Nichols' Accounts, 7 Jan. 1955.   **22** Nichols' Accounts, 2 Jan. 1930.   **23** Nichols' Accounts, 1 Jan. 1940.

may not have impinged on a family, is recorded in the funeral of an infant boy from the Bethany Home, a Protestant refuge for single mothers. His entry reads: 'Bethany Home, Orwell Road, Rathgar, Van. etc. 2.0 Elm coffin, shirt, for infant S. L., at Mount Jerome. Cost £1 10s. 6d.'[24]

The expanding range of services that Dublin families purchased from funeral directors is accompanied by increasingly detailed descriptions in the accounts. These enable us to see the costs of a variety of items, and to trace how elaborate some funerals had become by the final quarter of the century; for example,

> Mr A. S. W., Blackrock. Co. Dublin £171 6s. 0d. Hearse and cars at £7 10s. 0d. each Plain oak coffin £50 0s. 0d. New grave and interment fee £23 10s. 0d. in Deans Grange Cemetery. Removal from St Vincent's Hospital to St Brigid's Church Stillorgan, thence to Deans Grange. Paid £50. Sexton £20/- GD [grave diggers] 20/-; JCN 20/-. Organist 42/-. Irish Times 3/-; Independent 42/-; London Times £14 Daily Examiner £9. Phone calls London (4) 30/-. Acknowledgement notice I. Times 25/- Independent 38/-. 1 wreath £6 6s. 0d.; 3 wreaths £4 4s. 0d. each. Account to J. H. A. Esq, Foxrock Co. Dublin. Receipt to A. L. Goodbody, 31 Fitzwilliam Sq.[25]

Here we see the undertaker arranging for flowers, the church organist, death notices at home and abroad and a second set of notices acknowledging the condolences offered to the family. Floral wreaths appear in the accounts from the mid-1960s, and organists from 1970. Other items disappear from the list. Accounts entries for funerals from the 1920s sometimes list a burial sheet, or shroud, but these do not appear in the sample beyond that date. However, this apparent change in burial customs may be due to a changing terminology as a 'habit' is provided on a number of occasions between 1945 and 1985.

The importance of giving a loved one a decent burial is evident from the accounts, and the most expensive funerals do not necessarily come from the most prosperous addresses. One of the largest billings for 1960 relates to an elaborate funeral (six cars to the chapel for the removal, motor hearse, three cars and attendant to chapel on the day of the burial). This much-loved mother's funeral cost £50 14s. 3d., and was paid for by her daughter living in a newly developed public authority housing estate in Finglas.[26] In 1989, a

24 Nichols' Accounts, 23 Jan. 1945.   **25** Nichols' Accounts, 24 Nov. 1970.   **26** Nichols' Accounts, 15 Jan. 1960.

funeral costing over £1,880, well in excess of the average for that year, left from Pearse House, a neighbouring complex of flats built in the 1930s to rehouse families from the old tenements.[27] Bereaved families were faced with the shock of a death, but also with the sudden financial strain of a funeral. While many burials were provided for by life assurance policies, the records show most bills being paid by the immediate family. The relationship between the deceased and the person making the payment (son, daughter, widow etc.) is often mentioned but in other cases it is not clear whether the invoice is directed to a more distant relative or, perhaps, an accountant. Bills sent to solicitors acting on behalf of the deceased's estate are always clearly identified. In some instances it appears that a charity, or charitable individual, may have made the payment, 'Funeral of N. M. to Mount Jerome, paid by Rev. Ferguson of Dublin Central Mission, Lower Abbey Street, £31 3s.'[28] At least one funeral was paid for in advance by the deceased, 'Funeral of J. J. K. £65 0s. 0d. (paid for by himself), of Deerpark Road, Mount Merrion taken from St Kevin's Hospital to Andrew's Church, Westland Road, there to Deans Grange – removal motor hearse 3 cars and 1 attendant, funeral, m. hearse, 4 cars. Interment fee £2 10s. 0d.'.[29]

As with any business, funeral directors must face an occasional credit risk, and the social pressure on families to give the deceased 'a good send-off', and the emotional state of the bereaved client, has always placed the undertaker in a difficult position. Nichols', like other undertakers, gave their customers credit if required. This was a financial risk, but it seems that the strict social ethics that surround death and burial meant that almost all such funerals in the accounts books reviewed were finally paid off. Payment 'on tick' was an established practice for suppliers and customers in Dublin so, for example, the debt relating to a relatively expensive funeral in 1980 (£830) was cleared in twenty-five small payments over the following ten months. But not all such monies were paid in full. A modest burial ('Church offering £15, Motor Hearse [no cars], Priest £5') left a bill of £160.43 outstanding, this sum being written off three years later.

According to the sample examined, the monthly number of funerals handled by Nichols' across the period declined from 106 in January 1920, to 44 in January 1990 (Table A). While this general trend was reversed between 1940 and 1945, possibly due to the impact of the wartime economy on the

---

27 Nichols' Accounts, 12 Sept. 1989. 28 Nichols' Accounts, 15 Jan. 1965. 29 Nichols' Accounts, 30 Jan. 1965.

health of the inner city population, the tendency across the century reflects both an improving life-expectancy and the resettlement of families from the overcrowded tenements surrounding Lombard Street to the new suburbs of Coolock, Crumlin, Cabra and Finglas. During the period examined, the number of firms engaged in the trade in Dublin was relatively static,[30] so the fall in numbers is not accounted for by competition from other undertakers. The gradual expansion of undertaker firms into these suburban areas in subsequent decades reflects the link between commerce and population cycles.

TABLE A Number of funerals each January, 1920–90

Source: Nichols' Accounts Books, 1920–90

In contrast to the declining number of funerals, the average cost of burial increased slowly until the early 1970s, when a steep rise is evident (Table B). This dramatic leap in funeral prices illustrates the expanding range of services that undertakers offered as funeral practices changed but, perhaps more significantly, the price curve closely matches the trend in the Consumer Price Index, 1922–90, as compiled by the Central Statistics Office (CSO).[31] This

30 The editors are grateful to Orla Nolan of the Irish Association of Funeral Directors for this information.
31 CSO: http://www.cso.ie/multiquicktables/quickTables.aspx?id=cpm07_cpm02_cpa04_3, accessed 20 Nov. 2015.

national statistic records the cost of an extensive basket of goods and services (including funeral costs) which the average family might encounter in any given year (Table C). The comparatively small sample involved in this survey can only give provisional findings, but the close parallel between the rise in funeral costs seen in the Nichols' sample and the rise in national CPI figures suggests that funerals have not increased disproportionately in price. When prices are compared with the average industrial wage the figures show that a typical funeral in 1970 cost five times the average weekly industrial wage, while in 1990 this had dropped to 4.7 times the average weekly wage (Table D).[32]

TABLE B Average funeral cost, 1920–90

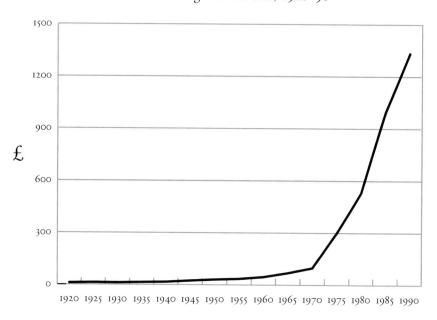

Source: Nichols' Accounts Books, 1920–90

32 CSO: http://www.cso.ie/en/releasesandpublications/er/elcq/earningsandlabourcostsq22013finalq32013 preliminaryestimates/#.UwwHLIV8oZk, accessed 20 Nov. 2015.

TABLE C Annual average consumer price index, 1922–90

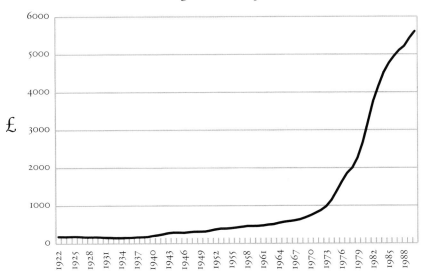

Source: CSO http://www.cso.ie/multiquicktables/quickTables.aspx?id=cpm07_cpm02_cpa04_3

TABLE D Average funeral costs compared with average industrial wage

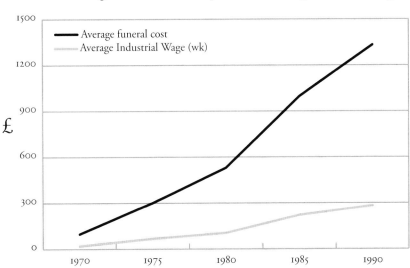

Source: Nichols' Account Books, 1970–90 and CSO

Undertakers' records are a valuable source for the researcher, they reveal much about the social and economic context, from the state of public health and attitudes towards death to the changing profile of the city's trades. In their accounting columns we can find evidence of what happened when times of crises led to the worst outcome – death. Undertakers were to the fore in assisting the bereaved during communal crises such as medical pandemics, war and revolution, but also during times of personal and family grief. Their records provide a unique window into the social aspirations, religious beliefs and economic status of Dublin families, across a wide time span and in a relatively consistent manner.

Using the quantitative and qualitative data buried in their pages we can also trace changes in society such as the gradual evolution from people dying at home, to people dying in hospitals and hospices, or the decline of the horse and the arrival of the motor car onto the streets of Dublin. The number of funeral directors in the city has remained fairly constant over a prolonged period, and some firms' records stretch back almost a century. Such a resource, rich in specific data and implied trends, merits further investigation by a variety of researchers.

Appendix 4: List of crypts, cemeteries and graveyards

(sourced from Dublin City Library and Archive's Graveyard Directory)

This list has been drawn from the DCLA database of Dublin (city and county) Graveyards, Crypts and Cemeteries. The listing is a free resource that can be found at http://databases.dublincity.ie/graveyards/search.php While the list below includes the name of the cemetery and the address the online listing also includes valuable details such as the period the graveyard was in use, who now takes care of the graveyard, if there are any burial records and where they are located, and other studies associated with the location. We would like to thank DCLA for allowing us to reproduce the list here.

NAME OF GRAVEYARD	ADDRESS
Abbotstown	Castleknock, Co. Dublin
Aderrig	Aderrig townland is two miles south-west of Lucan and the graveyard is on a secondary road linking Hazelhatch with Lucan
All Hallows	Grace Park Road, Drumcondra, Dublin 9
Arbour Hill	Stoneybatter, Dublin 7
Artane	Kilmore Road, Artane, Dublin 5
Balbrigan (St Peter and Paul's)	Balbriggan, Co. Dublin
Balbriggan (St Peter's)	Church Street, Balbriggan, Co. Dublin
Baldongan	Adjacent to Baldongan Castle, Skerries, Co. Dublin
Balgriffin	Balgriffin, Dublin 17
Ballyboghal	Ballyboghal, Co. Dublin
Ballybough	65 Fairview Strand, Dublin 3
Ballyfermot	Le Fanu Road, Ballyfermot, Dublin 10
Ballymadrough	Donabate, Co. Dublin
Ballymadun	Ballymadun, Co. Dublin
Balrothery	Balrothery, Co. Dublin
Balrothery Union	Oberstown, Lusk, Co. Dublin
Balscaddan	Balscaddan, Co. Dublin

NAME OF GRAVEYARD	ADDRESS
Balscaddan (Church of the Assumption)	Balscaddan, Co. Dublin
Baring Family Mausoleum	Lambay Castle, Lambay Island, Co. Dublin
Barrington's	Brennanstown Road, Cabinteely, Co. Dublin
Beresford Family Vault	Abbeyville House, Kinsealy, Co. Dublin
Beth Olam	Aughavanagh Road, Crumlin, Dublin 12
Blackrock College Vaults (also Holy Ghost Fathers)	Blackrock, Co. Dublin
Bohernabreena (Saint Anne's)	Bohernabreena, Co. Dublin
Bohernabreena (Saint Joseph's)	Bohernabreena, Co. Dublin
Brackenstown	Brackenstown Road, Swords, Co. Dublin
Bremore	Balbriggan, Co. Dublin. On the south side of Barnewall Castle
Bully's Acre	The Royal Hospital, Kilmainham, Dublin 8
Cabbage Garden	Cathedral Lane, off Kevin Street, Dublin 8
Carmelite Sisters	Carmelite Monastery, Firhouse, Dublin 24.
Carmelite Sisters (Monastery of the Incarnation)	Hampton, Grace Park Road, Drumcondra, Dublin 9
Carrickbrennan	Monkstown, Co. Dublin
Castle Avenue (Saint John the Baptist)	Clontarf, Dublin 3
Castleknock (Saint Brigid's)	Castleknock, Dublin 15
Challoner's Corner	Trinity College, Dublin 2 (behind the chapel on the Front Square of Trinity College)
Chapelizod (Saint Lawrence's)	Main Street, Chapelizod, Dublin 20
Chapelmidway	Killsallaghan, Co. Dublin
Charity of Saint Vincent de Paul, Daughters of	Saint Vincent's, North William Street, Dublin 1
Christ Church Cathedral Crypt	Christ Church Place, Dublin 8
Christian Brothers (Oratory of the Resurrection)	Oratory of the Resurrection, Kilmore Road, Artane, Dublin 5

NAME OF GRAVEYARD	ADDRESS
Christian Brothers (Saint Joseph's School for Deaf Boys)	Saint Joseph's School for Deaf Boys, Cabra, Dublin 7
Christian Brothers (Saint Mary's Training College)	Saint Mary's Training College, Griffith Avenue, Marino, Dublin 3
Christian Brothers (Saint Patrick's)	Saint Patrick's, Baldoyle, Dublin 13
Cloghran	Swords, Co. Dublin
Clondalkin (Saint John's)	Tower Road, Clondalkin, Dublin 22
Clonmethan	Oldtown, Co. Dublin
Clonsilla (Saint Mary's)	Clonsilla, Dublin 15
Colmanstown	Athgoe, Castlewarden, Co. Dublin
Coolock (Saint John the Evangelist)	Tonlegee Road, Coolock, Dublin 17
Cruagh	Rathfarnham, Dublin 16
Cruagh (Old)	Rathfarnham, Dublin 16
Crumlin (Saint Mary's)	Crumlin, Dublin 12
Dalkey (Saint Begnet's)	Dalkey, Co. Dublin
Dardistown	Collinstown Cross, Swords, Co. Dublin
Dean's Grange	Dean's Grange, Co. Dublin
Dominicans (Saint Mary's)	Dominican Priory, Tallaght Village, Dublin 24
Donabate (Ballalease)	Portrane Road, Donabate, Co. Dublin
Donabate (Saint Patrick's)	The Square, Donabate, Co. Dublin
Donabate (Saint Patrick's RC)	Donabate, Co. Dublin
Donnybrook	Main Street, Donnybrook, Dublin 4
Drimnagh (Bluebell)	Old Naas Road, Dublin 12
Drumcondra	Church Avenue, Drumcondra, Dublin 9
Drumcondra (Saint George's)	Whitworth Road, Drumcondra, Dublin 9
Esker (New – Saint Mary's)	Lucan, Co. Dublin
Esker (Old)	Lucan, Co. Dublin
Finglas (Saint Canice's)	Church Street, Finglas, Dublin 11

NAME OF GRAVEYARD	ADDRESS
Friend's Burial Ground	Temple Hill, Blackrock, Co. Dublin
Garristown	Garristown, Co. Dublin
Glasnevin	Finglas Road, Glasnevin, Dublin 11
Glasnevin (Saint Mobhi's)	Church Avenue, Glasnevin, Dublin 11
Glencullen (Old)	Glencullen, Co. Dublin
Glencullen (Saint Patrick's)	Glencullen, Co. Dublin
Goldenbridge	Saint Vincent Street West, Inchicore, Dublin 8
Grallagh	Naul, Co. Dublin
Grange Abbey	Grange Road, Donaghmede, Dublin 13
Grangegorman Military Cemetery	Blackhorse Avenue, Dublin 7
Hibernian Cemetery	Saint Mary's Hosptial, Phoenix Park, Dublin 20
Hollywood	Naul, Co. Dublin
Holmpatrick	Skerries, Co. Dublin
Holy Faith Sisters	Holy Faith Convent, Old Finglas Road, Glasnevin, Dublin 11
Howth (Old Abbey)	Church Street, Howth, Co. Dublin
Howth (Saint Mary's)	Church Street, Howth, Co. Dublin
Huguenot Cemetery – Cabbage Garden	Cathedral Lane, Upper Kevin Street, Dublin 8
Huguenot Cemetery – Merrion Row	10 Merrion Row, Dublin 2
Huguenot Cemetery – Peter Street	Peter Street, Dublin 2
Irishtown (Saint Matthew's)	Irishtown, Dublin 4
Jewish Community Graveyard	Ballybough
Jewish Progressive Congregation	Woodtown, Rathfranham, Co. Dublin
Kenure	Rush, Co. Dublin
Kenure Old Church	Rush, Co. Dublin
Kilbarrack	Dublin Road, Sutton, Dublin 13
Kilbride	Kilbride Townland, Co. Dublin

NAME OF GRAVEYARD	ADDRESS
Kilcreagh	Kilcreagh Road, Donabate, Co. Dublin
Kilgobbin	Enniskerry Road, Co. Dublin
Kilgobbin (Old)	Enniskerry Road, Co. Dublin
Kill O'The Grange	Clonkeen, Co. Dublin (formerly Saint Fintan's Church).
Killeek	Killeek, Swords, Co. Dublin
Killester	Killester Avenue, Dublin 5
Killiney, Old Churchyard	Marino Avenue, off Killiney Hill Road, Killiney, Co. Dublin
Kilmactalway	Castle Bagot, Kilmactalway, Newcastle, Co. Dublin
Kilmahuddrick (Saint Cuthbert's)	Deansrath, Bawnogue, Clondalkin, Dublin 22
Kilmainham (Royal Hospital Military Cemetery)	The Royal Hospital, Kilmainham, Dublin 8
Kilmashogue	Edmondstown Rd, Rathfarnham, Dublin 16
Kilsallaghan	Kilsallaghan, Co. Dublin
Kiltiernan	Kilternan, Co. Dublin
Kiltiernan (Old)	Bishop's Lane, Kiltiernan, Co. Dublin
Little Sisters of the Assumption	Mount Saint Joseph's, Monastery Road, Clondalkin, Dublin 22
Little Sisters of the Poor	Saint Patrick's House, South Circular Road, Kilmainham, Dublin 8
Loreto Abbey	Loreto Abbey, Rathfarnham, Dublin 16
Loughlinstown Workhouse	Loughlinstown, Co. Dublin
Loughtown	Newcastle, Co. Dublin (behind Peamount Hospital)
Lucan Chapel Hill (Saint Mary's)	Lucan, Co. Dublin
Lucan Demesne	Lucan, Co. Dublin
Lusk (Saint MacCulind's)	Lusk Village, Co. Dublin
Lusk (Saint MacCulind's RC)	Lusk Village, Co. Dublin

NAME OF GRAVEYARD	ADDRESS
Malahide (Saint Andrew's)	Church Road, Malahide, Co. Dublin
Malahide (Saint Sylvester's)	Main Street, Malahide, Co. Dublin
Malahide (Yellow Walls)	Malahide, Co. Dublin
Malahide Castle Demesne	Malahide Castle Demesne, Malahide, Co. Dublin
Merrion (Bellevue)	Merrion Road, Dublin 4
Moravian	Whitechurch Road, Dublin 16
Mount Anville	Mount Anville, Dundrum, Dublin 14
Mount Argus	Saint Paul's Retreat, Mount Argus, Harold's Cross, Dublin 6
Mount Jerome	Harold's Cross, Dublin 6
Mount Sackville	Sisters of Saint Joseph of Cluny, Mount Sackville Convent, Chapelizod, Dublin 20
Mount Venus	Rockbrook, Rathfarnham, Dublin 16
Mulhuddart	Ladyswell, Mulhuddart, Dublin 15
Mulhuddart (Saint Thomas')	Mulhuddart, Dublin 15
Naul	Naul, Co. Dublin
Newcastle	Newcastle, Co. Dublin
Newcastle (RC)	Newcastle, Co. Dublin
Newcastle-Lyons (Saint Finian's)	The Glebe, Main Street, Newcastle, Co. Dublin.
Newlands Cross Cemetery & Crematorium	Ballymount Road, Dublin 24
Oblate Fathers	Tyrconnell Road, Inchicore, Dublin 8
Old Connaught	Old Connaught Burial Ground, Little Bray, Co. Dublin
Our Lady of Lourdes'	Our Lady of Lourdes Church, Sean McDermott Street, Dublin 1
Palmerstown	Mill Lane, Dublin 20 (behind Stewart's Hospital)
Palmerstown	Kennelsfort Road, Palmerstown, Dublin 20
Palmerstown	Oldtown, Co. Dublin
Portmarnock	Strand Road, Portmarnock, Co. Dublin
Portmarnock (Saint Marnock's)	Old Portmarnock, Co. Dublin

NAME OF GRAVEYARD	ADDRESS
Portrane (Saint Catherine's)	Langstone Park, Portrane, Co. Dublin
Portrane (Saint Ita's Hospital)	Saint Ita's Hospital, The Quay Road, Portrane, Donabate, Co. Dublin
Presentation Sisters (Clondalkin)	New Road, Clondalkin, Dublin 22
Presentation Sisters (Terenure)	Saint Joseph's Convent, Terenure Road West, Dublin 6
Presentation Sisters (Warrenmount)	Warrenmount Convent, Warrenmount, Dublin 8
Raheny	Our Lady Mother of Divine Grace Church, Howth Road, Raheny, Dublin 5
Raheny (Saint Assam's)	Raheny Village, Dublin 5
Rathcoole	Main Street, Rathcoole, Co. Dublin
Rathfarnham	Rathfarnham Village, Dublin 16
Rathmichael Old Church	Rathmichael, Co. Dublin
Redemptoristines	Monastery of Saint Alphonsus, Saint Alphonsus Road, Dublin 9
Rowlestown (also Killossery)	Rowlestown, Co. Dublin
Rosminian Fathers	St Joseph's School for the Visually Impaired, Grace Park Road, Drumcondra, Dublin 9
Rush (Saint Maur's)	Rush, Co. Dublin
Saggart	Main Street, Saggart, Co. Dublin
Saint Andrew's	26 Suffolk Street, Dublin 2
Saint Andrew's Vaults	Westland Row, Dublin 2
Saint Ann's	Dawson Street, Dublin 2
Saint Audoen's	Cornmarket, Dublin 8
Saint Bride's	Bride Street, Dublin 8 (No longer extant)
Saint Catherine's	Saint Catherine's Park, Thomas Street, Dublin 8
Saint Doolagh's	Saint Doolagh's, Kinsealy, Co. Dublin
Saint Fintan's	Carrickbrack Road, Sutton, Co. Dublin
Saint George's	Hardwicke Place, Dublin 1
Saint James'	James' Street, Dublin 8 (behind 121 James' Street)
Saint John's	Fishamble Street, Dublin 8

NAME OF GRAVEYARD	ADDRESS
Saint Kevin's	Liberty Lane, Camden Row, Dublin 8
Saint Luke's	106A The Coombe, Dublin 8
Saint Margaret's	Saint Margaret's, Finglas, Dublin 11
Saint Mark's	42 Pearse Street, Dublin 2
Saint Mary's	Mary Street, Dublin 1
Saint Mary's Pro-Cathedral (Vaults)	Marlborough Street, Dublin 1
Saint Michan's	Church Street, Dublin 7
Saint Nicholas Within	Christ Church Place, Dublin 8
Saint Paul's	North King Street, Dublin 7
Saint Peter's	Aungier Street, Dublin 2 (the site of the YMCA building)
Saint Thomas'	Marlborough Street, Dublin 1
Saint Werburgh's	Werburgh Street, Dublin 8
Santry (Saint Pappin's)	Santry, Dublin 9
Shanganagh	Bray Road, Shankill, Co. Dublin
Sisters of Charity	Saint Mary Magdalen's, Sisters of Charity, Donnybrook, Dublin 4
Sisters of Mercy	Saint Vincent's Convent, Goldenbridge, Inchicore, Dublin 8
Sisters of Our Lady of Charity	High Park Convent, Grace Park Road, Dublin 9
Skerries (Saint Mobhi's)	Grange Road, Milverton, Skerries, Co. Dublin
Skerries (Saint Patrick's)	Skerries, Co. Dublin
Stillorgan (Saint Brigid's)	Stillorgan, Co. Dublin
Swords (Saint Colmcille's)	Chapel Lane, Swords, Co. Dublin
Swords (Saint Columba's)	Church Road, Swords, Co. Dublin
Tallaght (Saint Maelruan's)	Tallaght Village, Dublin 24
Taney (Saint Nathi's)	Churchtown Road, Dundrum, Dublin 14
Templeogue	Wellington Lane, Dublin 12
Templeogue (Old)	Wellington Lane, Dublin 12
Tully	Lehaunstown, Cabinteely, Co. Dublin
The Ward	The Ward, Co. Dublin
Westpalstown	Naul, Co. Dublin
Whitechurch	Whitechurch Road, Dublin 16
Whitechurch (Old)	Whitechurch, Dublin 16
Whitestown (Saint Maur's)	Rush, Co. Dublin
Woodtown	Woodtown, Rathfarnham, Co. Dublin

Select bibliography

Ariès, Philippe, *The hour of our death* (London, 1981).

Aytemiz, Pelin, 'Death photography in Turkey in the late 1800s and early 1900s: defining an area of study', *Early Popular Visual Culture*, 11:4 (2013), pp 322–41.

Barker, F., & J. Cheyne, *An account of the rise, progress and decline of the fever lately epidemical in Ireland*, vol. 1 (Dublin, 1821).

Bateson, Ray, *Memorials of the Easter Rising* (Dublin, 2013).

Bolger, Mary Ann, 'The ephemera of eternity: the Irish Catholic memorial card as material culture' in Linda King & Elaine Sisson (eds), *Ireland, design and visual culture: negotiating modernity, 1922–1992* (Cork, 2011), pp 235–51.

Browne, Alan, (ed.), *Masters, midwives and ladies-in-waiting: Rotunda Hospital, 1745–1995* (Dublin, 1995).

Bynum, W.F., *Science and the practice of medicine in the nineteenth century* (Cambridge, 1994).

Campbell Ross, Ian, *Public virtue, public love: early years of the Dublin Lying-in Hospital, the Rotunda* (Dublin, 1987).

Carey, Tim, *Hanged for murder: Irish state executions* (Cork, 2013)

Clark, M., 'Dublin piped water accounts, 1680', *Irish Genealogist*, 7 (1987), pp 201–4.

— 'List of principal inhabitants of the city of Dublin, 1684', *Irish Genealogist*, 8 (1990), pp 49–57.

Collins, Robert, *A practical treatise of midwifery containing the result of 16,654 births, occurring in the Dublin Lying-in Hospital, during a period of seven years, commencing November 1816* (London, 1835).

Connell, Carmel, *Glasnevin Cemetery, Dublin, 1832–1900* (Dublin, 2004).

Corcoran, M., *Our good health: a history of Dublin's water and drainage* (Dublin, 2005).

Cressy, David, *Birth, marriage and death: ritual, religion and the life-cycle in Tudor and Stuart England* (Oxford, 1997)

Crosby, Alfred, *America's forgotten pandemic* (Cambridge, 2003).

Cullen, L.M., 'Population trends in seventeenth century Ireland', *Economic and Social Review*, 6 (1975), pp 149–65.

Curl, James Stevens, *The Victorian celebration of death* (Stroud, 2000).

Davidson, Andrew H., *Clinical report of the Rotunda Hospital*, 1 November 1935–31 October 1936.

— *Clinical report of the Rotunda Hospital*, 1 November 1939–31 October 1940.

Dickson, D., C. Ó Gráda & S. Daultney, 'Hearth tax, household size and Irish population change, 1692–1821', *PRIA*, 82c (1982), pp 125–62.

Dickson, David, *Dublin: the making of a capital city* (London, 2014).

Fernandez, Ingrid, 'The lives of corpses: narratives of the image in American memorial photography', *Mortality: Promoting the Interdisciplinary Study of Death and Dying*, 16:4 (2011), pp 343–64.

Ferriter, Diarmaid, '"A figurative scramble for the bones of the patriot dead": commemorating the Rising, 1922–65' in Mary E. Daly & Margaret O'Callaghan (eds), *1916 in 1966: commemorating the Easter Rising* (Dublin, 2007), pp 199–219.

Fleetwood, John F., 'The Dublin body snatchers: part one', *Dublin Historical Record*, 42:1 (Dec. 1988), pp 32–40.

— 'The Dublin body snatchers: part two', *Dublin Historical Record*, 42:2 (Mar. 1989), pp 42–52.

Foley, Caitriona, *The last Irish plague: the great flu epidemic in Ireland, 1918–19* (Dublin, 2011).

Fitzpatrick, Orla, 'Portraits and propaganda: photographs of widows and children of the 1916 leaders in the *Catholic Bulletin*' in Lisa Godson & Joanna Brück (eds), *Making 1916: material and visual culture of the Easter Rising* (Liverpool, 2015), pp 82–90.

Fry, Susan Leigh, *Burial in medieval Ireland, 900–1500: a review of the written sources* (Dublin, 1999).

Garattini, Chiara, 'Creating memories: material culture and infantile death in contemporary Ireland', *Mortality*, 12:2 (2007), pp 193–206.

Gatrell, V.A.C., *The hanging tree: execution and the English people, 1770–1868* (Oxford, 1994).

Gillespie, Raymond, 'Funerals and society in early seventeenth-century Ireland', *JRSAI*, 115 (1985), pp 86–91.

— 'Irish funeral monuments and social change, 1500–1700: perceptions of death' in Raymond Gillespie & Brian P. Kennedy (eds), *Ireland: art into history* (Dublin, 1994), pp 155–68.

— *Devoted people: belief and religion in early modern Ireland* (Manchester, 1997).

Godson, Lisa, & Joanna Brück (eds), *Making 1916: material and visual culture of the Easter Rising* (Liverpool, 2015).

Gorey, Philomena, 'Managing midwifery in Dublin: practice and practitioners, 1700–1800' in Margaret M. Preston & Margaret Ó hÓgartaigh (eds), *Gender and medicine in Ireland, 1700–1950* (Syracuse, 2012), pp 123–37.

Gunnis, Rupert, 'Some Irish memorials', *Bulletin of the Irish Georgian Society*, 4 (1961), pp 1–15.

Hallam, Elizabeth, & Jenny Hockey, *Death, memory and material culture* (Oxford, 2001).

Hamlin, Christopher, 'Predisposing causes and public health in early nineteenth-century medical thought', *The Society for the Social History of Medicine*, 5:1 (1992), pp 43–70.

Hooper, C.B., 'Dublin anatomy in the 17th and 18th centuries', *Dublin Historical Record*, 40:4 (Sept. 1987), pp 122–32.

Igoe, Vivien, *Dublin burial grounds and graveyards* (Dublin, 2001).

Johnson, Niall, *Britain and the 1918–19 influenza pandemic: a dark epilogue* (Abingdon, 2006).

Jones, Greta, *The captain of all these men of death: the history of tuberculosis in nineteenth- and twentieth-century Ireland* (New York, 2001).

Jordan, Thomas E., '"The quick and the dead …" in late seventeenth-century Dublin', *Dublin Historical Record*, 61:1 (Spring 2008), pp 62–77.

— 'Quality of life in seventeenth-century Dublin', *Dublin Historical Record*, 61:2 (Autumn 2008), pp 136–54.

Kelly, James, & Mary Ann Lyons (eds), *Death and dying in Ireland, Britain and Europe: historical perspectives* (Sallins, 2013).

Kelly, James, *Gallows speeches from eighteenth-century Ireland* (Dublin, 2001).

— '"Glorious and immortal memory": commemoration and Protestant identity in Ireland, 1660–1800', *PRIA*, 94:C (1994), pp 25–52.

Kelly, Mary A., 'The development of midwifery at the Rotunda, 1745–1995' in Browne (ed.), *Masters, midwives and ladies-in-waiting, the Rotunda Hospital 1745–1995* (Dublin, 1995).

Kirkpatrick, T.P.C., *The book of the Rotunda Hospital* (London, 1913).

Kurti, László, '"For the last time": the Hiltman-Kinsey post-mortem photographs, 1918–1920', *Visual Studies*, 27:1 (2012), pp 91–104.

MacGiolla Phadraig, Brian, 'Speed's plan of Dublin', *Dublin Historical Record*, 10:3 (1948), 89–96; 10:4 (1949), pp 97–105.

MacThomáis, Shane, *Glasnevin: Ireland's necropolis* (Dublin, 2010).

— *Dead interesting: stories from the graveyards of Dublin* (Cork, 2012).

Marshall, Peter, *Beliefs and the dead in Reformation England* (Oxford, 2002).

McLellan, Anne, & Alice Mauger (eds), *Growing pains: childhood illness in Ireland, 1750–1950* (Dublin, 2013).

Mills, J. (ed.), *The register of St John the Evangelist, Dublin, 1619 to 1699* (Dublin, 1906).

Milne, Ida, 'Influenza: the Irish Local Government Board's last great crisis' in Virginia Crossman & Sean Lucey (eds), *Healthcare in Ireland and Britain, 1850–1970: voluntary, regional and comparative perspectives* (London, 2015), pp 217–36.

Minihan, John, *Shadows from the Pale: portrait of an Irish town* (London, 1996).

Murphy, Claire, 'What can an osteological investigation reveal about medical education in eighteenth-century Dublin?', *Archaeology Ireland*, 25:3 (Autumn 2011), pp 30–4.

Mytum, Harold, *Mortuary monuments and burial grounds of the historic period* (New York, 2003).

Nic Dháibhéid, Caoimhe, 'The Irish National Aid Association and the radicalization of public opinion in Ireland', *Historical Journal*, 55:1 (Sept. 2012), pp 705–29.

Nichols, Gus, & Paula Howard, *Past Nichols the undertakers; six generations of a Dublin family business, 1814–2014* (Dublin, 2014).

Ní Murchadha, M., *The vestry records of the United Parishes of Finglas, St Margaret's, Artane, and the Ward, 1657–1758* (Dublin, 2007).

O'Dwyer, Rory, '"The wilderness years": Kilmainham Gaol, 1924–1960', *History Ireland*, 18:6 (Nov./Dec. 2010), pp 41–3.

Ó Dúshláine, Tadhg, *An Eoraip agus litríocht na Gaeilge, 1600–1650* (Baile Átha Cliath/Dublin, 1987).

Ó Gráda, Diarmuid, *Georgian Dublin: the forces that shaped the city* (Cork, 2015).

— 'Infant and child mortality in Dublin a century ago', *Centre for Economic Research Working Paper Series* (Dublin, 2002).

O' Neill, Timothy P., 'Fever and public health in pre-famine Ireland', *JRSAI*, 103 (1973), pp 1–35.

O'Shea, Shane, *Death and design in Victorian Glasnevin* (Dublin, 2000).

Ó Súilleabháin, Seán, *Irish wake amusements* (Cork, 1967).

Petty, William, *Discourse concerning the use of duplicate proportion: the economic writings of Sir William Petty*. 2 vols (Cambridge, 1899).

— *Observations upon the Dublin bills of mortality 1681 and the state of that city*, (London, 1682).

— *Further observations upon the Dublin bills: or accompts of the houses, hearths, baptisms, and burials in that city* (London, 1686).

Phillips, Howard, & David Killingray (eds), *The Spanish influenza pandemic of 1918–1919, new perspectives* (Abingdon, 2003).

Porter, Katharine Anne, *Pale horse, pale rider* (Orlando, 1939).

Potterton, Homan, *Irish church monuments, 1570–1880* (Belfast, 1975).

Prior, P.M., *Madness and murder: gender, crime and mental disorder in nineteenth-century Ireland* (Dublin, 2008).

Refaussé, Raymond, 'Gone but not forgotten – the Church of Ireland graveyards of the city of Dublin', *Dublin Historical Record*, 68:1 (Spring/Summer 2015), pp 84–96.

Reynolds, Paige, *Modernism, drama, and the audience for Irish spectacle* (Cambridge, 2007).

Ridge, Anne, *Death customs in rural Ireland: traditional funerary rites in the Irish midlands* (Galway, 2009).

Ruby, Jay, *Secure the shadow: death and photography in America* (Cambridge, MA, 1995).

Seal, L., *Capital punishment in twentieth-century Britain: audience, justice, memory* (London, 2014).

Tait, Clodagh, *Death, burial and commemoration in Ireland, 1550–1650* (London, 2002).

Tarlow, Sarah, *Bereavement and commemoration: an archaeology of mortality* (Oxford, 1999).

Taylor, Lawrence J., 'Introduction: the uses of death in Europe', *Anthropological Quarterly*, 62:4 (1989), pp 149–54.

— 'Bás in Éirinn: cultural constructions of death in Ireland', *Anthropological Quarterly*, 62:4 (1989), pp 175–87.

Taylor, Mark C., & Dietrich Christian-Lammerts, *Grave matters* (London, 2002).

Timony, Mary B., *Had me made: a study of the grave memorials of Co. Sligo from c.1650 to the present* (Dublin, 2005).

Witoszek, Nina, & Pat Sheeran, *Talking to the dead: a study of Irish funerary traditions* (Atlanta, GA, 1998).

Worpole, Ken, *Last landscapes: the architecture of the cemetery in the West* (London, 2003).

Index

Compiled by JULITTA CLANCY

NOTE: unless otherwise indicated, places are in Dublin city and/or county;
page references in *italics* denote illustrations

233